Value Nets

Value Nets

BREAKING THE SUPPLY CHAIN
TO UNLOCK HIDDEN PROFITS

DAVID BOVET
JOSEPH MARTHA
Mercer Management Consulting

John Wiley & Sons, Inc.

New York • Chichester • Weinheim • Brisbane • Singapore • Toronto

This book is printed on acid-free paper. ∞

Published by John Wiley & Sons, Inc.
Published simultaneously in Canada.

This publication is designed to provide accurate and authoritative information
in regard to the subject matter covered. It is sold with the understanding that
the publisher is not engaged in rendering legal, accounting, or other
professional services. If legal advice or other expert assistance is required, the
services of a competent professional person should be sought.

Library of Congress Cataloging-in-Publication Data:

Bovet, David.
    Value nets : breaking the supply chain to unlock hidden profits / David
Bovet, Joseph Martha, Mercer Management Consulting ; with a foreword by
Adrian Slywotzky.
        p.   cm.
    Includes bibliographical references and index.
    ISBN 0-471-36009-0 (cloth)
    1. Business logistics.   I. Martha, Joseph.   II. Mercer Management
Consulting.   III. Title.

HD38.5 .B68 2000
658.7—dc21
                                                                99-088480

Printed in the United States of America.

10 9 8 7 6 5 4 3 2 1

Contents

Foreword   vii

Acknowledgments   xi

Introduction   xiii

Chapter 1   The Power of Value Nets   1

Chapter 2   Value Nets and Business Design   18

Chapter 3   Value Proposition: Crafting the Offer   34

Chapter 4   Scope: Deciding Where and How   74
            to Play

Chapter 5   Profit Capture: Casting the Net   117

Chapter 6   Strategic Control: Staying   157
            in the Game

Chapter 7   Design for Execution: Realizing   184
            the Net

Chapter 8   Lessons from the Innovators   225

Appendix   Value Net Self-Diagnostic   245

Index   259

Foreword

Customer expectations are exploding. Today, just about everyone wants customized products, and they want them right away and bundled with convenient services. Most Internet "e-tailers" understand this and promise convenient access to their products. But as web shoppers have discovered, the actual delivery experience often fails to measure up, destroying customer equity in the process. Meanwhile, many traditional manufacturers and retailers have yet to "get it" with regard to customer desires for superior service and tailored goods.

Yet there is an alternative to the traditional, unhappy mismatch of customer needs and supplier performance. Customers are gaining the ability to describe exactly what they want, and producers can deliver the desired product without compromise or delay. The catalyst for this shift is the *choiceboard,* an interactive tool that allows customers to design their own products by choosing from a set of components and service options. Customers' choices send signals to the supplier that set in motion the wheels of sourcing, assembly, and delivery.

This book is a practical guide to delivering exceptional convenience, reliability, speed, and customization. It is about the critical challenge that every business now faces: how to create an operations network that meets these new customer needs. This seamless web of customer choice and fulfillment capability is fast enough and flexible enough to respond to the rhythms of the market, and it adds service value beyond pure cost efficiency. The book's advice is aimed at young dot-coms and traditional businesses alike. Authors David Bovet and Joseph Martha have studied and worked with companies in many industries around the world that have succeeded in this challenge. This book describes what they have learned and presents it in a way that is readily applicable to any business.

Value Nets introduces an entirely new class of business designs—designs that deliver new and unique levels of service and personalized products to customers. Value nets integrate the essential front-end understanding of customer needs with the crucial back end that precisely delivers on the front-end promise. Value nets are digital, collaborative, agile powerhouses that unlock hidden profits for shareholders. They begin by capturing what is important to different customers and work back to physical production and distribution processes enabled by unifying information flow design.

Value Nets is a logical extension to the research published in a series of books that focus on value growth through innovative business design. That research began with *Value Migration* (1996), in which we revealed the flow of market value from obsolete business designs to new, more customer-relevant ways of doing business. The moral of that book was that business leaders must reverse the value chain to focus on customers and to stay ahead of the curve—by anticipating changing customer requirements, competitor moves, and fundamental shifts in industry economics. We extended our value migration thinking in two subsequent volumes, *The Profit Zone* (1998) and *Profit Patterns* (1999). These developed a business design methodology and identified a set of profitable business design patterns. Both books challenged executives to adopt a rigorous new approach to strategic thinking—one directly aimed at anticipating new customer needs and inventing ways to serve them profitably.

Value Nets takes Mercer Management Consulting's approach to business design to the next logical level, showing which design characteristics, both strategic and operational, distinguish tomorrow's winners. It applies business design methodology to the practical world of manufacturing, distribution, and retailing. And it redefines the challenges and opportunities in each of these activities in light of the e-commerce revolution. If you are looking for practical advice on using customer-based fulfillment models to drive company performance to previously unattainable levels, you will find it here.

Bovet and Martha provide readers with powerful, fresh examples of how executives can create value through value net designs: Mexican cement producer Cemex, furniture maker Miller SQA, Spanish fashion house Zara, automobile insurer Progressive, Internet grocer Streamline .com, telecommunications equipment maker Cisco Systems, and many more. Their stories bring to life the design decisions that have created a new breed of successful enterprises, and they illustrate (using a clear, implementable framework) how winning designs are crafted from elements available to all. Moreover, they present the dramatic results achieved by these innovative players.

Value Nets is a compelling read for any executive who hopes to realize the dream of customer satisfaction *and* profitable growth. It challenges and appeals to the strategic thinker and the pragmatic operations manager alike. It uniquely integrates a powerful business design framework with fresh operating models to create a virtual how-to guide for delivering service-differentiated value to customers and shareholders. Best of all, it captures the creativity of today's leading business models and provides a path that others can follow.

Adrian Slywotzky
Mercer Management Consulting

Acknowledgments

This book has truly been a team effort, and we extend our sincere gratitude to all who participated. The first and foremost of these are the many individuals at leading-edge companies who gave generously of their experience and insights. The stories told here flow from the innovative businesspeople who have lived them; those stories constitute the real core of this book.

We would also like to acknowledge the contributions of our Mercer Management Consulting partners Adrian Slywotzky and David Morrison. The business design framework they developed is widely applied in this work. We also benefited from the intellectual engagement of our book steering committee, which was led by David Morrison and included Pat Pollino, Les Artman, and Paul Katz.

Mercer partners around the world contributed client experiences, valuable perspectives, and thoughtful feedback. We wish especially to thank Peter Baumgartner's Manufacturing team, Hugh Randall's Transportation team, and our MercerDigital colleagues. Individual partners who devoted their time and talents to conducting interviews for the book include Kirk Kramer in Hong Kong, Ambrosio Arizu in Madrid, Andros Payne in Zurich, Les Artman in Cleveland, Vasco Fernandes and Jack Dougan in Washington, Bob Martin and Chris Lange in San Francisco, and Eric Vratimos in Chicago.

Our deep thanks go to our research and analysis team, without whom this book would not have been possible. Skillfully led by Kamenna Rindova, with key contributions by Christoph Knoess and Kimberly Mills, the team consisted of Taisir Anbar, Denise Auclair, Terry Cauthorn, Keanne Henry, Alex Reichert, and Kathryn Yung. Therese Lapitino provided valuable administrative support.

Dick Luecke of Salem, Massachusetts, also played a critical role in the book-building process. Thanks as well to Jeanne Glasser and the editorial staff of John Wiley & Sons.

Last but never least, we would like to thank our families for their steady and loving support during this extended effort.

David Bovet and Joseph Martha
Mercer Management Consulting

Introduction

If your company is like most, substantial profits are locked away where you'd least expect to find them—in those activities commonly called the *supply chain*. Whether yours is a young dot-com company or a seasoned incumbent, enormous new value can be found and unlocked in the operating end of the business: handling orders, sourcing components, building products, and getting them to customers.

This book will introduce you to a new form of digital business design built around superb supply chain performance. The old supply chain got the job done but did not provide the basis for true marketplace differentiation. The new design can set you apart by making your company fast, reliable, and highly flexible.

The new design delivers service and customized products to customers in ways that delight them and keep them coming back for more. It begins with customer needs and seamlessly links back to a carefully designed fulfillment engine. It draws many of its capabilities from collaboration across a network of providers. It is agile and scalable, accommodating short-term fluctuations and long-term growth. It produces speed—both in bringing new products to market and in delivering orders to end customers. And it uses digital technology to create new information flows that span layers of production and distribution, thus eliminating mountains of aging inventory.

We call this new business design a *value net*. Value net companies are succeeding in many industries, and the model will migrate to many more soon. Perhaps yours.

Companies that implement value net design are often the best in their industries. Yet only a few progressive CEOs or senior executives understand how these new designs create shareholder value. A value net operates at the speed needed to satisfy real customer demand. It reliably and precisely delivers on promises made to customers. And it has the agility to change as customer priorities change. As speed, reliability, convenience, and customization become increasingly important to customers across industries, we believe that a growing number of CEOs and senior executives will realize how this new business design can please both customers and shareholders.

Value net design combines both strategic thinking and recent advances in supply chain management. In this sense it bridges the gap between two very distinct cultures: the executive culture, which speaks the language of strategy and business reinvention, and the operational world of procurement, manufacturing, and logistics. The chasm between these cultures is seldom crossed—which is why so many profits remain hidden. It is our hope that the CEOs, corporate planners, and operating executives who read this book will learn a new and common language that will help them treat business design and the supply chain in a unified and strategic way.

The stories are the best part of this book. We searched long and hard for powerful examples of innovating companies that have adopted value net design. Everyone has heard of Dell Computer's ability to custom-build personal computers through a virtual network of suppliers and deliver them to customers' doorsteps in a few days, all with little inventory and a negative cash conversion cycle. But we have found other examples that are equally compelling and that illustrate a broad range of value net designs.

Our primary research sought the best examples of supply chain innovation in the Americas, Europe, and Asia, and we interviewed over 30 companies (Figure I.1). We have presented many of these as full-length or abbreviated case studies. Though not every one of these companies is a

Company	Industry	Company	Industry
AirLiance Materials	Aircraft maintenance	Keystone Fulfillment	E-commerce
Apple Computer	Computer	Li & Fung	Clothing, toys
Becton Dickinson	Medical equipment	Miller SQA	Office furniture
Biogen	Biotechnology	Nike	Footwear
Cat Logistics	Logistics	OrderTrust	E-commerce
Celarix	E-commerce	Philips Components	Electronics
Cemex	Cement	Progressive Insurance	Auto insurance
CIBA Vision	Contact lenses	SOHO Inc.	Office furniture
Cisco Systems	Telecommunications equipment	Streamline.com	Home delivery
Daimler-Chrysler	Automotive	Sun Microsystems	Computer
Español.com	E-commerce	The Limited	Clothing
Fingerhut	E-commerce	Toyota	Automotive
FooFoo.com	E-commerce	UPS	Logistics
Ford	Automotive	Volkswagen	Automotive
Gateway	Computer	Weyerhaeuser	Forest products
Hewlett-Packard	Computer	W.W. Grainger, Inc.	Maintenance supplies
IBM	Computer	Zara	Clothing
Intel	Computer		

Figure I.1 Primary research database.

complete value net, each offers a valuable lesson and demonstrates opportunities for profitable differentiation using value net design. Readers are invited to learn more about these firms on our web site, www.ValueNets.com, which also includes an online version of our self-diagnostic tool.

Our Mercer colleagues set the stage for business design thinking in a series of recent books: *Grow to Be Great, Value Migration, The Profit Zone,* and *Profit Patterns.*[1] We owe an enormous debt to their work. We have taken their conceptual platform and combined it with our field research to show how modern value net capabilities can unlock hidden profits by aligning operations with customer needs for speed, reliability, and convenience.

This book is organized into eight chapters. Chapter 1 provides an extensive definition of a value net and discusses its key characteristics. It features an example of a company that has achieved breakthrough results by adopting a value net design, and it illustrates the outstanding results that value net innovators have produced for shareholders.

Chapter 2 explains the conditions that make business redesign so necessary today: escalating customer demands for service, the rise of digital technology, new competitive pressures, and globalization. It then supplies the framework we use for business design.

Chapters 3 through 7 are the core of the book, explaining why and how value nets are created. Each chapter covers one of the five elements of business design: (1) value proposition, (2) scope, (3) profit capture, (4) strategic control, and (5) execution. We include case studies and examples of companies that have built (or are in the process of building) value nets. You'll see how this new business design has helped them achieve superior profitability and customer satisfaction.

Chapter 8 draws out key lessons from the innovative companies presented in the preceding chapters. An appendix provides a self-diagnostic tool designed to help executives think through the applicability of value net concepts to their own companies.

■ NOTE

1. See Dwight L. Gertz and João P.A. Baptista, *Grow to Be Great* (New York: The Free Press, 1995); Adrian J. Slywotzky, *Value Migration* (Boston, MA: Harvard Business School Publishing, 1996); Adrian J. Slywotzky and David J. Morrison, *The Profit Zone* (New York: Times Books, 1998); and Adrian J. Slywotzky, David J. Morrison, Ted Moser, Kevin A. Mundt, and James A. Quella, *Profit Patterns* (New York: Times Books, 1999).

Chapter

The Power of Value Nets

A new business model is emerging. If you've ordered a computer over the Internet, you've probably come into contact with this model without quite realizing what it was. As a businessperson, you may be bumping against it in the course of day-to-day competition. This model links increasingly stringent customer requirements to flexible and cost-effective manufacturing. It uses digital information to move products rapidly, bypassing costly distribution layers. It connects providers who work in concert to deliver tailored solutions. It elevates operational design to the strategic level. It adapts to constant change. We call this new model a *value net*.

Firms like Cisco Systems, Gateway, furniture-maker Miller SQA, home delivery innovator Streamline.com, and others are in the vanguard of creating value nets. These companies allow customers to configure their own orders, then build and deliver them to the customers' doorsteps in a matter of days. No hassles. No mistakes. No excuses. And they are beating competitors who cannot do the same.

Value nets are a quiet revolution—but savvy executives are starting to pay attention. The Internet and e-commerce provide a special impetus to value net business designs. As customers gain experience with this type of commerce, they begin to ask other, more traditional companies questions like these:

> "Why can't I buy an automobile the way I buy a Gateway computer?"
> "Why does it take two months or more to design and deliver furniture for our new office?"
> "Why can't my supplier tell me when the material will arrive at our receiving dock?"
> "Why do I have to deal with four suppliers to solve a single business problem?"

Few traditional manufacturers or service providers can answer these questions or provide better solutions. Even creative new dot-com companies that have developed slick front ends often lack back ends capable of consistently delivering high-level service. Can you meet tomorrow's customer needs? If not, the door of opportunity is open to others.

■ VALUE NET DEFINED

A *value net* is a business design that uses digital supply chain concepts to achieve both superior customer satisfaction and company profitability. It is a fast, flexible system that is aligned with and driven by new customer choice mechanisms.

A value net is not what the term *supply chain* conjures up. It is no longer just about supply—it's about creating *value* for customers, the company, and its suppliers. Nor is it a sequential, rigid chain. Instead, it is a dynamic, high-performance network of customer/supplier partnerships and information flows. The traditional supply chain manufactures products and pushes them through distribution channels in the hope that someone will buy them.[1] In contrast, a value net begins with customers, allows them to self-design products, and builds to satisfy actual demand. Although the idea of demand-pull systems is scarcely recent, the disappointing reality is that most companies still maintain heavily push-driven and sequential supply chains.

The old supply chain is tactical, and its primary mission is cost efficiency with "acceptable" service. It works hard to optimize this goal within a variety of constraints. It is built on conventional (and often antagonistic) supplier–purchasing agent relationships. Most senior executives rightly view it as a back-office activity, the concern of specialized managers. A value net, on the other hand, is strategic. It seeks solutions beyond the old constraints. It is a new form of business design that leverages operations and customer choice to drive strategic advantage. It merits a place in the boardroom.

A traditional supply chain is designed to meet customer demand with a fixed product line, relatively undifferentiated, one-size-fits-all output, and average service for average customers. A value net views every customer as unique. It allows customers to choose the product/service attributes they value most. Manufacturing, delivery, and associated services are differentiated to meet the needs of each customer segment—and to do so profitably.

In a traditional business design, materials flow slowly and sequentially down the supply chain (Figure 1.1). Information moves, often erratically, back up the chain. Time delays and multiple handoffs are endemic. As a result, supply and demand rarely match. Inventories pile up all along the chain as buffers against supply failures and

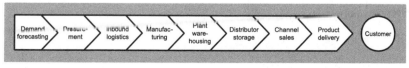

Figure 1.1 Traditional supply chain.

demand forecasts that are rarely accurate. Working capital burdens the balance sheet, and inventory carrying costs eat into profits. Salespeople are forever apologizing for how long it takes to fill an order.

In contrast, a value net forms itself around its *customers,* who are at the center (Figure 1.2). It captures their real choices in real time and transmits them digitally to other net participants. Pathways for information and material flows are aligned with the service needs and priorities of distinct customer segments. The customer-provider relationship is symbiotic, interactive, and value enhancing.

The *company* (or business unit) creating the value net is the inner concentric circle surrounding the customer. It controls the customer touch points by accessing customer information, nurturing the relationship, and managing satisfaction through digitally integrated service and support. At the same time, it manages its network of providers to ensure rapid and cost-efficient fulfillment.

The outer circle of the value net in Figure 1.2 represents the constellation of *providers* that perform some or all of the

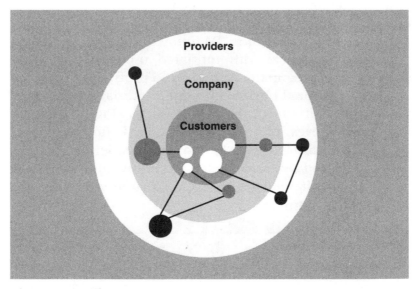

Figure 1.2 Value net.

sourcing, assembly, and delivery activities. They may be connected directly to customer order information, and they may furnish products and services directly to customers, thus bypassing traditional layers in the value chain.

Two very different games, croquet and soccer, can be used as metaphors for the differences between traditional supply chain operations and value nets. In the game of croquet, each player acts alone, planning his or her moves and focusing on accurate execution. Rapid movements are few. Players take turns. The ball progresses sequentially from hoop to hoop. In soccer (football), on the other hand, team play is foremost. Each team moves forward in concert, passing the ball quickly from player to player. Motion is rapid and continuous. Signals fly between teammates. The ball is kicked from the left wing to the striker, who shoots and scores.

The differences in the two games are very apparent. Soccer is based on collaboration and speed. It has individual heroes, but the real value is bound up in the team.

■ FIVE CHARACTERISTICS OF A VALUE NET

The following five characteristics distinguish a value net business and give it the edge over a traditional business design relying on supply chain thinking (Figure 1.3):

➤ *Customer-aligned.* Customer choices trigger sourcing, building, and delivery activities in the net. Distinct customer segments receive customized solutions with customized service "wraps." The customer commands the value net; he or she is not a passive recipient of supply chain output.

➤ *Collaborative and systemic.* Companies engage suppliers, customers, and even competitors in a unique network of value-creating relationships. Each activity is assigned to the partner best able to perform it.

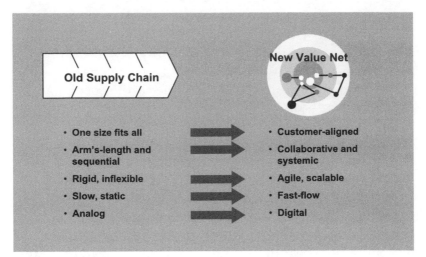

Figure 1.3 Key business design differences.

Significant portions of operational activities are delegated to specialist providers, and the entire network delivers flawless results thanks to collaborative, systemwide communication and information management.

➤ *Agile and scalable.* Responsiveness to changes in demand, new product launches, rapid growth, or redesign of the supplier network are all assured through flexible production, distribution, and information flow design. Constraints imposed by bricks and mortar are reduced or eliminated. Working capital shrinks. Process time and steps are collapsed, sometimes eliminating entire echelons of the traditional supply chain. Everything in the value net, physical or virtual, is scalable.

➤ *Fast flow.* Order-to-delivery cycles are fast and compressed. Rapid delivery goes hand in hand with reliable and convenient delivery. That means on-time, complete orders delivered to the customer's plant, office, or home. Time is measured in hours or days, not weeks or months. At the same time, it means drastically lower inventories for the company.

➤ *Digital.* E-commerce is a key enabler. But beyond the Internet, it is the information flow design and its intelligent use that lie at the heart of the value net. New digital information pathways link and coordinate the activities of the company, its customers, and its providers. Rule-based, event-driven tools take over many operational decisions. Distilled real-time analysis enables rapid executive decision making.

Together, these five characteristics constitute a competitively differentiated business design. Add a healthy dose of vision and leadership, a high-velocity organization, and zealous attention to flawless execution, and you have a powerful engine for generating shareholder value.

To be sure, building a value net is not a simple matter. For both established businesses and young dot-coms, success requires real commitment and involves substantial cost and effort. For Internet start-ups, the challenge lies in integrating effective and differentiated fulfillment capabilities with a powerful customer interface. Established companies need to learn new ways of relating to customers and suppliers, to redesign internal processes, and to digitize them as well. The work of some functions may have to be eliminated or outsourced. Changes like these are difficult in large, mature organizations.

■ MILLER SQA AS VALUE NET

Aware of these challenges, office-furniture-maker Herman Miller created a new unit, Miller SQA, that provides an excellent example of value net design. Like its parent, Miller SQA makes office furniture, but with a twist. Its product and the entire furniture-buying experience are designed to be "simple, quick, and affordable" (hence SQA).

➤ SQA's entire manufacturing and delivery system is *customer-aligned* with the demands of specific purchasers: small businesses and others who value speed and simplicity more than unlimited choice. SQA also customizes the product for each buyer through a configure-to-order digital interface.

➤ *Collaborative* arrangements with suppliers allow Miller SQA to hold minimal inventory (one to two days' worth in mid-1999), and supplier hubs located near SQA's manufacturing facility deliver components on a just-in-time basis. Activities occur in parallel rather than in sequence. As orders arrive, relevant information is transmitted to suppliers four times a day so that parts replenishment, order assembly, and logistics arrangements can begin almost simultaneously.

➤ Supply and manufacturing processes are geared to minimize handling and to maximize *speed*. Order-to-delivery time can take as little as two days, compared with the industry norm of two months.

➤ *Digital* information flows—between customers, SQA, and suppliers—orchestrate seamless production and allow the company to make firm delivery commitments at the time of order.

➤ SQA has kept its product line simple, ensuring that it is *agile* in matching customer demand.

The clarity of Miller SQA's vision, the value net design just described, and its exemplary execution have been hugely successful. Orders are being shipped 99.6 percent on time and complete. Profitability is excellent, and sales are growing at 25 percent a year.

SQA is not alone. Our interviews with more than 30 companies confirm that the value net concept is spreading. Some of the best examples we see are new, often Internet-based, companies that enjoy the luxury of creating their business designs on a clean slate. Others, like

SQA, introduce the new concepts through a single division of a large corporation. But even entire enterprises with established supply chains can adopt a value net design to good effect. Consider the case of Apple Computer.

■ APPLE COMPUTER GETS IT RIGHT

During the mid-1990s, Apple was selling lots of products but losing money hand over fist—nearly $1.9 billion in the period from 1996 to 1997. Its share price had dropped into the cellar, and some industry analysts were already writing its obituary as a player in the personal computing industry.

A look behind the gloom and doom reveals a key cause of the computer company's woes. Despite its state-of-the-art products and legions of die-hard followers, Apple's operations were in shambles. It had finished 1996 with close to $700 million in inventory, and technological obsolescence was making the value of that inventory melt like ice cream on a hot day! Inventory was turning over at an anemic 13 times per year. By comparison, Dell's inventory was turning over at a rate of 41 times a year.

"Apple's problem," observed one analyst, "was a supply chain management problem."[2] And one source of that problem was consistently poor demand forecasting. The company was, in fact, notorious for being out of stock on hot new products and overloaded with everything else. Being out of stock on hot items, particularly during key selling seasons, frustrated Apple's distributors and drove potential customers into the arms of its competitors, who had plenty of new machines at lower prices.

Being overloaded with inventory wreaked havoc on Apple's bottom line as obsolete components and finished goods were dumped at big discounts. "Huge Mac Blowout!" was a recurring theme with Apple's direct mail distributors. As new, faster Macintoshes were introduced, prices on mountains of older finished goods inventory had to be slashed to the bone, producing profitless sales.

Apple's fortunes began to brighten in 1997 when Steve Jobs returned to lead the company he had co-founded decades earlier. They brightened again when the company launched its highly successful iMac family in the rapidly growing low end of the market. By 1999, Apple had pulled itself out of its death spiral, and the business press was busy writing about the company's sudden new vitality.

Jobs and iMac did wonders for Apple, but a supply chain makeover deserves much of the credit for its new lease on life. One of Jobs's key moves was to lure Tim Cook away from Compaq and assemble a team of executives to grapple with Apple's supply chain problems. "We set out to beat Dell," recalls Cook. "We didn't want to deliver products like theirs—we have our own unique design, look, and feel—but we did want to emulate them in operations."[3]

Jobs, Cook, and the rest of the team rolled up their sleeves and reinvented Apple's supply chain. Tim Cook recalls those exciting times: "There was no one thing. It was a series of things." Cook stresses the following elements:

➤ Jobs streamlined the product plan from more than 15 models to four basic products. "This greatly reduced the number of parts. We were able to focus more on customizing a few products rather than carry lots of inventory for lots of products. This was the umbrella move that set the stage."

➤ Many warehouses and all country distribution centers of the company were closed. "Warehouses tend to collect product. . . . We started to deliver directly from manufacturing to the customer, be it the channel or the end user."

➤ An enterprise resource planning tool (from SAP) was installed.

➤ Apple launched an Internet strategy to let customers configure to order. "We began to take orders directly from educational institutions and consumers over the Internet, via the Apple Store (www.apple.com), and configured products directly for them."

➤ The number of suppliers was reduced dramatically to a small core set.

➤ Apple and its suppliers began to work together in very different ways. "We began to pass very frequent forecasts to them. And we asked them to supply us from a nearby hub, forming a very focused supplier network."

➤ The company began to outsource manufacturing. "We were still building motherboards in 1998. We looked around and saw that many suppliers were building good motherboards. So we sold off the business."

➤ The existing global supply chain was reexamined. "Our laptops were built in Cork, Ireland. Components manufactured in Asia were being shipped to Ireland for assembly, and then a significant portion of finished product was shipped back to Asia. So we began to assemble PowerBooks in Asia."

These reforms were far-reaching, and their effects were quickly felt. By September 1998, within a year after Cook's hiring, inventory had been reduced 82 percent from its previous high. Inventory collapsed from 27 days in 1996 to just 6 days—lower than Dell's by a day at the time! By September 1999, inventory held by Apple had shrunk to less than two days, including raw materials, work in progress, and finished goods. "I consider any internal inventory to be a defect," Cook told a reporter.[4] When we spoke with Cook in September 1999, he was able to claim, "No one else is flipping inventory like we are. . . . Our supply chain is now fundamentally different. It's responsive, and it has a lot less cost in it."

Apple's aim had been to please customers and reduce costs by making the company operationally faster and more responsive to the rapid technical and market changes that roiled the personal computer industry. And it succeeded. By September 1999, Apple was able to report an eighth consecutive profitable quarter, breaking its previous two-year string of losses (Figure 1.4). The hemorrhaging had been stanched. And its stock price had rocketed to over $100 (end of December 1999) from $13 just two years earlier.

In effect, Apple had built a value net. Following a radical course of reform, Apple strategically reconfigured its entire supply chain—reducing the number of suppliers and distributors, better integrating their activities, and developing rapid linkages between them, Apple, and its customers. These feats were painfully won—the company spent over $500 million in restructuring costs, and many long-term employees had to be furloughed. And it wasn't a one-shot deal. "It is a journey," says Cook. "It wasn't done overnight. And it isn't finished." But the company has been brought back from the brink.

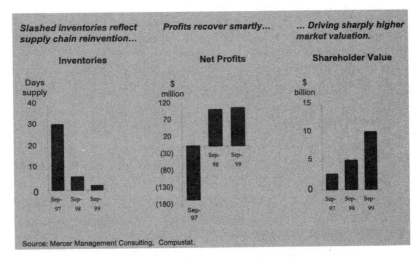

Figure 1.4 Apple's reinvention as a value net.

■ VALUE CREATION

Value creation success stories like Apple's are emerging among both start-ups and established companies. The value net concept is touching companies in many industries, as we'll see through the cases and examples provided in subsequent chapters. In each instance, value nets have produced more than mere cost savings. They have generated customer satisfaction and altered the terms of competition, causing rivals to change or lose out. Many value net designs are so new that their full effects on profits and shareholder value have not yet been felt. Others have already made dramatic contributions.

These new designs add value in a variety of ways. Benefits derived from faster, nimbler operations include greater profits, better capital efficiency, and shareholder value growth. The innovators you will meet throughout this book illustrate the power of value nets. These companies include the following:

➤ Zara, a Spanish apparel manufacturer and retailer, zips fashion clothing from sketch to stores in just 10 to 15 days.

➤ Biogen, a young biotech firm, brought its new multiple sclerosis drug to market in record time with minimal fixed assets, capturing a profitable leadership position.

➤ Cemex, a Mexican cement company, achieves net cash flow of 31 percent of sales, 10 percentage points higher than major rivals, and profitability 50 percent higher than top competitors with its digitally managed, fast, reliable delivery.

➤ Weyerhaeuser's door-building operation increased on-time and complete deliveries from the 60 percent level to 97 percent and returned the plant to profitability.

➤ AirLiance Materials, a multi-airline parts management venture, saves both its partners and its competitors money by acquiring replacement parts cost-effectively and eliminating duplicate inventories, potentially industrywide.

➤ OrderTrust, an order-processing network for e-tailers, lets merchants focus on their web sites and merchandising while ensuring dependable and customer-pleasing fulfillment of massive order volumes through digital connectivity.

Companies that back compelling customer solutions with powerful value nets are winning in the marketplace. Consider the shareholder value growth of exemplary value net players versus that of their respective industries (see Figure 1.5). While many factors influence corporate performance and stock market valuations, we believe that value net design has a great deal to do with the rising fortunes of these companies.

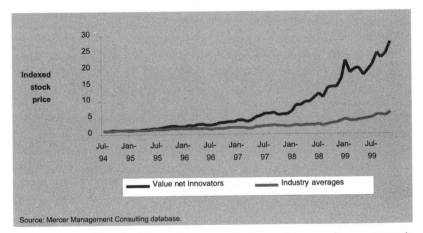

Source: Mercer Management Consulting database.

Figure 1.5 Shareholder value growth for value net innovators.*
*Value net innovators include (beginning in): Apple (7/97), Biogen (5/96), Cisco (11/94), Dell (11/94), Gateway (11/94), Grainger (11/94), Li & Fung (11/94), Sun (11/94).

■ HOW DOES A VALUE NET APPLY TO YOUR BUSINESS?

Should you begin thinking about a value net design for your company—or for one of its units? What are the warning signs of impending change? Look for these indicators and answer the tough questions they raise:

➤ *Your business isn't meeting customer demands for speed, reliability, and convenience.* A good product is no longer sufficient for success. Good products are merely your admission ticket to the game. Today's customers want rapid fulfillment, on-time delivery, and convenience in doing business with you. And they won't settle for less. How can you leapfrog current service standards in your industry to differentiate your offering?

➤ *Your customers are defecting.* There is no such thing as an average customer, yet most companies serve a wide range of customers through a single set of production and distribution processes. The most profitable customers, however, want their offerings customized and will shift their spending to companies designed to meet their requirements. Are your most profitable customers being plucked away by rivals?

➤ *You worry about being "Amazoned!"* The tentacles of e-commerce are reaching into more and more industries, shaking the grip of traditional participants. Established players are scrambling to meet the Internet challenge, and new entrants are racing to develop the means of delivering on their promises. Do you view e-commerce technology as an opportunity or a threat?

➤ *Profits are migrating elsewhere.* Profits migrate from outmoded business designs toward those that are better designed to satisfy customer priorities.[5] This is true in all industries. And the Internet is intensifying the competitive challenges for all players—incumbents and dot-coms—hence the need for companies to renew their business designs. Are your revenues per customer stagnating? Are profits moving away from your business to others with more compelling value propositions and superior execution and delivery?

➤ *You equate "customer-centric" with a good marketing department.* Marketing and strategic planning staff members often overlook the value of a superb service wrap and don't understand how it can be provided. They aren't looking to operational capabilities for customer-pleasing solutions. Did you design your supply chain *after* the product and service mix decisions were made? If so, don't expect high marks from customers.

➤ *Your managers view suppliers as enemies.* Traditional supplier relationships are often adversarial. Beating up suppliers, or playing one off against another, can drive down purchasing costs and enforce deadlines in the short run, but in the long run, supplier distrust limits your ability to develop powerful new products and services. Could collaborative initiatives with your suppliers open up new opportunities for you?

➤ *Senior executives view the supply chain as an operational issue.* A purely functional perspective limits the potential of supply chain concepts to reshape the business. Does your team view the supply chain as the domain of purchasing and logistics specialists? Are your supply chain expectations limited to cost cutting and fire fighting?

If any of these indicators apply to you and your company, it's time to think about a business design change. Your current supply chain may have made you vulnerable, and it certainly won't help you in a faster-paced future. Reshaping your business as a value net will open the door to strategic opportunities—and you don't have to be an e-commerce start-up to do it.

■ NOTES

1. The *supply chain* is the set of inter- and intracompany processes that produce and deliver goods and services to customers. It includes activities such as materials sourcing, production scheduling, and the physical distribution system, backed up by the necessary information flows. Procurement, manufacturing, inventory management, warehousing, and transportation are typically considered part of the supply chain organization. Marketing, sales, finance, and strategic planning are not. Product development, demand forecasting, order entry, channel management, customer service, and accounts payable and receivable lie in a gray area; in theory, they are part of the supply chain process, but they are seldom included within the supply chain organization.
2. Tom Grace, senior manufacturing analyst for AMR Research, Inc., quoted by Doug Bartholomew, "What's the Reason for Apple's Recovery," *Industry Week,* March 15, 1999, 36.
3. Tim Cook. Interview with author, September 29, 1999.
4. Bartholomew, "Apple's Recovery," op. cit., 36.
5. Adrian Slywotzky, *Value Migration* (Boston: Harvard Business School Publishing, 1996), 3–4.

Chapter

Value Nets
and Business Design

The value net concept couldn't be more timely. The world is changing faster than ever, creating major opportunities and challenging companies to maintain their relevance. Change requires businesses to adapt and to reinvent themselves. And the greater the external change, the greater the reinvention required.

In this chapter, we will examine how innovators are responding to dramatic market changes through smart value net design.

■ CHANGE DRIVERS

To understand why many companies are ripe for business reinvention, consider the factors that are driving change in today's world of commerce: (1) more demanding customers, (2) the Internet and digital technology, (3) growing competitive pressures, and (4) globalization.

➤ More Demanding Customers

Consumers and business customers today want it all. They want speed, service, and customization, all at a low price.

People want things sooner, and they want absolute commitments to delivery timetables. Overnight and even instant availability is becoming the norm for a growing spectrum of goods and services. Books, clothing, and built-to-order personal computers arrive on consumers' doorsteps in just a few days. Business-to-business customers expect the same or better treatment. Since 1978, when FedEx shipped its first overnight package, the express package industry has exploded, handling over 1.5 *billion* shipments per year. Time-sensitive deliveries in the United States grew three times faster than the economy as a whole from 1991 to 1998. And their reliability has increased as well—UPS, for example, achieved over 99 percent on-time reliability in its next-day air service in 1998.[1] These advances are raising buyer expectations across all product and service categories.

People are also demanding a richer mix of services tailored to their individual needs. In the world's wealthiest economies, where leisure time is scarce, customers want— and will pay for—timesaving convenience, customized delivery, installation support, ongoing maintenance, and ultimate disposal (e.g., removal, recycling, or scrapping) of a wide range of products. For example, many U.S. consumers are doing business with companies that provide direct "home replenishment." Busy, affluent households are attracted by the speed and convenience promised by these vendors. The statistics on consumer-direct commerce, in fact, are striking. During the second half of the 1990s, direct sales (catalog, phone, TV, and Internet sales) grew at an annual rate of 30 percent, compared to 11 percent for the retail industry overall. Convenient direct-to-consumer sales are expected to grow by an average of 81 percent a year through the year 2004.[2]

Customers want these services provided in seamless fashion. While each supplier specializes in its own core activities, the entire offering—selection, design, building, delivery, installation, and maintenance—must be fully integrated. Customers want to deal with a single, trusted agent. A single phone call must result in quick satisfaction or problem resolution.

Growing family incomes in many markets around the globe have reached levels that cause customer priorities to shift from basic product functionality to convenient, service-intensive solutions. In the personal computer industry, where product customization is taking hold, companies that allow buyers to customize their purchases grew at 37 percent a year between 1994 and 1998 versus 11 percent for the traditional made-to-stock producers.

As these examples indicate, customers are becoming more demanding, particularly with respect to the service "wraps" that few companies can efficiently deliver. This has created opportunities for those willing and able to fill the void with high-performance fulfillment capabilities.

► Digital Technology

Digitization of the economy—the Internet, growing bandwidth capacity, skyrocketing computing power—is revolutionizing the way companies do business. And it's having positive effects. Federal Reserve Board chairman Alan Greenspan acknowledged as much when he declared: "Technology has driven significant advances in companies' operating capabilities, enabling them to better track product orders, supplies, deliveries, and other aspects of their businesses, which allows them to meet customers' needs more quickly and at lower cost."[3]

The Internet is the most visible manifestation of digitization and the catalyst for thousands of new businesses, many of which are in the process of creating value nets. These companies provide just about every type of product and service via the web—and their numbers continue to grow (Figure 2.1). Will e-commerce account for 10 to 20

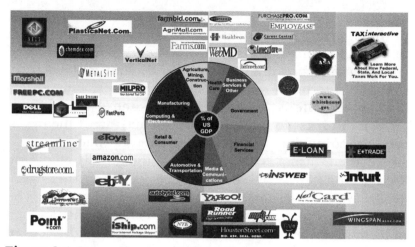

Figure 2.1 Internet companies in the new economy.

percent of retail sales 10 years from now, as some predict? Fully $100 billion in annual sales revenue could pass through this new channel by 2002 alone. And business-to-business e-commerce, already estimated at $30 to $50 billion, is projected to reach between $400 and $800 billion by 2002.[4]

Unfortunately, many Internet ventures have been more successful at designing slick web pages than at fulfilling their larger potentials, including profits. As a Levi's spokesman said, "We dumped a lot of money into the Internet. . . . It didn't pay out. . . . [I]t is very costly to run a truly world-class e-commerce business."[5] Second, speedy, accurate e-fulfillment is a chimera that eludes many Internet businesses. Stories of missed and late deliveries abound. A video game purchased as a Christmas gift arrives in August. A customer has to make five attempts to order a book over the Internet before succeeding. Even some of the biggest and best-known players continue to experiment. Amazon's 1999 investment in HomeGrocer.com, an Internet home delivery venture, reflects its interest in refining its approach to effective e-fulfillment. The dot-coms have unwittingly highlighted the need for value net capabilities.

Whole industries are being transformed by the power of the Internet. The Internet is not just about connecting and communicating. It can rewrite the rules. Postage stamps and recorded music can now be delivered instantly over the Internet. Companies like Chemdex.com (an exchange for life sciences supplies) and FastParts.com (which brokers computer components) are fundamentally changing the ways customers fill their needs.

Yet the Internet is just one side of the rapidly changing digital landscape. Digital technology is impacting every aspect of business, creating opportunities for growth. The challenge for managers and strategists is no longer a lack of technology, but how best to harness digital advances to make profitable, event-driven decisions. For example,

➤ Software can now connect customer orders directly to shop floor activities.

➤ Algorithms from vendors such as i2 Technologies or Manugistics optimize production automatically.

➤ Advanced protocols, such as extensible markup language (XML), create cross-system compatibility, giving all players the advantages previously enjoyed only by large companies with EDI (electronic data interchange).

➤ Communications technology, such as the wireless global positioning system (GPS) used by Cemex, enables trucks to be dynamically dispatched and rerouted.

➤ Remote sensors, such as those used by Caterpillar to monitor heavy equipment performance, transmit critical data to trigger timely machine maintenance.

In short, the rise of e-commerce is dramatically affecting many aspects of business—and none more so than the traditional supply chain. The Internet has raised the bar for fast and reliable delivery. At the same time, new digital capabilities are enabling progressive firms to offer revolutionary levels of responsiveness and efficiency.

➤ Competitive Pressures

Competition is emerging from unexpected quarters. The near-universal availability of computer technology, skilled staff, and venture capital is making it possible for entrepreneurs to launch new ventures that very suddenly threaten established businesses. Stratospheric Internet stock prices give these entrepreneurs substantial war chests.

Venture capital investments in Internet-based companies are skyrocketing. They doubled in 1998 and doubled again in the first six months of 1999. By mid-1999, money was pouring into Internet start-ups at a rate of nearly $4 billion per quarter.[6] And the talent is following the money. Thirty percent of the 1998 graduating class of Harvard Business School, for example, took jobs with high-tech or venture capital firms, compared to only 12 percent just four years earlier.[7] These lower barriers to entry for newcomers place additional pressure on incumbents to find new ways to protect and lead their markets.

We also see that innovations in one industry are triggering rapid shifts in unrelated industries. Supply chain innovators like Dell Computer and Miller SQA are providing the inspiration (and the models) for new business designs across industries. Fast-declining price levels and constant obsolescence due to shrinking product life cycles provide the impetus for innovation. The digital technology, risk capital, and required supply base exist in many fields to bring these new business models to life in a very short period of time. Incumbents face the threat of being blindsided by unforeseen competitors.

➤ Globalization

The appearance of burgeoning new markets and supply sources in once-undeveloped corners of the world is the fourth factor driving the shift to value nets. Accessing these regions efficiently with traditional supply chains has been frustrating. Goods often seem to fall into a "black hole" somewhere between continents.

Recent economic development has transformed emerging markets into geographically dispersed pockets of modern business activity. Low-cost labor is located in one nation, state-of-the-art contract assembly plants in another, and a pool of technically specialized workers in yet another. A senior executive at The Limited explains, "Most apparel products have been in two or three countries by the time they are manufactured. It's rare to find everything in one place—the fabric, skills, and machinery."[8] A global operations manager needs to call on the best of these resources, regardless of their locations, and knit them into a fast and cost-effective network. Suppliers must be managed in ways that neutralize problems caused by distance, language, time zones, business practices, tariffs, and other impediments to the efficient flow of materials and information. They need to deliver as though they were right next door.

Business leaders are aware of the challenges of growing globalization. A 1998 survey of large company CEOs by the Foundation for the Malcolm Baldridge National Quality Award indicated that three of the top five issues for responding CEOs revolved around globalization (Figure 2.2).[9]

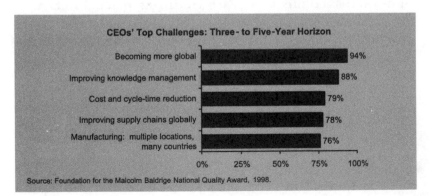

Figure 2.2 Globalization as a top CEO issue.

Clearly, CEOs are concerned about designing and operating global supply chains that can serve worldwide customers effectively.

Advances in information and communication technology, the Internet, lower costs for transportation, and the convenience of global communication are breaking through the barriers of physical distance. Speed, agility, and digital connectivity are making value net designs the favored structures for tapping into such far-flung global markets of customers and suppliers.

■ VALUE MIGRATION AND BUSINESS REDESIGN

The change drivers just described cause *value migration*®— that is, the flow of profits and value away from outmoded business designs toward others that are better designed to maximize utility for customers and profits for companies (Figure 2.3). For example, in the computer industry, value has shifted rapidly toward innovative, customer-direct, build-to-order manufacturers and away from traditional manufacturing and distribution models. Dell Computer and Gateway together benefited from this shift to the tune of $134

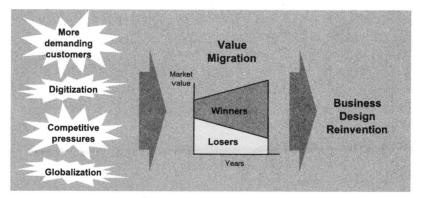

Figure 2.3 Value migration.

billion in added market value between 1990 and November 1999. During that time, more traditional computer manufacturers Digital Equipment and Compaq collectively created only $22 billion in market value. Value migrations like these illustrate the importance of timely business redesign.

To understand the elements that power successful business designs, Mercer Management Consulting conducted extensive research with the securities analysts who have so much to do with establishing market valuations. These analysts process hundreds, if not thousands, of pieces of information about a company's products and services, its internal operations, financial structure, competitive position, and so forth. But in the end, we found that they are overwhelmingly concerned with just three things:

1. The growth rate of profits
2. Capital efficiency
3. The ability to sustain profitable growth

Mercer used these factors to develop a framework that defines a value-creating business design.[10] This model, which is described in detail in *The Profit Zone,* has five elements (see Figure 2.4):

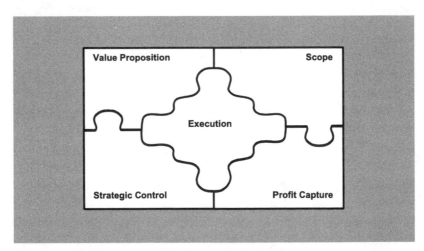

Figure 2.4 Elements of business design.

1. *Value proposition.* What the company will offer to potentially profitable customers.
2. *Scope.* Which activities need to be performed, and by whom (ownership, outsourcing, and partnering arrangements).
3. *Profit capture.* How the company aims to earn a compelling return on shareholder capital.
4. *Strategic control.* The ability to protect the profit stream over time through sustainable advantages.
5. *Execution.* The human capabilities and digital technology that, like a keystone, hold all the other elements together.

The first and third elements represent the company's ability to grow profitably. The second element represents the efficiency with which capital is employed. The last two elements determine a company's ability to sustain profitable growth over time.

Innovative strategic and operational thinking, applied to each of the five puzzle pieces of business design, constitutes a value net. Let's examine the meaning of each piece and how value net concepts drive business design.

➤ Value Proposition

How can a value net enhance or redefine the offer for each targeted customer segment?

The choice of customer segments to be pursued is a necessary starting point in developing a value proposition. Successful businesses choose their customers wisely, knowing that some are much more profitable to serve than others. The profitability of customer segments is based on both the products they purchase and the service features that go with those products. Cost to serve is an essential element in understanding segment profitability.

A value proposition is the utility a company provides through its products and services to the customers whom it chooses to serve. Value nets make it possible for companies to enhance their value propositions with important service attributes, such as fulfillment speed, precisely timed delivery, and convenience, among others. Fast and agile operating designs also allow companies to offer customization of the product/service at the segment or individual level and at a reasonable cost. Finally, well-tuned value net capabilities can respond to a broader spectrum of customer priorities.

Alignment of the value proposition with the needs of selected customer segments is a critical part of business design. Consider Streamline.com, a Boston-based home replenishment service. It targets a narrow customer segment of busy, well-heeled suburban families who value convenient ordering and delivery. Exact alignment of this value proposition with the right customer segment is so critical that the company turns away customers who do not fit its target profile. Streamline's service offering (scheduled weekly resupply of groceries, laundry services, film development, video rentals, and other items to customer homes) is enabled by an innovative fulfillment and delivery design. The close alignment of the value proposition and these customers' needs results in customer loyalty of over 90 percent.

Chapter 3 presents several value propositions uniquely enabled by innovative value net business designs.

➤ Scope

What are the essential activities in a value net? Which activities should a company perform internally, and which should it outsource to others? How can a value net leverage its partners and customers?

Traditionally, companies focused on product development and marketing to generate value. Supply chain operations were relegated to a tactical role and were not closely linked to the customer. A value net's notion of "essential activities" includes customer choice, production, and delivery, all broadly defined. In a value net, where customers are at the center, any activity that touches customers is a critical element of scope. Innovative companies create interactive choice mechanisms to capture real demand, as Gateway and Miller SQA have done. And they leverage the delivery experience to please the customer. Activities hidden from the customer's view, such as sourcing, manufacturing, and assembly, also take on a different character. The chief concern shifts away from high-volume, low-cost production. Instead, companies knit together combinations of capabilities (some internal, some external) that support each unique customer value proposition.

Many CEOs once believed—and some still do—that the vast majority of value-creating activities should be performed internally. This belief is being challenged in many industries—and rightfully so. In maturing industries, such as personal computers and automobiles, sophisticated suppliers can now handle parts of the value chain more reliably and flexibly, at lower cost, and with fewer assets. Value net companies in these industries leverage outside capabilities to their advantage.

Some companies are challenging traditional scope definitions by taking outsourcing to the extreme. E-tailers like FooFoo.com, a high-end virtual store for urban professionals, rely on other companies for most operating activities other than their web site management. These virtual merchants have created strong demand for an entire category of business services that assure physical fulfillment (e.g., Fingerhut's Business Services division and Hanover Direct's Keystone Fulfillment) and order processing (e.g., OrderTrust routes customer orders between 600 merchants, suppliers, and fulfillment houses). The same explosion of third-party services has occurred in the business-to-business world. Contract manufacturing, for example, has become extremely popular. In the PC industry, revenues for contract manufacturers Solectron, SCI Systems, Jabil Circuits, and Celestica have grown from a total of $4 billion in 1992 to $17 billion in 1998, creating $11 billion of shareholder value in the process. These business models are spreading to medical equipment manufacturing, garments, pharmaceuticals, and many other industries.

Chapter 4 explores the key activities of a value net, examines who can best perform them, and discusses the growing role of collaboration among networked parties.

➤ Profit Capture

How can a company enhance its ability to generate profits? Can returns be leveraged through higher asset efficiency?

A value net's unique contribution to superior profitability lies in its ability to increase revenues through either premium pricing or faster growth in a profitable market. For example, Mexican cement producer Cemex offers delivery reliability in an industry that is chronically unreliable. It meets its delivery commitments 98 percent of the time versus the 34 percent commonly achieved by its competitors. This superreliability allows Cemex to charge a premium in most markets, contributing to operating profit levels 50 percent higher than those of its key competitors.

Value nets also help companies minimize operating costs and raise asset efficiency. The ability of PC-maker Gateway to digitize operations and reach customers while bypassing the retail channel (and its required 10 to 12 percent margin) is just one example of how a value net can radically redefine the cost equation. On the asset side, value net design can support growth by substantially shrinking the fixed assets and working capital employed in the business.

Chapter 5 discusses how value nets raise revenues and cost/asset efficiency to capture profits.

➤ Strategic Control

How can a value net help a company sustain its competitive advantage and protect its profit stream over time?

Strategic control is the aspect of the business design that allows a company to protect its profit stream for as long as possible—until it is time to redesign. It is the hook that keeps customers loyal and competitors at bay. It is the acid test of true differentiation.

A design that offers truly innovative service (such as low-cost customization where none was available before, or next-day delivery in an industry where six weeks is the norm) gives a company first-mover advantage. A significant lead in value net innovation, much like a new product, can become a source of strategic differentiation. In fact, outstanding service levels can be harder to copy than product features, providing a longer-lasting advantage. Exceptional service can even lead to brand recognition, a familiar source of strategic control in the product-centric world. For example, Herman Miller's SQA unit has created a service-rich value net brand whose staying power is reflected in high margins and high customer retention.

Chapter 6 explores these and other value net–based sources of strategic control.

➤ Execution

What are the essential underpinnings for smooth execution of the value net design? What does it take to realize the potential performance of a value net?

None of the design elements described—the four corner pieces of the puzzle—benefit a company that cannot execute well. Good execution is the linchpin of business design.

The value net innovators we interviewed all stressed the importance of the right business culture in execution. The *right* culture, in their collective view, is characterized by visionary leadership, entrepreneurial teams, and clear goals. Remarkably, these innovators downplayed the importance of organizational structure.

Value net implementation draws heavily on information technology, which today delivers results not possible just a few years ago. The Internet, *intra*nets, *extra*nets, groupware, and resource planning software all facilitate rapid and effective decision making by multiple value net constituents. They imbue value nets with speed, agility, and opportunities for collaboration.

Chapter 7 treats in detail the unique execution aspects that make a value net successful.

■ HOW DOES BUSINESS DESIGN APPLY TO YOUR BUSINESS?

A value net business design is very different from one based on a traditional supply chain. A supply chain is an operational appendage to a company's business design; it simply makes and moves products. A value net, in contrast, *is* the business design.

Is your company ripe for a business redesign? Are the forces of change narrowing the incremental gains you can achieve from your current ways of doing business? What role does your supply chain currently play in enhancing the customer experience or improving your profitability? Could operations become the means to differentiating your company? Are you vulnerable to being roundly outmaneuvered by a competitor who adopts the new design first?

The next five chapters will examine each of the five elements of business design in detail and illuminate key points with case studies of successful value net companies.

■ NOTES

1. Don McMackin, UPS public relations manager. Private communication, November 15, 1999.
2. Valerie Seckler, "Direct Sales Predicted Rising to 6.25% in 2004—Report on At-Home Shopping," *Women's Wear Daily*, May 18, 1999, 2.

3. John Berry, "Greenspan Now a Technology Believer," *Washington Post*, May 7, 1999, 11.

4. Retail sales in 1998 were over $2.7 trillion (source: Bureau of the Census, www.census.gov/svsd/www/adseries.html). Sources of 2002 e-commerce: IDC/Link, 1998; *Resizing On-line Business Trade*, November 1998, Forrester Research; *Retail's Growth Spiral*, November 1998, Forrester Research; Web Week Electronic Commerce Trend Study, 1998.

5. Kevin McSpadden, former director of Levi's e-commerce and retail marketing, quoted by Bradley Johnson, "Levi's Goes Offline to Plug Web Stores," *Advertising Age*, June 14, 1999, 2. Levi's spokesperson quoted by Andrew Edgecliffe-Johnson, "Levi's to Shut Down Unaffordable Website," *Financial Times*, October 31, 1999, 1.

6. George Anders and Kara Swisher, "Venture Capitalists Focus on the Net in New Approach," *Wall Street Journal*, August 18, 1999, C1.

7. Betsy Morris, "MBAs Get .com Fever," *Fortune*, August 2, 1999, 62.

8. Nicholas LaHowchic. Interview with Les Artman (Mercer Management Consulting), July 20, 1999.

9. The Foundation for the Malcolm Baldrige National Quality Award commissioned Louis Harris & Associates to conduct a survey of a nationally representative cross section of CEOs of companies with revenues of $100 million or more. A sample of 308 respondents were interviewed by mail. Interviewing took place between February and April 1998.

10. For an extended discussion of business design, see Adrian Slywotzky, *Value Migration* (Boston: Harvard Business School Press, 1996), and Adrian Slywotzky and David Morrison, *The Profit Zone* (New York: Times Books, 1998).

Chapter

3

Value Proposition:
Crafting the Offer

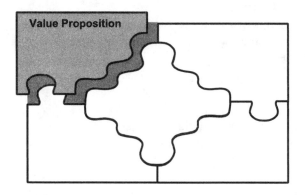

Value Proposition

"Knowing our clients and serving their needs is absolutely everything at Gateway,"[1] declares Jeff Weitzen, Gateway's president and COO. Though his statement sounds simple, understanding customer needs and serving them with unique products and services that respond to each segment's most relevant priorities is no simple matter. These tasks constitute the first piece of the business design puzzle.

The *value proposition* is the utility-creating product and/or service that a company offers to customers. In many cases, product and service are tightly bound together. A growing number of purchase decisions are determined by the service and information attributes that enhance tangible products: a pleasing store ambiance, next-day delivery,

34

expert assistance in making a selection, or after-sale technical assistance. We call these the *service wrap*.

In the developed world, the demand for services has grown enormously in recent decades. Much of the economic growth in the United States over the past 20 years has occurred in the service sector. The service share of U.S. gross domestic product grew from 30 percent to 40 percent during that period, whereas traditional manufacturing activities declined from 33 percent to 28 percent. Leading companies are capitalizing on the growing demand for services. Services as a share of IBM's revenues, for example, more than tripled between 1995 and 1999, climbing from 10 percent to 36 percent of total revenues.[2]

The shift toward services at the consumer level is being driven by demographic forces and changing social values. For example, in the United States, expanding household incomes and shrinking leisure time have a great deal to do with the increased demand for services and service wraps related to manufactured goods. Over the past 20 years, the number of dual-income families increased from 52 percent of the U.S. population to 60 percent as mothers with young children have joined the labor pool. Between 1985 and 1998, the percentage of mothers working grew from 62 percent to 72 percent.

Shrinking leisure time and larger household incomes have boosted demand for all types of services, from housecleaning to personal chefs. They have also spurred demand for timesaving conveniences such as home shopping and home delivery. Busy people do not like to spend scarce leisure time doing routine errands or milling around in crowded shopping malls. For these people, the Internet has become a very popular medium. They value the Internet primarily as a way to gather information for better decisions and to save time, according to a recent Mercer Management Consulting consumer survey.[3]

At the same time, innovation and competition have whetted the public appetite for fast and reliable service. Express deliveries have mushroomed. Faxes and e-mail have provided even faster communication for documents. Throw in cell phones, pagers, ATMs, one-hour photofinishing, 10-minute loan approvals, downloadable software, and drive-through liquor stores and you have a culture in which people expect that anything can—and should—be available anywhere, anytime.

The innovators we studied have capitalized on these important trends by offering three powerful value propositions:

1. *Super service*—prominently including speedy and reliable delivery.
2. *Convenient solutions*—complete and targeted services addressing a broad set of customer needs.
3. *Customization*—uniquely customized products and services.

These are high-value concepts whose attractiveness will rise in the years ahead. In a world where many products have reached near parity in terms of features, quality, and price, each of these concepts is capable of setting one company apart from the herd. Each, however, depends on a level of operational elegance that only value net business designs make possible. If you adopted any one of these value propositions as your offer to customers, could your existing supply chain support it?

The sections that follow will examine each of these value propositions in detail and show how they have been successfully applied. We must emphasize, however, that every value proposition must be *customer-aligned*—that is, the offer must be made to the *right* group of customers. The right customers are those who (1) place a high value on the offer and (2) are profitable to serve. The key is to stay focused on the needs of specific profitable customer segments, develop a proposition they value highly, and design a value net that is capable of profitably delivering on that proposition.

■ SUPER SERVICE

We define *super service* as a quantum leap in the service offering or performance level deemed critical by the customer. Breakthrough service delights the customer and differentiates the provider. It may take the form of product availability, related information, quality service, or easy return. The two most powerful forms of super service, however, are rapid and reliable product delivery. In some cases, both attributes are equally important to the customer, whereas in other cases the customer greatly values one over the other. At the same time, the customer expects these at no extra cost. Few companies have risen to the challenge of super service, and this presents a great opportunity for innovators to create value for customers through super service.

Let's consider the two key aspects of super service: speed and reliability.

➤ Speed

What do we mean by speed? Speed can mean receiving an urgent letter overnight, settling an insurance claim at the accident scene, getting a special-order book in 15 minutes, or downloading tonight's video rental instantly. But speed can also mean introducing new fashions to store shelves within a week or the newest computer technology within days. Speed means both instant gratification and high-velocity response.

Operating speed is generally a function of design. This is true of both mechanical systems and organizations. In the 1940s, aeronautical engineers found themselves bumping up against the limits of propeller-driven aircraft. Airspeeds of 400 to 450 miles per hour represented the practical, if not theoretical, maximum. The only effective way to reach higher speeds was through redesign using jet propulsion. A similar barrier was encountered with straight-wing jets, which quickly gave way to swept-wing designs.

We see a similar phenomenon in business operations. Here, maximum speed is a function of supply chain design. If you want to achieve a major breakthrough in operating speed, you have to change your business design. Obsessive tinkering with the current design will produce marginal improvements at best.

Progressive Insurance, the fifth largest U.S. auto insurer, changed its service delivery design when it determined that its existing design was too slow to give it an edge in its highly competitive industry. Prior to the early 1990s, Progressive, like all other auto insurance companies, took days or weeks to settle a claim. As Moira Lardakis, process leader at Progressive, recalls:

> We used to be open Monday through Friday, 8:30 A.M. to 5:15 P.M., and closed on weekends. We spent all of Monday, and sometimes Tuesday, simply taking loss reports. The rest of the week we would batch all of the losses and send claim representatives out on the road to meet with people who had been in accidents. It was a never-ending cycle of being swamped with phone calls in the beginning of the week and trying to play catch-up during the rest of the week. . . . If someone called and said, "Can you come right now?" the likelihood that we could do that was slim to none. We were not set up that way.[4]

Then Progressive's CEO Peter Lewis had a vision: "We will design our organization to respond *immediately* when the customer calls." According to Lardakis, this "was a visionary shift. . . . It was a major turning point for us as a company. Up to that point, the word *customer* was not even in our vocabulary."

The company was responding to the growing demand for speed. Progressive's director of consumer marketing noted: "In the mid-1990s, you could get new glasses in 60 minutes and have a pizza delivered in 30 minutes. It was time to bring that kind of service attitude and urgency to insurance."[5] Accordingly, Progressive adopted an on-the-spot system for settling accident claims. Dubbed Immediate Response®, the system's fleet of 1,500 Ford Explorers equipped with cell phones, laptops, and wireless modems makes it possible for claims adjusters to access the company's databases 24 hours a day, seven days a week and, if appropriate, settle claims on the spot.

Immediate Response claim service was a radically different way of doing business. Claims office hours were extended on weekdays and weekends, and a national call center was set up to dispatch Immediate Response vehicles around the clock. Claims adjusters can now check a customer's coverage and assess minor damages in real time. The key performance metric for the company became the number of responses within nine hours of a loss report.

Rapid delivery of service has produced a number of benefits for this insurer: increased customer retention, increased referrals, reduced risk of fraudulent activity, reduced car rental costs, and rising insurance premium revenues. Progressive has, in fact, grown profitably (at a 9 percent net margin), increasing revenues from $1.8 billion in 1993 to $5.3 billion in 1998, a 24 percent annual growth rate, compared to 5 percent for the auto insurance industry as a whole.

A traditional supply chain is generally incapable of supporting the speed necessary for super service. Like the vintage prop-driven aircraft of the 1940s, its structure imposes limits beyond which it cannot deliver greater operating speed. Sequential processes, multiple layers, and information flows that move as *atoms* (paper, phone calls, and faxes) rather than as *bits* (data via the Internet or electronic data interchange) result in slow and unresponsive service. The chain is laden with error-prone communications and poor information visibility. As an example, consider the case of a large U.S. electronics manufacturer. It was experiencing delays in moving its Asian-made components through customs. The root cause of these delays was revealed to be its antiquated information system (illegible faxes of vendor invoices) and the fact that its freight forwarders went home every night before passing on critical paperwork to the customs broker. Slow-moving information in the supply chain was in turn delaying critical material flows.

Value nets use digital design to break through speed barriers. Information sent electronically and simultaneously to supply partners results in greater speed, flexibility, and responsiveness. Many information transfers are automatic. Supply chain management software analyzes incoming customer orders and translates them automatically into component requests that flow automatically and digitally to suppliers. Advance shipping notices are triggered by the manufacturer's systems, alerting retailers of products on the move. Bar-coded shipments and individual items make tracking easy and electronically available to customers. Fast, real-time information enables rapid response to customer demands.

Spain's Zara is breaking speed records in producing fashion for masses of young and hip urban consumers. Zara can take new fashion ideas from the drawing board to the store shelf in 10 to 15 days. And customers love it. They queue up in long lines at Zara's stores on designated delivery days—a phenomenon dubbed "Zaramania."

Zara's value net design begins with customers and their fast-changing tastes. Store employees gather comments from consumers on clothing designs and colors and report them regularly to headquarters-based designers. The designers tour plazas, discos, cafés, university campuses, boutiques, competitor stores, and catwalks—all of which are clientele hot spots—always on the lookout for new trends. The product of this market intelligence is what Zara calls "interactive and democratic" fashion—fashion that originates with customers and to which customers can have direct input.

Knowing that what's *in* today may be *out* next week, Zara is organized to move a design concept from the drawing board to retail stores at a lightning pace. Fabrics are sourced globally—from Italy, France, the United Kingdom, China, the Netherlands, Morocco, India, Turkey, and Korea. Capital-intensive steps—creating patterns, cutting, and color treatment—are executed in factories owned by Zara's parent company, Inditex, in Galicia, Spain's northwestern province. Labor-intensive tasks such as sewing and assembly are outsourced to small shops with which Zara has collaborative and exclusive arrangements in Galicia, neighboring Castile, León, and northern Portugal. Zara provides these shops with the technology and logistics needed to get the job done on time and with the required quality. In return, it enjoys control of the end-to-end process, ensuring speed, quality, and cost efficiency.

Rapid information flows are a critical component of Zara's high-velocity operation. All stores are electronically linked to the company's headquarters, and information is channeled to those who need it. The entire production system—from design to final retail—is digitally linked and controlled. Information sharing binds together the separate pieces of Zara's operation. It is shared openly across business units and flexible work centers that are highly adaptable and that have decision-making responsibility.

Customer alignment, speed, agility, and digital information—all important value net attributes—have paid off for Zara. The company holds much less inventory than its rivals—36 days' worth of supply versus 94 for Cortefiel, its direct Spanish competitor, and 52 days for Sweden-based Hennes & Mauritz. The reason is that most fashion retailers design garments to last an entire season. To achieve cost efficiency, they produce the season's designs in bulk and then hold the inventory. Zara's ability to bring new designs to stores in less than two weeks allows it to carry less inventory and minimize accumulations of stock due to supply-demand mismatch.

Zara's revenues and profits both grew by more than 30 percent in 1998, faster than competitors like Benetton, Cortefiel, and Adolfo Dominguez. And the French newspaper *Le Figaro* has identified Zara as the best-known Spanish firm abroad.[6]

There are, of course, many ways to increase velocity. Dell and Gateway deliver computers with the very latest technology and hottest features in just a few days by compressing both time-to-market and the order-to-delivery cycles. The key elements used to drive higher speeds include technology partnerships with select suppliers, simplification of the component mix, building supply hubs near assembly plants, merging orders in transit, and eliminating distributors' warehousing and retail shelf time.

Most traditional supply chains provide ample opportunities for accelerating the pace of business. For example, consumer goods often pass through multiple layers of warehousing and distribution, and they are frequently shifted between locations as well, adding unnecessary weeks to the total pipeline. Process industries, such as pulp and paper, operate with lengthy time frames and are generally unable to answer customer needs quickly. Transportation equipment manufacturing is also slow; an order for an 18-wheel truck, for example, is typically custom-made and takes months to fill and deliver. Ditto for aircraft. Digital collaborative value nets could drastically reduce cycle times in these industries and provide differentiation for individual companies.

Speed for speed's sake, however, should never be the objective. The objective should be to provide the kind of performance that creates value for a particular customer or customer segment. As Jeffrey Trimmer, DaimlerChrysler's director of operations and strategy, recently explained, "There is a probability distribution [with respect to customers' views of ideal service speed]. Some customers are willing to wait forever; others ran into a tree yesterday, so they want the car right now."[7] For many customers, what's most relevant is the accuracy and reliability of service delivery. Trimmer elaborates: "If we can tell people that the car will be delivered in 15 days, then there's no problem. We think the ideal time is 12 to 15 days. But the key is accuracy."

➤ Reliability

Reliability is an important dimension of super service. Reliability means predictable, on-time delivery of perfect orders, as expected by the customer. A *perfect order* is one that is shipped on time and complete, but more important, one received at the customer's desired location within a precise time window, in excellent condition, and ready to use. It also includes the flexibility to respond to last-minute changes by the customer at equally high service levels.

Cemex, the world's third-largest cement producer, is one company that has made reliability its trademark. Headquartered in Monterrey, Mexico, Cemex produces and sells cement, ready-mix concrete, aggregates, and clinker, primarily to the construction industry. It maintains operations in 10 countries and markets cement in 60 countries worldwide. Over half the company's revenues come from outside Mexico.

Reliability is an important virtue in the ready-mix business, because delivery delays or delivery of the wrong type of concrete can wreak havoc with construction schedules. At the same time, reliability is difficult to achieve because customers—who are unable to control their own schedules—frequently cancel or reschedule orders.

Until the late 1980s, Cemex's operations center looked like that of any other cement company—chaotic. Dispatchers took orders for 8,000 different grades of concrete and passed them on to regional mixing plants, each of which controlled its own truck fleet. Half of all orders were changed by customers prior to delivery—often repeatedly and sometimes at the last minute. The company's response was to require longer delivery lead times and to charge penalties for order changes. Cemex was setting three-hour delivery windows—"We'll have a ready-mix truck at your site today between 1:00 and 4:00 P.M."—as was the competition. This response, however, lacked the precision that customers really needed.

Cemex's CEO Lorenzo Zambrano realized that this situation was serving neither his customers nor the company, and he began to rethink the entire operation. In 1987, he hired Gelacio Iniguez as head of information technology and charged him with evaluating the problem. Judging that Cemex could not change customer behavior, Iniguez concentrated on developing a system that would work *with* customer unpredictability rather than against it.

Iniguez and his team looked far and wide for possible solutions. They visited the Memphis, Tennessee hub of Federal Express to understand the processes behind its guarantee, "It's on time, or it's on us." They also traveled to Houston, Texas, and that city's emergency services dispatch center (911), where they observed how center personnel responded quickly and reliably to life-threatening situations, sending ambulances and police cruisers to the right places at the right time.

Cemex realized the potential for a whole new approach to its business. It envisioned using state-of-the-art communications and information systems to respond more profitably to the natural chaos of the industry. The new Cemex motto became, "Quality cement available anywhere, anytime." This vision recognized two important facts about the cement business:

1. Customers need the flexibility to make order changes, but they require reliable delivery.
2. On-time delivery is imperative for Cemex because a load of concrete is never more than 90 minutes from spoiling.

Three technology-based initiatives—CemexNet, Dynamic Synchronization of Operations, and Global Digital—were responsible for the transformation. CemexNet established satellite connections between the company's production facilities and automated back-office functions. Dynamic Synchronization of Operations, which began in the early 1990s, incorporated GPS and computer technology into the logistical system. Company trucks were linked in as well. Dynamic Synchronization now controls plant production, tracks the movement of delivery vehicles, and automatically optimizes routing. Using information on truck locations, speed, and direction, as well as customer locations, order specifications, mixing-plant capacities, and traffic patterns, the central control system constantly optimizes order fulfillment.

The final stage of Cemex's transformation—Global Digital—began in the late 1990s with the goal of linking Cemex's entire global operations by wire, satellite, and the Internet. Cemex is now moving into e-commerce through a pilot program designed to link clients, suppliers, customs agents, and Cemex personnel. When complete, Global Digital will enable Cemex to provide FedEx-like tracking of orders and payments.

Cemex's new operational design has translated into features that its customers value: guaranteed on-time delivery and the ability to make unlimited order changes up to the last minute at no additional charge. The company now boasts 98 percent on-time performance, which is all the more impressive given its 20-minute delivery windows versus the three- to four-hour standard used by competitors. It aims to cut that 20-minute window in half and, eventually, to eliminate all charges when and if orders are delivered late.[8]

The Cemex makeover was not cheap. The company invested $200 million over a 10-year period in its effort to create a seamless flow of information on inventory, delivery schedules, quality records, and so forth. But this investment has paid off. Cemex now commands a 60 percent share of the cement market in Mexico, and it outperforms all major competitors globally. In 1998, Cemex's ratio of earnings (before interest, taxes, depreciation, and amortization) to sales was 35 percent versus 21 percent on average for its five major global competitors.[9] And in mid-1999, Cemex commanded the highest market value–to-sales ratio of the world's six largest cement producers.[10] The company has been rated "Most Admired Company in Mexico" (1998, *Expansion* magazine) and has appeared on *Industry Week*'s list of the world's "100 Best-Managed Companies" in every year since the list began to be published in 1996.

■ CONVENIENT SOLUTIONS

Convenient solutions is the second powerful value proposition—and again, one that value nets are uniquely able to support.

Customers today do not seek *things* as much as they seek *solutions*. The more convenient the solution, the better. With rising demands on people's time, the need for convenience and for complete solutions grows more acute.

Companies that intend to offer convenient solutions must do two things well: (1) pinpoint the convenience needs of the customer and (2) deliver the solution without a slip. Value nets pinpoint need by capturing critical customer information at each of many *touch points* (i.e., points at which a company interacts with its customers), such as the ordering and selection process, tracking of order status, the delivery process, and ongoing maintenance. Attention to these touch points is a company's best guarantee of being in tune with customer needs. Each touch point represents an opportunity to understand and meet a broader set of customer needs.

Progressive Insurance provides an instructive example of a company that listened to the customer voice and that is evolving from its initial focus on fast-response service to a total customer solution. As process leader Moira Lardakis explains:

> *The whole thing is evolutionary. We have concluded that responding immediately is terrific, but we need to extend our concern and our measurement to include*

how long it takes before the car is back in the cus-
tomer's driveway. . . . A couple of years ago, we would
have agreed that it's all about speed, but today we're
saying speed is only one element of it. Doing the right
thing for the consumer at the right time—that's really
the ultimate goal.

In practical terms, Progressive's evolution has moved it beyond the initial goal of fast response to the total resolution of claims within seven calendar days and to helping customers get duplicate titles, arrange for car rental, and other time-consuming chores. Customers love it. According to Lardakis, Progressive gets "some amazing e-mails from consumers saying, 'I can't believe what just happened—you delivered a rental car, you made sure mine was in the shop, I had no out-of-pocket expense, and the thing is done!'" A total and convenient solution. "The whole approach when you talk to the consumer has a lot of appeal," says Lardakis.

In the business-to-business world, W.W. Grainger, Inc., provides an equally powerful example of a convenient solutions provider. Grainger is an MRO (maintenance, repair, and operations) supplier, distributing thousands of maintenance items such as mechanical components, tools, cleaning fluids, work uniforms, and lightbulbs. This could be another commodity business, like cement, but Grainger has made *solutions*—not boxes of materials—the key element in its value proposition. Its solutions include taking responsibility for procurement, inventory management, logistics, reporting, and accounting reconciliation functions—services that allow Grainger to differentiate itself from its competitors.

This wasn't always the case. Prior to 1990, Grainger didn't stand out in its field; it was one of many suppliers of commodity products. To change this situation, it created Grainger Integrated Supply, a unit dedicated to addressing a broader set of customer needs, such as lower materials costs and superior supply chain management. Its vision was clear: "To be the primary source for customers through breadth of products/services offered, with a focus on the lowest total cost solution."

"We saw a market niche," says President Pete Torrenti. "It was the underpinning of a supply chain revolution. It's like the minivan concept. No one knew that the customer was asking for a minivan. All they knew was that the customer was asking for something beyond what was currently being offered."[11]

In describing what Grainger Integrated Supply offers today, Pete Torrenti clarifies the value proposition: "We offer lower prices, better service, inventory buyback, site support, etc., [not] cleaning solutions or work uniforms. . . . Grainger is in the business of keeping other businesses running."[12] Group president Wes Clark is also emphatic: "We are selling speed and convenience, not just a hammer and a lightbulb."[13]

Grainger Integrated Supply has taken a number of steps to ensure superb execution of its value proposition:

➤ Its representatives are stationed on-site, at the headquarters of customers such as Procter & Gamble, American Airlines, and DaimlerChrysler, to ensure service coverage 24 hours a day, seven days a week.

➤ Grainger maintains total customer focus and an attitude that it will do anything for the customer, solve any problem. "Once we get customers," says one company executive, "we very rarely lose them because of our service package. When they call in and want something, it's there when they need it. No questions asked."[14]

➤ It maintains electronic linkages between customers, partner-suppliers, and itself, but provides customers with a single MRO point of contact. This single interface is both more convenient and more cost-efficient for customers. Customers place one order for many products from many suppliers, but they receive one delivery and one bill—and make one payment.

➤ Integrated supply offers customers potential savings of up to 35 percent.

➤ The company extended its one-stop shopping concept to the Internet with the May 1999 launch of OrderZone.com.

Demand for Grainger Integrated Supply services has grown rapidly. In 1998, the unit's sales grew 56 percent versus 5 percent for Grainger overall. First- and second-quarter 1999 sales grew 25 and 37 percent, respectively, versus 3 and 2 percent for Grainger overall.

Demand for convenience and single-point solutions underlies the value propositions of a growing number of Internet companies. VerticalNet, for example, offers a single aggregation point for information and supplier contacts for 38 different industries. CarPoint provides a one-stop solution for car buyers—from price comparisons to getting tags and car insurance. Both companies rely on a network of partnerships—a value net—to create the broader or deeper solution customers seek.

At the end of this chapter, we examine Streamline.com, another value net company that has based its future on convenience and customer solutions. Streamline.com has tightly aligned its operations with the needs of its target market and has harnessed a delivery system capable of providing a total "lifestyle solution" for its customers.

■ CUSTOMIZATION

Product and service customization is the third major category of innovative value propositions for which we foresee a bright and expanding future. Industrialization largely displaced the output of artisans (skilled cobblers, watch-makers, weavers, brewmasters, and hundreds of other tradespeople) with standardized, but cheaper, mass-produced goods. Standardization and low cost marched to the same beat. Long production runs lowered unit costs, but also imparted sameness to most of the things that people purchased, from automobiles to apparel.

Then came the movement known today as *mass customization*—custom output at mass-produced prices. Dell was in the early wave of this movement. It broke the mold when it offered individually customized computers at or below mass-production prices. It showed that computerized controls, digital information flows, and close coordination among supply partners could make manufacturing more flexible. An evolution was set in motion toward value net operations that could rapidly and cost-effectively produce the exact products and services desired by customers.

Customization is still novel and differentiating, but it is catching on fast. The Personal Pair program of Levi Strauss sews jeans to order. Ford has invested in Microsoft's CarPoint venture to develop an Internet-based customer interface on which auto buyers will be able to configure their own cars. "We think customers want to specify their own cars," says Ming Yeh, new business development manager at Ford Motor Company. "There is an opportunity to exceed expectations."[15] DaimlerChrysler is developing its own customization capabilities. Meanwhile, Amazon.com customizes shopping recommendations, and MP3 allows music lovers to customize their own CDs. And the list goes on.

Customization enhances purchasers' utility by allowing them to choose their preferred product/service attributes from a set of extensive but controlled choices. An easy-to-use digital choice mechanism (see Chapter 4) is a critical element of the customization proposition.

Mass customization benefits both customer and provider. The customer benefits by getting exactly what he or she wants. The provider benefits by avoiding the costly consequences of traditionally inaccurate demand forecasting and building to stock. "In high-tech industries with hot products, forecasts are always wrong," says Mel Friedman of Sun Microsystems. "The only good forecast is the actual purchase by the customer."[16] As with classic job shops, mass customizers do not respond to forecasts but to actual demand. They configure and build to order, eliminating most inventories in the process.

Some companies are trying to get ahead of customer orders by offering individually crafted purchase recommendations based on accumulated customer data. New technologies, such as the recommendations generator introduced by NetPerceptions, help companies to develop individualized product and service offerings *before* customers have requested them. Amazon.com uses NetPerceptions' Book Matcher software to create recommendations for customers based on their indicated preferences and past choice patterns.

Mass customization has tremendous customer appeal. Anyone who can deliver products and services designed to the unique requirements of each customer, and at a reasonable speed and cost, stands to win. The challenge, of course, is achieving speed *and* cost efficiency.

The purest form of mass customization is build-to-order. *Build-to-order* (BTO) manufacturing is triggered by actual customer orders. Products and services are produced to exact customer specifications. DaimlerChrysler's Jeffrey Trimmer highlights the benefits of BTO designs:

> *Build-to-order definitely has advantages over building to stock. Building to stock creates problems because you are not seeing the true customer orders. If you could see the customer orders, you could maximize what they want. There is also a huge inventory cost. Cars, unlike wine and cheese, don't get better with age.*

Well-designed BTO models can actually be cheaper than traditional mass-production models, especially in industries with high rates of product obsolescence. The lack of finished goods inventory can also create tremendous financial benefits. Gateway is one notable example of BTO manufacturing, and one of the benefits it enjoys is a *negative* cash conversion cycle (discussed in detail in Chapter 5), which means that customers and suppliers effectively finance Gateway's growth.

Companies that do not build to order can achieve a certain degree of customization through channel assembly or postponement. *Channel assembly* is a BTO equivalent to customization for manufacturers who sell through channel partners. This model offers fewer options than pure BTO, but allows manufacturers to complete final product assembly at the reseller level or in the store. Sun Microsystems, Compaq, and IBM began channel assembly when customers familiar with Dell and Gateway's capabilities began to expect customization. Sun treats its resellers as an extension of its manufacturing system and provides the training they need to perform final assembly of customer-configured systems on their own premises.

A milder form of customization, called *postponement,* is also used to better match supply with demand. Postponement is the strategy of differentiating or customizing the partially completed product as close to the customer as possible, where knowledge of actual demand is more accurate. Hewlett-Packard's European printer operation saw postponement as the solution to chronic demand-supply imbalances. Because of differences in electric currents and languages across European countries, printers produced for England are slightly different than those made for Italy. When HP stocked ready-to-ship printers, unanticipated demand fluctuations in individual countries created serious overstock and stockout problems. HP's solution was to postpone installation of the power converter and inclusion of the language-specific instructional manual until the very end, when actual customer orders were in hand. Postponement strategies like this help companies stay as responsive as possible to real demand while maintaining flexibility and low inventories.

■ HOW DO THESE VALUE PROPOSITIONS APPLY TO YOUR BUSINESS?

We have described three powerful value propositions that value nets uniquely support: super service, convenient solutions, and individually customized products and services. Do any of these apply to your business? If so, what are the signs that the moment is ripe to offer them? And which of the three is best for you?

We see a pattern that suggests where a particular business may be in the time frame of converting from the old supply chains to the new value nets. The world's leading innovators in this arena—the Dells, the Gateways, and the Ciscos—developed their value nets in the early to mid-1990s. Whole industries (personal computers and apparel, for example) are moving fast in the value net direction. Other consumer goods are likely to follow, with heavy industries bringing up the rear (Figure 3.1). What this means is that companies in the PC industry, for example, are almost required at this point to have a value net in place. In other industries, the requirement is less immediate, but the potential for differentiation is greater, as the Cemex example shows.

The question to consider is whether you can get ahead of the curve. As with other business designs, you can make the most of a value net proposition when you are on the cutting edge of change. The trick is to spot the opportunity before your competitors do and to make your move while others still believe it can't be done.

Can you leap ahead of your industry? Absolutely. Are there serious hurdles to overcome? Of course. Customizing to order and delivering in just a few days are far more dif-

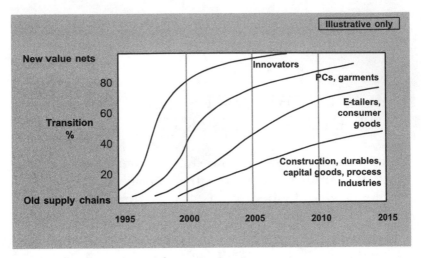

Figure 3.1 Expected value net adoption pattern.

ficult for makers of automobiles and massive telecommunications switches than for purveyors of personal computers and fast food. But the potential advantages are so great that companies should make the effort.

The list of indicators in Figure 3.2 will help you determine if one of the value propositions we have described is timely for your business. *Super service* aligns well with rapidly changing customer demand and short product life cycles. Customer demand for many product variations suggests a *customization* approach. And multitiered distribution could offer the chance for a breakthrough with a *convenient solution*. Other indicators, such as commoditization or declining margins, suggest that any of the value net propositions may be appropriate.

As you consider adopting a value net business design, framing the right value proposition is the critical first step. Would one of these three value propositions allow you to leapfrog others in your industry and achieve competitive differentiation? Would the value proposition work best for particular product lines? Is the targeted customer segment large enough to support the concept?

Key Business Indicators	Value Proposition		
	Super Service	Convenient Solutions	Customization
Volatile demand	✓		
Rapid technological change	✓		
Product perishability	✓		
Multiple product variations		✓	
Increasing product returns		✓	✓
Multitiered distribution		✓	
Product commoditization	✓	✓	✓
Declining margins	✓	✓	✓

Figure 3.2 Value proposition selection.

The right offer. The right customers. The best way to connect them. Think through this piece of the business design puzzle and you will have taken the first step toward creating a value net. The case study that follows will show you how one company has already done it.

■ STREAMLINE DELIVERS

Streamline.com is one of a new breed of companies that provides convenient, Internet-enabled home delivery of goods and services. From its beginnings in the Boston area, Streamline has aspired to take its concept nationwide, and the company has used its June 1999 initial public offering to fund the first leg of that expansion. Its story is important for three reasons:

1. *It illustrates how a value net design provides a convenient solution—one of the three value propositions discussed in this chapter.*
2. *It shows the power of careful customer selection and close supply chain alignment with the needs of those customers.*

3. *It exemplifies a consumer-direct business design for home delivery—a model that many companies will attempt to perfect in the coming years.*

Many companies, particularly in the United States, are now adopting consumer-direct/home delivery business models—and several are in direct competition with Streamline.com. Each is experimenting, trying to determine what works and what does not. In this embryonic period, none of these home delivery businesses has yet achieved profitability. As a consequence, Streamline's ultimate success is far from assured. Nevertheless, the particular design developed by Streamline in creating a value net offers important lessons for executives in other businesses.

Streamline was created as a service enterprise, offering weekly scheduled home delivery of groceries, personal care products, dry cleaning, and other home replenishment items to a carefully defined segment of households in its operating areas. In late 1999, these included Boston and Washington, D.C. (an acquisition in Chicago subsequently occurred in January 2000). Streamline's aim is to simplify the lives of busy families by eliminating the need to make frequent trips to many different stores: the supermarket, the dry cleaner, the florist, the post office, the video store, and others. "Consumers want simplicity in their lives," says former marketing VP Frank Britt. "The Streamline brand has always been about lifestyle efficiency for consumers. It's not about groceries, it's about simplification and efficiency."[17]

Streamline is the brainchild of Timothy DeMello, an experienced entrepreneur who observed the interplay of important macroeconomic and consumer trends that to him spelled opportunity. These included a healthy economy, an increasing number of time-pressed, dual-income families, a trend among consumers to reduce the number of "suppliers" with whom they did business, and the growth of the Internet. DeMello borrowed his concept from category killers such as Home Depot, Toys 'R' Us, and Staples—merchandisers who aggregate products into one-stop-shopping opportunities for customers—and extended it to services, creating a home delivery "solutions killer."

The home delivery model is spreading. In the United States, companies like UPS, FedEx, and the Postal Service provide home delivery of nonperishable items for thousands of catalog and Internet retailers, and a number of firms have entered the grocery home delivery field with different business designs. Though home grocery shopping is estimated to account for less than $400 million of the $449 billion grocery industry, delivery of groceries to the home is expected to grow rapidly.[18] Different grocery home delivery models are being developed by Peapod, ShopLink, Home-Runs, Webvan, NetGrocer, HomeGrocer, Greatfood.com, and even Wal-Mart. In the United Kingdom, Tesco and Somerfield are also offering home delivery services. Each is racing to perfect a profitable home delivery model.

What is most interesting about Streamline's value net business design is its laser-sharp definition of its target customer segment, its alignment of the value proposition with the needs of that segment, and the operating design that delivers on its promise to customers.

➤ The Streamline Model in Brief

Streamline's targeted customers are busy suburban families (BSFs) with children, high incomes, and, initially, with homes in certain contiguous suburbs that can be served from a central distribution facility. The set of products and services offered to these customers is designed to appeal to their desire for quality, selection, and convenience. These include both food and nonfood items—groceries, videos, dry cleaning—that would normally require shopping trips to many different stores and locations. The broad selection constitutes a convenient solution for time-pressed customers.

To support this system, DeMello and other Streamline executives have developed a carefully engineered value net geared to deliver convenience. This network addresses customer expectations for accuracy and timeliness as well as the constraints of product perishability and cost-effectiveness. Excellent coordination of fulfillment between Streamline and its food and service providers, combined with precision delivery, is essential.

The Streamline value net is illustrated in Figure 3.3. A customer order is placed, usually via the Internet, to the company's order entry system and then routed to the warehouse management system. That warehouse is supplied by dry grocery vendors, a local bakery, a top-of-the-line meat supplier, UPS package service, Blockbuster Video, and dozens of others. Many deliver to the Streamline distribution center on a just-in-time basis.

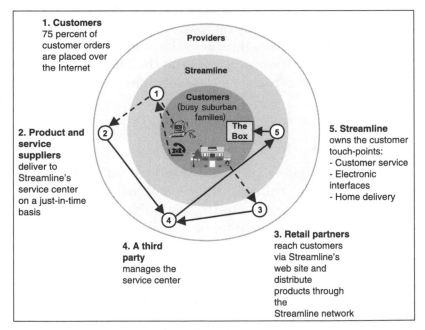

Figure 3.3 How Streamline does it.

Every subscriber is on a fixed weekly delivery schedule, a unique feature of Streamline's design. At least one day prior to delivery, the customer selects the items he or she wants and sends an order to Streamline. Currently, almost 75 percent of customers select and order through the company's web page, and this percentage is growing. The customer's Personal Shopping List indicates items that he or she will receive on a regular basis as part of the Don't Run Out program (e.g., a pound of butter, a pound of Starbucks coffee, a gallon of low-fat milk). The customer can then click on other product categories to order nonautomatic replenishment items for the upcoming week (e.g., four fresh rainbow trout for Friday night's dinner; a selection of gourmet cheeses, crackers, vegetables, and steaks for Saturday night's dinner guests; a movie from Blockbuster Video).

On the day a customer order is scheduled for delivery, picked and packed items are placed aboard a temperature-controlled truck whose route is optimized to make the most deliveries in the fewest miles possible. The truck's driver has access to the subscriber's premises (usually a locked garage), where the order is left in a special unit ("The Box") provided by Streamline (see Figure 3.4). Temperature-sensitive products are placed in either the unit's freezer or its refrigerated section. Canned goods, videocassettes, and other nonperishables are placed on shelves or in bins within the unit. As the driver leaves, he or she picks up outgoing dry cleaning, video returns, or empty bottles and cans. Subscribers needn't be present, nor must they schedule other activities around the timing of the Streamline delivery. In the parlance of the home delivery industry, Streamline's delivery is "unattended," an important value to busy subscribers.

Subscribers are charged a $30 monthly fee for this weekly service, plus the price of purchased goods, which are about the same as those purchased in supermarkets. As an operating model, it seems simple and logical. Customer support has been encouraging. According to company officials:

Figure 3.4 "The Box"—Streamline's unattended home delivery unit.

➤ About 94 percent of current customers look to Streamline as their primary provider of groceries and household goods and services.

➤ The average subscriber receives over 40 deliveries per year, more than twice the rate of competing services.

➤ Customer retention is over 90 percent.

➤ Streamline enjoys a 75 percent "share of wallet" among its 3,000-plus customers in the Boston area.

➤ A Closer Look

Though the Streamline operating model may be simple, the details of making it work are devilishly complex and have taken the company years (since it first opened in 1993) to develop. That development continues. In this section, we'll take a closer look at the company's operation—in particular, its approach to customer selection, the product/service offering, and its innovative delivery design.

Customer Selection

Streamline's founders aimed to create a complete solution for a narrowly defined set of people: busy suburban families with children. The company recognizes that it is serving only a tiny fraction of the households in its geographic areas that might find value in home delivery, but this narrow targeting is quite deliberate. According to Frank Britt:

> *If you are going to be a "solution killer," you need to select a customer segment and be the best in the world for that customer segment. Unfortunately, you cannot provide a solution that is equally good for everybody. So we decided very explicitly that busy suburban families are our focus. We are not serving single people, senior citizens, or city dwellers. We just want to be great at what we do, and to be great, you need to be targeted. The whole business is designed around that targeted customer segment. Unattended delivery, for example, doesn't work for everyone, but it works for busy suburban families with dual incomes and kids.*

Approximately 90 percent of current subscribers fit Streamline's target profile: family incomes of $75,000 or more, children under age 18 living at home, located in adjacent suburban communities (currently, west of Boston and in certain sections of the Washington, D.C., area), and, ideally, having Internet access. Streamline finds that these BSFs place large weekly orders—about $104 worth of groceries, dry cleaning, and other services per order. Streamline monitors its marketing success on a daily basis, through a "BSF index," which reports the percentage of deliveries destined for its ideal customer segment. This monitoring is an example of how performance measures and business strategy need to be linked.

The Value Proposition

Streamline provides a useful example of a customer-aligned value proposition. It allows its customers to take a wide range of chores off their to-do lists. And it conveniently delivers to their homes items traditionally purchased from grocery supermarkets and other stores, a task that requires considerable personal logistical effort (Figure 3.5).

The fact that every one of the items available to subscribers is obtainable elsewhere underscores the point that service and convenience, not products, are what attract subscribers to Streamline and companies like it. In all, Streamline makes some 10,000 stockkeeping units (SKUs) available to its subscribers, roughly one-third the number stocked by a typical grocery supermarket. This smaller

Basic Groceries	Convenience Services
❏ Brand-name groceries and dairy products	❏ Dry cleaning pickup and delivery
	❏ Videos and video games
❏ Quality meats, seafood, and gourmet cheeses	❏ Firewood
	❏ Film processing and photo supplies
❏ Fresh baked goods and deli products	❏ Package pickup and delivery
	❏ Shoe repair
❏ Specialty pet foods	❏ Bottled water and cooler delivery
❏ Prepared meals, restaurant meals	❏ Deposit redemption for bottles and cans
❏ Fresh flowers and seasonal items	
❏ Cleaning supplies and health/beauty products	❏ Postage stamps

Figure 3.5 Streamline's solution-killer offerings.

number, according to the company, is more than adequate. "Customers don't care about 27 kinds of pickles," says former VP of operations Dave Blakelock, "but they do have to believe that the order they get tomorrow night is exactly what they ordered, and they have to trust that the 10 kinds of pickles available are the good kinds."[19] Streamline also carries national and local premium-brand goods not normally sold through grocery stores (e.g., Legal Sea Foods, Iams pet foods, and Boar's Head deli meats).

About 70 percent of items delivered by the company, on a dollar basis, are groceries. Groceries are traditionally characterized by low margins, but Streamline claims a blended gross margin of 29 percent and anticipates continued improvement as it adds more nonfood items to its product mix. That product mix is bound to change in the months and years ahead.

Strategically, the company doesn't view itself as a grocery delivery service but as an innovator in the emerging consumer-direct merchandising field. It is less concerned with *what* it delivers through its customer-direct pipeline than it is with the pipeline itself. As merchandising VP Bill Paul states, "The emotional tie with our lifestyle solution consumer is at a whole different level than it is in traditional retailing."[20]

So, why groceries? Groceries are, in the company's view, the key to its hope for profitability in home delivery. Every one of its subscribers needs groceries on a regular basis. The same is not true to the same degree for *any* of the other products or services offered by the company. Groceries form a solid and predictable baseload for the company. With that volume in place, other, higher-margin products and services can be profitably added. And with the growing role of the Internet, home delivery companies like Streamline may play an important part in the new economy.

Nordstrom was an early investor in the company (along with Intel, GE Capital, and SAP), and it is not difficult to imagine why. For Nordstrom, Streamline could develop into a new, low-cost distribution channel. A link from the Streamline web page to a Nordstrom page, for example, could feature "Nordstrom's Special Sales Items" for Streamline subscribers on a weekly basis. A simple click on a sweater would add the item to the customer's regular bill, and the item would be included in the next scheduled delivery. "The incremental cost of adding something on the truck is nominal," as Frank Britt puts it. But adding the Nordstrom sweater would increase the order's dollar size by close to 50 percent. And returns improve with increased order size.

Streamline's business design has also led it into unique strategic relationships with consumer packaged goods manufacturers—Campbell Soup, Nestlé, Procter & Gamble, Nabisco, Gillette, and others. These companies compensate Streamline for research it generates from its proprietary panel of consumers, located throughout the United States, who are frequent users of consumer-direct services. And Streamline's own customers form quarterly focus groups that provide rich, qualitative feedback to the manufacturers. Dubbed the Consumer Learning Center, this initiative builds directly on Streamline's special access to consumer knowledge and highlights the value of such information for the company and its suppliers.

Streamline's value proposition and delivery are tightly intertwined. Its business design began with its chosen set of customers. "We started with the customer, knowing nothing about the supply chain," says Blakelock. "So we first asked, what does the customer want?" Streamline sought to determine which goods and services customers wanted, how they wanted to buy them, how they wanted to receive them, and how they wanted to pay for them. Once they had the answers, DeMello and his associates created a value net that aligned itself with those needs. According to Blakelock:

> *Luckily, we did a lot of things early on that were best for the consumer and best for the company from a supply chain perspective. Scheduled delivery [for example]—a huge benefit. Having the service box—great*

for the customer and great for the company. These were decisions made at the very beginning, done for the customer. We put the service box in the garage because the customer didn't want to have to schedule around us—"Honey can you be home between 4 and 6? . . ." The customer wanted to place an order and not worry about it. So we designed the service box to deliver to them, and it turned out great from a supply chain perspective, though a little expensive on the acquisition/customer setup.

The Box was a major benefit from a supply chain perspective because it enabled unattended delivery and, combined with scheduled delivery, allowed Streamline to aggregate orders and optimize its routes. Unattended delivery pleased customers, and the combination improved the economics of home delivery.

Another win-win element of the design has been the automatic replenishment program. The customer doesn't run out of the basics, and the company enjoys predictable repeat business. According to Streamline officials, rival Peapod enjoys roughly the same order size but makes only nine deliveries per year to a particular customer, no doubt the consequence of its on-demand model versus the weekly scheduled delivery and automatic replenishment of Streamline.

The Delivery

The Streamline customer perceives a simple, straightforward transaction. He or she places an order over the Internet, and a truck delivers it to the home. Behind that simple transaction, however, is a complex logistical challenge—one that any aspiring e-tailer must face and overcome. Says Dave Blakelock, "You can have a beautiful web site and marketing materials, but unless you get the right product to the right customer, you're not in the game." Frank Britt echoes this view:

The ability to consistently pick and deliver perfect orders is rapidly becoming the single most important factor affecting consumer-direct channel adoption, customer loyalty, and business-model economics. . . . For these reasons, it may be the investment in logistical capability rather than on-line shopping competencies that ultimately differentiates the winning providers.[21]

The challenge is that everything ordered by a customer must be part of the shipment and must be in excellent condition: no melted ice cream or bruised peaches; no navel oranges when Valencias were specified; no whole milk when the customer asked for low-fat; no "Sorry, we are temporarily out of stock on that item." Streamline checks every fresh produce item and throws out the 20 percent that might be even slightly damaged. According to Blakelock, Streamline customers value accuracy and getting what they ordered more than they value bargains.

Backstock, out-of-stock, and substitutions just aren't acceptable. So we have thrown away all standard industry benchmarks, such as 10 percent out-of-stock and a 1 percent mis-pick rate. Unlike retail, we are going to the customer's home! So in designing the supply chain, quality was more important than cost—not that cost isn't a priority. That's why we operate refrigerated trucks to maintain the "chill chain." That's why we double-scan every product into the bin to make sure that the product ends up in the right bin.

The logistical arrangements for picking, packing, delivery, and billing for the 60 or so items in the average customer order are carefully engineered and highly automated. Everything is driven by customer orders, which typically enter the company's warehouse management system via the Internet. The rest (a declining number) come in by fax or phone and are manually keyed into the system.

The heart of the Streamline logistics system for its Boston-area customers is a 56,000-square-foot distribution facility called the Consumer Resource Center (CRC). Management of the CRC is outsourced to a third party. The company retains in-house those processes that directly touch customers. These include customer service, electronic customer interfaces, marketing, and, most important, carrying groceries and other items into the homes of subscribers. By design, Streamline performs these activities itself.

Streamline's CRC offers several advantages. According to Frank Britt,

A dedicated fulfillment center, rather than store-picked fulfillment, has emerged as the preferred approach. In contrast to stores, which are designed primarily for merchandising and for customer convenience, a fulfillment center can be optimized for peak logistical performance. Moreover, service levels such as picking accuracy, order customization, fill rates, and operational flexibility are dramatically enhanced in this setting.[22]

Within the CRC, order pickers have the benefit of handheld computerized devices that direct them to the right items in the most efficient patterns, even as they maintain accuracy through bar coding. Fresh bakery items, dry cleaning, photofinishing, and other orders supplied by third-party providers are added through just-in-time cross docking.

Streamline's supply arrangements for basic groceries are fairly traditional—and hold considerable opportunity for enhancement. "We are looking at how to better utilize *all* the resources of our suppliers, including assortment planning and research," says Bill Paul. Although the company has a slick customer interface, supplier interactions are still dominated by fax and phone. EDI is used only with Streamline's largest supplier, national food wholesaler SuperValu. Streamline's information flow design does not yet encompass total network visibility. It is in the process of implementing SAP, an enterprise resource planning system.

Even so, Streamline achieves a 99.5 percent order fill rate for its subscribers. Stockouts are currently resolved through manual substitution procedures, but the company aims to replace these procedures with real-time availability advice and rule-based substitution programs.

The Final Mile

The final mile (i.e., delivery from the CRC to the subscriber's home) is both a challenge and an opportunity. Dave Blakelock stresses, "We have to own the delivery to the customer, because 25 to 30 percent of the time, we may actually run into a customer. It's a very important customer touch point for us." This is why Streamline does not outsource its delivery fleets, whereas other consumer-direct businesses often do.

Management of the final mile must run like clockwork. At 7 A.M., warehouse staff begin consolidating individual orders, pulling them from staging areas in each of three temperature zones. These are loaded aboard Streamline's fleet of refrigerated trucks. Streamline uses "a 16-foot cab-over design," according to Blakelock. "We looked at different options . . . and have changed the interior design many times to make delivery as efficient as possible," he says.

By 9 A.M., the trucks are ready to leave the loading dock, and each sets out on a carefully optimized route that may involve 30 to 50 home deliveries. Servicing a house takes no more than three to four minutes.

Dave Blakelock emphasizes that Streamline must contend with multitemperature product orders delivered all the way to the house. "So it's a very complicated operation," he says. "That's why incumbent grocery companies haven't done it. They don't have the logistics skills. Stop & Shop doesn't pick 'eaches.' They move pallets and boxes, and they certainly don't commingle 50 of them at a time, customize it at a household level, and deliver it to your house."

Streamline has thoughtfully addressed this last important part of the consumer-direct business model. Its strategy of controlling all customer touch points and outsourcing the rest puts it in a position to understand its subscribers and to use that understanding to improve its offerings and the means of their delivery. The Box and automatic weekly delivery reduce the chance that a subscriber will switch to a me-too competitor.

For companies that aim to be in the consumer direct business, Frank Britt advises: "The whole deal [of future Internet home delivery] is going to be in the last mile to the house."

➤ Dueling Designs

A number of companies are now offering home grocery delivery in the United States. There are both significant differences and remarkable similarities in their business designs (see Figure 3.6 for a thumbnail sketch).

The model of a central warehouse or staging facility for each metropolitan market seems to be generally accepted. Peapod, one of the pioneers in the field, initially used pickers who walked the aisles of a grocery store to assemble orders for home delivery. Peapod has since evolved to the centralized distribution facility model as well. The scale and investment in distribution facilities does vary, however. Webvan, whose initial public offering took place in November 1999, bases its design on huge, automated warehouses. Its first facility, in Oakland, California, is 330,000 square feet (six times as large as Streamline's CRC in Westwood, Massachusetts). Webvan has a $1 billion contract with Bechtel to build 26 such facilities nationwide.

Streamline appears to be unique so far in adopting a fixed weekly delivery schedule. Competitors are pursuing on-demand delivery, which appeals from an instant gratification perspective but may not be as attractive in terms of

	Stream-line	Webvan	Peapod	Shop-Link	Net-Grocer	Home-Grocer
Design Features						
Targets customers	Yes	No	No	Yes	No	No
Services beyond groceries	Yes	No	No	Yes	No	No
Unattended delivery	Yes	No	No	Yes	FedEx	No
Scheduled delivery	Yes	No	No	No	No	No
Non-Internet order taking	Yes	No	Yes	No	No	No
Automation of central DC	Low	High	Low	Low	Low	Low
Results						
Customer base	4,000	21,000	90,000	3,300	60,000	50,000
Order size	$104	$71	$120	$98	$60	$110
Orders/year	40	NA	8–9	NA	NA	NA
1999 revenue ($M)*	$13	$4	$69	NA	NA	NA
IPO capital raised ($M)	$45	$375	$64	NA	NA	NA
Date of IPO	Sept. 99	Nov. 99	1997	NA	NA	NA
Market value ($M)	$231	$7,800	$157	NA	NA	NA

Source: Mercer Management Consulting; Greg Lindsay, "Will the Net Really Bring Home the Bacon," *Fortune*, November 22, 1999, 354.

Figure 3.6 Grocery home delivery models.
*Streamline data for trailing 12 months through October 2, 1999, based on Streamline quarterly reports. Webvan data for trailing 12 months through September 30, 1999 based on Webvan quarterly reports. Peapod data for trailing 12 months through September 30, 1999, based on Peapod quarterly reports.

repeat business or logistics efficiency. Most companies require attended delivery—that is, they have not invested in a temperature-controlled unit at the home to permit unattended delivery. One exception is ShopLink, a direct Streamline competitor in the Boston suburbs, which installs a unit but delivers on demand. In fact, many of ShopLink's practices are uncannily similar to those of Streamline—its facility is in the same town, its trucks are similar, and it charges a similar monthly fee, highlighting Streamline's challenge to maintain strategic control in this space.

Access to capital may be one of the determinants of success in this emerging business. Most contestants assert that they have national rollout plans. In the race to sign up customers, players with the greatest financial backing may be able to capture customers sooner. This is particularly significant in an industry where none of the players are yet generating income from operations. In this regard, Webvan's IPO raised $375 million, which provides a substantial war chest for its nationwide expansion. Its aggressive approach reflects the vision of its creator, Louis Borders, the entrepreneur who cofounded the Borders bookstore chain.

The other factor that has yet to fully play out is the role that traditional grocers will play in this small but fast-growing sector. Grocery retailers have dipped their toes in the market. Hannaford Brothers owns HomeRuns, a Boston-based Internet grocery service. Albertsons, another large retail chain, serves the Dallas/Fort Worth Internet market and has announced plans to open a web site and an albertsons.com store in the Seattle area. Ultimately, it's likely that large retailers will become significant players, following the hybrid strategy we see emerging in other industries. Termed *clicks and mortar,* such a strategy could combine the advantages of Internet ordering with the supply economies of an established retail chain.

➤ The Lessons from Streamline

The Streamline story reveals four broad lessons regarding the development of a successful value proposition:

- ➤ *Precise customer selection.* Streamline focuses on one tightly defined customer segment. Although some companies may wish to serve multiple segments, it is important to be clear about which customers you are trying to serve and to define their distinct needs.

- ➤ *Value proposition alignment.* Streamline's home delivery design provides a convenient solution aimed squarely at the needs of its targeted customer base. Convenient solutions are increasingly popular value propositions for consumers and business customers.

- ➤ *Dogged attention to the customer touch points.* This means delivering the goods in ways that are efficient, pleasing, and convenient for customers. It includes creating an efficient order process, ensuring accurate fulfillment, and managing the delivery experience.

➤ *Building customer loyalty.* Streamline invests in its customer relationships (e.g., The Box). In addition, it has created switching costs through its automatic replenishment feature and by charging for removal of The Box. These elements have successfully yielded a high customer retention rate.

Streamline exemplifies the power of the new value propositions to appeal to busy consumers. Effective home delivery of groceries and many other items is bound to find an important niche in the years ahead, particularly as Internet businesses expand. The experiences of Streamline and similar firms will inform consumer-direct concepts of the future.

■ NOTES

1. Jeff Weitzen, *Gateway Annual Report,* 1998, 5.
2. John B. Jones, Jr., Salomon Smith Barney analyst report, June 3, 1999, 2.
3. In a consumer online survey conducted by Mercer Management Consulting (summer 1999), 82 percent of online users indicated that the value of the Internet is in providing information that helps them make better decisions and 75 percent indicated that the value is in saving time. The Internet's value as a cost-saving tool was important to less than half of responding consumers—49 percent. Source: Mercer Management Consulting Press Release, September 13, 1999.
4. Moira Lardakis. Interview with author, November 8, 1999.
5. Tom Stieghorst, "Aggressive Progressive: Fast-Growing Auto Insurer Aims to Boost Awareness by Sponsoring Today's Super Bowl Halftime show," Fort Lauderdale *Sun-Sentinel,* January 31, 1999, 1G.

6. "Zara, la empresa española más conocida en el extranjero," *Gaceta de los Negocios,* June 22, 1998; other figures obtained from the companies' annual financial reports.
7. Jeffrey Trimmer. Interview with Denise Auclair (Mercer Management Consulting), August 25, 1999.
8. Oren Harari, "The Concrete Intangibles," *Management Review,* May 1999, 30.
9. *Deutsche Bank Research Analyst Report,* March 22, 1999, 11.
10. *Interacciones Analyst Report,* March 1, 1999, 9. The market value–to–sales ratios for the five main cement producers are as follows: Lafarge, 1.7; Holderbank, 1.3; Blue Circle, 2.3; Heidelberger, 1.1; Cemex, 2.8.
11. Pete Torrenti. Private company communication, October 1999.
12. Pete Torrenti. Interview with Denise Auclair (Mercer Management Consulting), August 25, 1999.
13. Wes Clark, quoted by Judann Pollack, "Grainger Debuts on TV to Tout Industrial 'Stuff,' " *Advertising Age,* November 10, 1997, 20.
14. John Rozwat, VP Sales, quoted by Andy Cohen, "Practice Makes Profits," *Sales & Marketing Management,* July 1995, 24.
15. Ming Yeh. Interview with Kamenna Rindova and Keanne Henry (Mercer Management Consulting), October 14, 1999.
16. Mel Friedman. Interview with Chris Lange (Mercer Management Consulting), July 9, 1999.
17. Frank Britt. Interview with author, June 23, 1999.
18. Chris Reidy, "Westwood On-Line Grocer Plans $30M Acquisition," *The Boston Globe,* October 20, 1999, E2 (estimate of less than $400 million of online grocery revenues); *Progressive Grocer Sixth Annual Report of the Grocery Industry* ($449 billion in 1998).
19. Tim Blakelock. Interview with author, June 23, 1999.
20. Bill Paul. Interview with author, December 2, 1999.
21. Frank F. Britt, "The Logistics of Consumer-Direct," *Progressive Grocer,* May 1998, 39.
22. Ibid., 39.

Scope: Deciding Where and How to Play

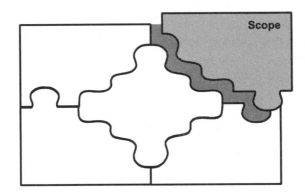

Every business must define the critical activities it will perform to create value for customers, to maintain strategic control of the customer interface, and to capture the profits it needs to prosper. These activities represent the *scope* of the business design. Scope decisions determine *what* activities must be performed to deliver on the company's value proposition and *who* will perform them—the company or outside partners.

■ VALUE NET ACTIVITIES

Broadly speaking, three categories of scope must be incorporated into the value net design: customer choice, production, and delivery (Figure 4.1).

Treating *customer choice* as an operational activity may strike readers as unusual. Customers are normally viewed as the receiving end of the supply chain, with the front end entrusted to sales and marketing. The Internet has rewritten the role of the customer. No longer a passive recipient, the customer has been transformed into an active participant in a company's operating processes. The Internet's ubiquity demands that every company consider creating an interactive customer choice mechanism, which we call a *choiceboard*. It allows companies for the first time to capture real demand and transmit choices directly to the fulfillment engine of the value net.

Delivery, broadly defined, constitutes the other major customer touch point. The potential for creative design of the delivery experience remains largely untapped. Many companies relegate this set of activities to a standardized, often outsourced, solution. In contrast, Mercer research reveals that value net companies leverage delivery to fulfill the winning value propositions discussed in Chapter 3.

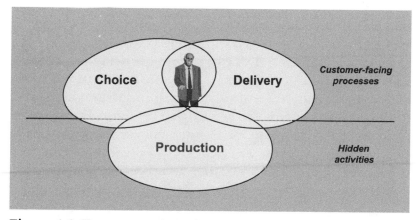

Figure 4.1 Key scope categories.

While choice and delivery are customer-facing processes, *production* constitutes the back-office functions, which are largely invisible to customers. Production must be designed to enhance flexibility, reliability, speed, and efficiency. Every company works to improve its internal effectiveness. A value net, in addition, seeks high performance and flexibility through outsourcing and collaboration with external providers.

While production and basic delivery are elements in all supply chains, value nets uniquely do the following:

➤ Create *choiceboards,* the interactive mediums through which customers can indicate their preferences.

➤ Develop *value-enhancing delivery* processes.

➤ *Synchronize* production activities with the customer-facing processes—choice and delivery—and partners across the value net.

➤ Employ strategic, and sometimes extreme, *outsourcing,* particularly of production functions.

➤ Establish *collaborative relationships* with partners to enhance customer value and capture profits.

This chapter examines each of these five points.

■ CHOICEBOARDS

The choiceboard is a new phenomenon made possible by the Internet. It has made it possible for companies to enjoy real-time, two-way interactions with their customers. Choiceboards are being used by a growing number of e-commerce companies. If you've never interacted with one, connect to www.dell.com or www.gateway.com and follow the routine for configuring and ordering a personal computer.

Generally, an effective choiceboard has four key elements, as shown in Figure 4.2.

Element	Choiceboard	Traditional choice options (catalog, e-catalog, retail shelf)
Communication process	Real-time, interactive	Sequential, iterative
Demand capture	Event-driven, based on revealed preferences	Forecast-driven, based on choice from available stock
Choice management	Real-time, active	Limited or none
Product definition	Configured-to-order	Predefined finished products

Figure 4.2 Key elements of a choiceboard.

➤ Communication Process

The choiceboard enables a fast, two-way conversation between the company and its customers. It is particularly useful for complex product decisions such as computer configuration, office furniture design, or even aircraft acquisition. The choiceboard developed by Weyerhaeuser's door division, for example, collapses a month-long process for custom-made doors to a 15-minute series of clicks.

➤ Demand Capture

Unlike a traditional supply chain, a value net does not push products. Nor does it operate to satisfy demand forecasts. It aims to fill *real* demand. But it can do this only if it knows what customers want and if it can link their desires to its operating design. A choiceboard overcomes these two constraints.

Real demand is elusive. A traditional supply chain allows customers to choose only from a predetermined set of in-stock, finished products. This creates a situation in which what customers purchase can be confused with what customers really want. Streamline's Frank Britt provides this example from the grocery industry:

> *Grocery stores have no idea what true demand is. Here's what happens in a grocery store. You go looking for the 12-ounce bottle and you can't find it, so you*

buy the 16-ounce one. If I am the planner, I look at the
demand and say, "Gee, there is a lot of demand for the
16-ounce bottle, so I'll order less of the 12-ounce ones
and more of the 16-ounce ones." You get into this vi-
cious circle because you are altering your inventory
mix based on bad data. You have no way of capturing
true demand.[1]

A choiceboard, on the other hand, allows a company to observe buyer reactions and obtain accurate insights into exact customer preferences. This encompasses specific products, product features, and services, such as requests for predelivery notification, postinstallation follow-up, training manuals, or express delivery. From the provider's perspective, a choiceboard creates efficiency in getting to know customers and their needs, thus eliminating the costs and guesswork associated with traditional demand forecasting.

➤ Choice Management

Customers can choose exactly what they want on a choiceboard, but the provider can manage the choice set. This benefits both parties. Experience with mass customization has shown that an excess of choice does not create value for customers—it merely creates confusion and decision gridlock. Smaller choice sets are actually preferred. For the provider, fewer component choices reduce inventory complexity and costs. Creative companies like Gateway are using choiceboards to actively manage demand and steer customers to components that are in better stock positions. Both result in lower inventory levels and contribute to superior profits.

The role of choiceboards in business-to-business commerce is potentially enormous. Dell's Premier Pages allow a customer (e.g., the central procurement department at a large corporation) to create its own customized choiceboards. Procurement can establish different options for various employees within the organization. The potential for consistency and control represents a significant benefit for the large corporate customer.

➤ Product Definition

The traditional option set—a catalog or retail shelf—presents customers with predefined finished products, which may not respond exactly to their needs. With a choiceboard, each customer can configure the product or service to his or her requirements. The ability to connect these customer choices directly to the assembly line enables efficient customization, the powerful value proposition discussed in Chapter 3.

The Internet provides an extremely efficient medium for choiceboards, but not all choiceboards must be confined to the net. The first choiceboards, in fact, were not built on the Internet. Dell and Gateway launched real-time, interactive order configuration over the telephone. Today, Gateway supplements its phone and Internet choiceboards with direct assistance at its wide network of Gateway Country® stores. The lesson is that the medium for registering customer choice should match the preference of targeted customers.

■ VALUE-ENHANCING DELIVERY

In conventional practice, delivery is an afterthought to product, pricing, and marketing decisions; it is simply the process of getting stuff to the customer. In a value net design, however, delivery is the business equivalent of crossing the goal line! Far from being an afterthought, delivery is an important opportunity to enhance the value of the offer, to delight the customer, and to make money. That opportunity should be considered early in the business design cycle.

In our definition, *delivery* includes the physical movement of materials, the intercompany processes that get the goods to the customer, the installation and training that may be necessary, ongoing support, product returns, and end-of-life retrieval. Many of the value propositions discussed in Chapter 3—speed, reliability, convenience, and customization—depend on a well-designed delivery process. Delivery therefore has to be an integral part of the scope design for a value net.

Many value net companies pay close attention to delivery as a customer touch point. For example,

➤ Cemex made a significant investment to digitize its delivery process. The high return from that investment demonstrates that fast and reliable delivery can create differentiation in an otherwise featureless product category.

➤ Streamline has chosen to own the truck fleet and deploy its own drivers (customer field reps) in order to control the customer experience at the delivery touch point.

➤ Xerox surrounds the mundane act of delivering a new office machine with activities that benefit it and its customers. Xerox delivery/removal contractors do not simply deliver a piece of equipment; they schedule it, install it, train the operators, seek feedback on customer satisfaction, and remove the old machine. This delivery system is unique in the office equipment business and contributes, Xerox believes, to higher customer loyalty.

The possibilities for adding value through a broadly defined delivery process are practically limitless. Here is an opportunity to take the ever changing pulse of the customer and fuel the overall relationship, making delivery an important element of value net scope.

■ SYNCHRONIZED PRODUCTION

Although production is largely hidden from the customer and may even be outsourced, these activities must be closely tied to the *choice* and *delivery* customer-facing processes and synchronized across the value net. Traditional production processes react blindly to customer orders and release batches of product in accordance with a manufacturing-driven schedule. In a value net, however, customer choiceboard selections and delivery requirements are immediately reviewed against the current production capacity and inventory situation. An available-to-promise date is instantly determined, driving all subsequent production activities and schedules. For value net companies, production is key in simultaneously setting and delivering on the customer promise.

Value net flexibility, reliability, speed, and efficiency are enhanced by close synchronization of production activities among in-house plants, in-transit merging centers, subcontractors, and suppliers. By *synchronization,* we mean that the company's production network, even if dispersed geographically or organizationally, is effectively operating together as one integrated, highly responsive system. For example, outsourced subcomponent manufacturing and deliveries are systemically tied to finished goods assembly schedules; a change to a customer delivery date immediately ripples through the value net, impacting material and labor requirements, priorities, schedules, and transportation modes; a parts shortage automatically triggers a requirement for an alternative supplier and expedited delivery.

Synchronized production tied to the choice and delivery processes is a hallmark of value net companies. For example,

> ➤ Zara, the fashion retailer, electronically links together its stores, headquarters, and global production network. Information binds and synchronizes

the separate pieces of its value net, enabling it to respond quickly and efficiently to the changing tastes
of the fashion-conscious consumer.

➤ Cemex uses its CemexNet information technology
to dynamically synchronize its operations at multiple mixing plants with the constantly changing
order stream—supporting its hallmark rapid and reliable deliveries with a flexible and efficient production process.

➤ Gateway works closely with its suppliers, coordinat-
ing production and delivery activities with the aid of
IT systems that provide visibility to customer orders
and inventory stocks within its value net. Early
identification of a parts shortage prompts the company to suggest alternative choiceboard selections to
customers, to offer free upgrades to an in-stock part,
or to launch an expediting process.

■ OUTSOURCING

Value net companies face the question, "Which activities
should we outsource to others?" Companies with traditional operating designs generally try to hold onto as
many activities as possible, limiting outsourcing to what
they view as noncore competencies. Value nets, however,
are redefining the notion of core competency. They are
placing greater emphasis on managing overall performance rather than on each of the transactional activities.
Transactions, in their view, should be carried out by
whomever has the ability to execute them with superior efficiency and with the highest potential for adding value.
Our rules of thumb on outsourcing are as follows:

1. Control the customer touch points—ordering, customer service, and delivery.

2. Own the information, the knowledge, and the relationship—not the transactions.
3. Own the visionary, analytical, relationship-building, and partner-management skills.

Everything else is fair game for outsourcing.

But what degree of outsourcing is right for a given firm? It depends on a company's value proposition, the maturity of suppliers in the industry, and the stage in a company's own life cycle. Outsourcing often provides flexibility and scalability—ideal characteristics for a young start-up. An entrepreneur with a vision for a new product or service can take that concept to market faster—and with less cash—by outsourcing production, distribution, and other functions. At one extreme, a start-up may engage in maximum outsourcing—debuting as a virtual company that performs none of the operating activities itself. Such a firm needs to be able to tap into a well-established set of suppliers to succeed.

At the other extreme, consider large corporations that have traditionally performed all manufacturing in-house. These firms are starting to reassess their basic make-or-buy decisions in favor of outsourcing. Sara Lee Knit Products, for example, announced in 1997 that it was selling its knitting mills in order to reduce its asset intensity. As we saw in Chapter 1, Apple Computer did the same during its 1997–1998 transformation. When Hewlett-Packard entered the home PC business in 1995, it never even considered manufacturing the machines itself. HP relied on contract manufacturers like SCI from the start.

The value net innovators we studied all use some form of outsourcing, especially for back-office operations that their customers don't directly see. Long-established incumbents would do well to consider doing the same. The ability to outsource has been aided in many industries by the rise of highly competent suppliers. Computer production, for example, has spawned a massive contract manufacturing business. In the pharmaceutical industry, clinical trials were traditionally conducted by the large drug companies themselves. Today, that activity is largely outsourced to companies like Quintiles (with sales of $1.2 billion in 1998) and others, few of which existed five years ago.

To explore the spectrum of outsourcing options, we begin at one extreme—the virtual company. Firms that follow this model are effectively separating the "sizzle" of product development and marketing from the "steak" of operations. We then continue with the notion of strategic outsourcing that characterizes many value net innovators. And we include an example of an outsourcer, Li & Fung, that supports its customers with a worldwide network of supply partners.

► The Virtual Company

Some companies have taken the concept of outsourcing to an extreme, contracting for most, if not all, operational activities. These are known as *virtual* companies. They sell products or services but own few, if any, production or delivery fixed assets; instead, they leverage the assets and strengths of business partners. Unburdened by assets, these companies can adapt quickly to changing market conditions and operate with little or no working capital.

The Internet is a hotbed of virtual companies. Its ease of entry, at least for selling, is immensely attractive to start-ups. E-tailer eToys.com's fixed assets, for example, amounted to $0.07 for each sales dollar in fiscal year 1999 versus $0.38 per dollar of sales for bricks-and-mortar competitor Toys 'R' Us. In grocery retailing, Peapod's fixed assets represented 6 percent of 1998 sales versus 21 percent for bricks-and-mortar grocer Safeway. Others such as eBay and FastParts are pure intermediaries; they do not manufacture or even take title to products. Entrepreneurs with new product and service ideas will continue to flock to the Internet's virtual world in the years ahead.

To succeed, virtual companies need three things: (1) an expansive vision, (2) a narrowly defined scope, and

(3) brilliantly executed value net operations. SOHO Inc., a California start-up and maker of ergonomic computer desks, has these three qualities. Founder Mahmoud (Max) Ladjevardi had little more than a patented idea in 1994. By 1999, however, his company had achieved $8 million in annual sales and was on a trajectory to continue its strong sales growth. Ladjevardi shared with us his views on the advantages of a virtual company:

> *The virtual design allowed us to use our capital to focus on the areas to grow the company, like sales and marketing. If we didn't use the virtual model, we'd have to develop manufacturing capabilities and world-class practices through years of experience. Nowadays, you can harness subcontractors to gain this expertise.*[2]

Minuscule capitalization is one of SOHO's striking features. The initial capital—$100,000—came from Ladjevardi's savings. Instead of paying millions for a factory, machinery, warehousing space, financing, and training, he brought together 14 suppliers and six retail partners from around the United States. He chose his partners carefully—a wood fabricator in North Carolina, a bracket supplier in Ohio, a metal manufacturer in Georgia, a warehouse in Chicago where ready-to-assemble components could be boxed and shipped to SOHO's retail and catalog partners.[3] Careful orchestration of these partners allows SOHO to set a high standard for delivery. As Ladjevardi told us, "We can guarantee to our customers a 48-hour turnaround time from order to delivery. As far as I know, there's no one in the competition that can match or better that."

Partners do everything except marketing, order entry, and customer service—the key customer touch points that SOHO jealously keeps for itself. Ladjevardi is emphatic about retaining control over the customer relationship: "We don't outsource customer service; we'd never outsource that. That's our direct link to the customer. That's the map that allows us to navigate where we want to go."

SOHO's virtual design allows it to operate at extremely low cost—only $400,000 per year of working capital and fixed costs combined. SOHO does no advertising. Instead, it offers retailers promotional discounts in return for premium shelf space or full-page catalog space. The company's only fixed costs are rent, insurance, and salaries for Ladjevardi, his wife (marketing VP), and two other employees. Says Ladjevardi, "The virtual model allows you to be reliable *and* turn a profit, even when you're small."

For new product developers, the virtual model offers advantages, and capable suppliers are emerging to make adoption of that model possible. In the medical device field, for example, TriVirix International of Chapel Hill, North Carolina, was formed in 1998 to offer a full outsourcing solution. "There are a number of virtual medical device companies out there—with technology and a CEO—but no intent of ever building a manufacturing or distribution capability," says Doug Suna, TriVirix's vice president of business development.[4] "These companies are looking for someone to take charge of operations. We're betting that the outsourcing wave we've seen in areas like clinical trials will reach devices soon." By focusing on information control to meet regulatory requirements and by managing the entire sourcing, manufacturing, and logistics process, Suna hopes that TriVirix will glean its fair share of the estimated $5 billion medical device manufacturing business.

For e-tailers, new product developers, and other startups, the virtual model offers advantages. It allows these firms to pursue what they do best—typically, product design, marketing, and brand management—even as they achieve superb execution through their supply partners. It enables companies to quickly launch their products and to scale output in tune with demand. It lets them capitalize on the experience and economies of scale of larger partners and helps overcome the need for major up-front investment in plant and working capital.

Lack of strategic control (the subject of Chapter 6) is the Achilles' heel of virtual companies. If one shifts the operating burden onto others, how can profits be captured and protected over time? It is revealing that Amazon, which began as a virtual bookseller with no distribution network of its own, changed its distribution strategy as it grew. As this book went to press, the company, which had thus far failed to earn a penny in profits, was in the midst of a $300 million distribution center construction program.[5]

➤ Strategic Outsourcing

Not every company can or should become virtual. However, every company needs to understand that the best place to play in the interconnected world of customers and suppliers does not remain constant. As companies acquire, divest, or extend their operations across borders, the best place to play in the chain of value-adding activities varies. It also changes as company and supplier capabilities evolve, as the ability to communicate in real time improves, and as intercompany relations become more open and collaborative. Hugh Aitken, vice president of operations for Sun Microsystems–Europe, gave us this example:

> In 1993, we were doing printed circuit boards in-house with our surface-mounting technology to build the BGA [ball grid array] capability. At the time, no suppliers could offer to build that capability reliably. Three to four years later, in 1997, suppliers caught up, and what had been a core competency for us had become a commodity. So we outsourced printed circuit board manufacturing to Solectron and retrained our employees for different tasks further up the supply chain. . . . The thing about supply chains is that they need to change dramatically, as supplier capabilities, products, customers, and technology change every two and a half to three years.[6]

E-tailers face the critical question of establishing an infrastructure that can do the job and scale quickly. Once up and running, though, there is a constant trade-off—the scope issue—of whether to use drop shippers or bring physical distribution in-house. Español.com, incorporated in November 1998 to offer culturally relevant products to Latino shoppers in U.S. and Puerto Rican markets, currently uses five fulfillment partners and one facility of its own to handle nearly 3 million SKUs. Kyle McNamara, CEO of Español.com, explains:

> *The toughest question, when you're talking about drop shipment, is the uniformity and dependability of the consumer experience. It's a great way to launch, but it may not be the ultimate solution. If you look at Amazon, they started out with a hybrid model—mostly drop ship and some warehouse—like we have. Now they're at the other end of the spectrum, doing almost all [their own] warehousing. Drop shipping, while cost-effective in some ways, isn't ideal because you're dealing with organizations that perhaps don't have your business at the center of their universe. . . . There's always this natural battle between not wanting to have a huge warehouse infrastructure and all the associated costs, but also not wanting to lose the uniformity of the customer experience. I can tell you it's something we talk about all the time. Right now, we're just tightening our drop-ship relationships as much as possible.[7]*

The growth of virtual companies like SOHO and many e-tailers is just one indicator that times have changed and that traditional (even successful) definitions of *scope* quickly become obsolete. As most products mature, capable and specialized suppliers grow up around them, offering efficient external manufacturing solutions.

The practicality of outsourcing has also grown as a more collaborative business culture and supporting technologies spread. In the past, companies avoided outsourcing for fear of losing control or service quality. As they saw it, outsourcing was a trade-off between lower cost *or* better service. However, collaboration, better management, and technology have made it possible to have both lower cost *and* better service.

One company that offers its customers a global outsourcing solution is Hong Kong–based Li & Fung.

➤ A Value Net with Global Scope: Li & Fung

Li & Fung Trading is positioned as the strategic outsourcing partner for leading apparel and toy companies that seek to tap global manufacturing resources. Its carefully defined scope of operations has evolved and been perfected over three generations. With nearly $2 billion in revenues and $60 million in profits (1999), Li & Fung Trading is Hong Kong's largest export trading company, serving several hundred major retailers from more than 45 offices in 30 countries in Asia, Africa, Europe, and Latin America.

Background

Li & Fung Trading does not own a single production plant or employ any factory workers, yet it orchestrates production of apparel, toys, and other consumer items through a worldwide network of 7,500 suppliers—factories, carriers, and financiers—with such finesse that it can deliver high-quality goods to European and North American retailers in a matter of weeks.

Li & Fung was founded in Canton, China, in 1906 by the grandfather of Victor and William Fung, the current chairman and CEO, respectively. At the time, it was the only Chinese-owned company in an export economy dominated by foreign-owned trading houses. Its value-added service, according to Victor Fung, was his grandfather's ability to speak English. The company earned its way by being a broker—bringing buyers and sellers together.

Victor Fung was teaching at the Harvard Business School and his young brother William was a recent graduate of the same institution when both were called back to Hong Kong in the mid-1970s to take over the family business, which was experiencing a major margin squeeze. As the Western buyers and Chinese factories became larger and more sophisticated and as information became more available, the company's role as a broker began to lose value. To compound its problems, the Asian "tigers" emerged as major rivals to the Hong Kong manufacturers for whom Li & Fung acted as matchmaker. Before long, Hong Kong was no longer competitive in manufacturing and contract assembly.

"My grandfather worked on 15 percent [margins]," Victor Fung explained to us. "My father worked on 10 percent, and we were working on 3 to 5 percent. . . . People were saying 'this is going to be marginalized to zero.' "[8]

Changing Scope

Something had to change if the house of Li & Fung expected to survive through another generation. The traditional scope of the company's activities was being eclipsed; it had to find a new place to play in the continuum of value-adding activities that placed finished goods on the shelves of U.S. and European retail stores.

The Fung brothers saw a new role as a global strategic outsourcer. They decided to take responsibility for customer orders, delivering finished products at the lowest cost and with the highest efficiency. Instead of acting as a go-between for Western retailers with orders for garments and other items as they had in the past, Victor and William Fung would dissect each order into its component parts (e.g., material, cutting, sewing, dying, packaging, and shipping) and then determine how best to complete that order in terms of customer requirements for cost, quality, and rapid delivery. For The Limited, Avon, and more than 300 other major retailers, Li & Fung would act as a fully outsourced supply network, taking orders and handling all of the details from end to end.

Long experience in Asian manufacturing has provided the company with a matchless knowledge (now in an electronic database) of the capabilities and resources of materials suppliers and factories throughout Asia. That knowledge base has kept pace as manufacturing dispersed to Thailand, Korea, the hinterlands of China, and more recently, South America and Eastern Europe. Chairman Fung explains:

> *Say we get an order from a European retailer to produce 10,000 garments. . . . For this customer, we might decide to buy yarn from a Korean producer but have it woven and dyed in Taiwan. So we pick the yarn and ship it to Taiwan. The Japanese have the best zippers and buttons, but they manufacture them mostly in China. Okay, so we go to YKK, a big Japanese zipper manufacturer, and we order the right zippers from their Chinese plants. Then we determine that, because of quotas and labor conditions, the best place to make the garments is Thailand. So we ship everything from there. And because the customer needs quick delivery, we may divide the order across five factories in Thailand. Effectively, we are customizing the value chain to best meet the customer's needs. Five weeks after we have received the order, 10,000 garments arrive on the shelves in Europe, all looking like they came from one factory.*[9]

Key Characteristics

How does Li & Fung excel as a strategic partner? Value net principles guide its approach.

➤ *It's customer-aligned.* In true value net form, Li & Fung begins with its customers, aligning its activities with theirs. With approximately 80 divisions, Li & Fung aligns its organization into customer-facing units. In some cases, these divisions even handle product development for customers. In 1999, for example, Li & Fung's Avon division helped to design, develop, source, and deliver 300 to 400 different products to Avon's units in North America, Australia, Germany, Japan, China, and Britain.[10]

➤ *It's agile.* Li & Fung's relationships with thousands of suppliers provide customers with the flexibility they need. In turn, a policy of not owning production facilities keeps Li & Fung agile and adaptable, encouraging its constant search for more highly quality-conscious and cost-effective producers and allowing it to assemble customized supply chains for each customer order.

➤ *Its agility is supported by its nimble organizational design.* Each of its 80 divisions is run as an independent, entrepreneurial business. Each has its own P&L and the authority to make decisions needed to respond to changing customer requirements. But although the divisions operate like entrepreneurial units, they avoid the typical small company headaches; they are supported by common finance, IT, and corporate administrative systems. A policy of "freedom with support" makes it possible for each division to respond with the speed and flexibility required by its customers.

➤ *It's fast.* The company has cut order delivery times on many apparel items from three months to four or five weeks. The secret lies in its ability to orchestrate its supplier network.

➤ *Close ties to supply partners are nurtured.* The company maintains close long-term relationships with its many suppliers and makes a point of providing them with a fairly steady and substantial volume of business. This in turn allows Li & Fung to maintain its own service reliability. The company is gradually reducing its strategic vendor base, and it now works most actively with perhaps 1,500 of its 7,500 partners. Why so many suppliers? Li & Fung must source each order from multiple handicraft factories, each employing less than 200 workers. To fill large customer orders quickly while respecting import quotas, Li & Fung uses numerous vendors around the world. Managing this web of supplier relationships is one of the company's core competencies and sources of value as a strategic outsourcer.

The Future

What about the future? Will the Internet and other linking technologies put the squeeze on the scope of Li & Fung's role as supply chain orchestrator, just as greater information did to the broker business of earlier generations? Chairman Fung is not worried. To him the Internet linkage between vendor and customer is merely the front end of the business:

> We want to be the quiet utility in the background, doing all the fulfillment. Frankly, I don't care if the Internet goes this way or that way . . . at some point someone must get the stuff manufactured and delivered. Most customers do not regard [what we do] as their core competence. As they should, they are focusing on the front end, which is how they generate the order. The fulfillment function is something that they want to contract out. That trend is very much in our favor.

■ COLLABORATIVE RELATIONSHIPS

All value net participants—suppliers, customers, and even competitors—represent opportunities to create leverage through collaboration. The idea of collaborating with these entities is still a radical one for most companies, so let's examine each in some detail.

➤ Suppliers

Traditionally, supplier leverage has been measured in terms of cost savings. Because spending on suppliers accounts for over half of many companies' total spending, the leverage potential here is substantial. Wal-Mart has created one classic approach to supplier leverage. It works closely with suppliers and demands changes that squeeze out costs, making Wal-Mart the paragon of low-cost, low-priced business designs.

Collaboration, however, should create value for everyone in the net. Supplier collaboration enables better product development, service design, and inventory management.

A reduction in the number of suppliers is generally a precondition for collaborative supplier relationships. No company can maintain close and effective relationships with more than a small set of other parties. Once the number of participants exceeds an optimal level, collaboration gives way to transactions.

For Sun Microsystems, 20 suppliers account for 90 percent of its $5 billion annual spending. Sun formed a council with the top five of these suppliers to jointly attack important problems—specifically, time compression in the procure-to-pay cycle of its operations and the creation of a scalable information architecture to help all partners respond to changing market conditions. It now views these collaborative initiatives as critical to its competitive position in the marketplace.

The U.S. auto industry provides another instructive example of the benefits of working with fewer suppliers. There, supplier rationalization, which began in the 1980s, has had a dramatic impact—reducing the number of parts suppliers in North America from 30,000 in 1988 to 4,000 in

1998. That number is expected to drop to under 3,000 by 2003.[11] The outcome of this contraction has been positive: greater information sharing, a higher level of collaboration in product development, stricter standards, and process improvements that have reduced inventories, costs, and cycle times.

The Internet is revolutionizing supplier collaboration. The growth of concurrent design technologies, virtual offices, and supplier-buyer networks allows companies to work together more seamlessly than ever before. At the same time, online auctions may challenge the trend toward long-term supplier partnering. Will this lead us back toward transaction-based procurement? Not really. Transaction-based procurement is and will remain appropriate for the 90 percent of suppliers that account for 10 percent of a company's spending (though it will be automated). For the top-tier suppliers that account for 90 percent of the spending, however, the name of the game will be collaboration and mutual value enhancement.

➤ Customers

While most companies continue to interact with customers in time-honored ways—through selling and follow-up service—few have pursued opportunities for two-way collaborative initiatives. Yet such opportunities abound. Procter & Gamble, for example, has set up incentives for customers who agree to take delivery of shipments within two hours or less at least 80 percent of the time. The reason for P&G's program is clear: The average unloading time for those shipments is 94 minutes, as opposed to the usual average of 211 minutes.

Becton Dickinson (BD), a major medical equipment company, has also looked to customers for help in developing more cost-efficient and value-enhancing services. In 1998, it hired Michael McDaid as vice president of operations for its Healthcare Services Division, a unit responsible for supply chain operations, distribution, finance, and sales across many of BD's brands. McDaid came with a grocery background and participates on a team that is exploring the applicability of grocery logistics to the healthcare industry. The grocery industry uses pricing based on *cost to serve* and fulfillment complexity. It defines several tiers of customers. The most desirable customers, logistically speaking, communicate entirely via EDI. Because these customers interact digitally and order full pallets or full tiers of products, they cost the least to serve; and therefore receive the lowest prices. Other grocery customers have a primarily digital relationship, with nonelectronically handled exceptions such as credit memos and returns. These customers order full tiers or full cases of products. The most costly customers to serve are those making minimal use of electronic ordering— they order "each-picks" (single units) instead of full tiers. The BD team hopes that an analysis of these principles can help create a new pricing model for the delivery of medical equipment and supplies—one that will allow prices to reflect the overall cost of doing business. Such innovative service pricing options can encourage customers to develop digital interfaces that are cost-efficient, fast, and accurate.

Philips Components also uses customer collaboration to gain market advantage. Its new Customer Linked Innovation and Commercialization program helps bring flat display systems (FDS) technology to market quickly. Philips seeks strategic relationships with original equipment manufacturers (OEMs) likely to emerge as winners in the marketplace, thus assuring quick popularization of its new technology. Mazy Sehrgosha, sales vice president for Philips Components, explains: "Time to volume is the name of the game. Whoever gets there first has the advantage. We bring the FDS technology. But we need strong sponsors."[12] With Hewlett-Packard and Compaq as its collaborators, Philips is able to bring its leading technology to volume fast. This type of collaboration shifts the dialogue between supplier and customer from traditional price bidding to the joint development of new, innovative products and platforms.

➤ Competitors

The least intuitive and least explored context for collaboration is that which occurs among competitors. Collaboration with competitors *can* be mutually beneficial in some cases. Ford, for example, gained scale efficiencies and cost savings through a distribution arrangement with Daimler-Chrysler's Mopar division. By agreement, the two automakers ship parts to dealers on the same delivery trucks, managed by Exel Logistics. A pilot of this program was launched in January 1998, with 11 U.S. dealerships participating. It was so successful that the two companies are rolling it out to other suitable dealerships.

Direct collaboration among competitors, however, is difficult and unlikely to become widespread in the foreseeable future. *Indirect* collaboration through third parties or joint ventures is more promising. Airlines and railroads are already pursuing opportunities for third parties to manage duplicate inventories and assets held by competitors in the same geographic locations. For example, why should each airline maintain its own inventory of replacement parts for the same Airbus aircraft at a major airport when a third-party inventory provider could keep a single stock at the same location at much lower cost?

The benefits accruing from competitors working together are illustrated by the emerging success of AirLiance Materials, a joint venture company formed in 1998 by United Airlines, Air Canada, and Lufthansa Technik. In early 1998, these three airlines were carrying $2 billion of parts inventories. The surplus parts were turning over less than once a year. In search of a better solution to this parts inventory problem, the airlines formed AirLiance Materials for the purpose of providing joint management of technical maintenance materials.

AirLiance was not constrained to serve only its three founding air carriers, but was given leave to expand its parts service to a wider circle of competing airlines. In this it has been very successful. As of late 1999, more than 100 airlines were on the AirLiance customer list. Says David Sisson, AirLiance's CEO, "We buy and sell from archcompetitors of our founding partners. . . . It's all money, isn't it?"[13]

The main benefit of the AirLiance venture for the industry as a whole is cost savings resulting from the increased use of pre-owned parts, which AirLiance sells at approximately a 30 percent discount relative to new OEM list prices. In addition, AirLiance partner airlines achieve higher yields on the sale of their surplus parts, reductions in overall inventory holdings, and lower prices from economies of scale on joint purchasing of new material. AirLiance's information systems also create value for customers and partners by answering parts pricing and availability queries in real time, by allowing order tracking, and by providing online access to critical parts documentation and certification.

By leveraging e-commerce and technology, AirLiance aspires to broaden the scope of its value-added services and to become a total supply chain integrator for the airline industry, offering repair management, inventory management, and logistics services. According to Sisson, "The general expectation among our partners . . . is that they will outsource more of their supply chain management tasks to [us]." The broader the scope of AirLiance and other ventures like it, the greater the potential benefits of collaboration among competitors in the airline industry.

Industrywide clearinghouses can provide similar benefits among competing companies. FastParts.com, a clearinghouse for excess computer inventories, is an interesting example of a third-party facilitator that benefits competing OEMs in the PC industry. Because many components in the computer industry are standard, an OEM like IBM can use the FastParts web site to anonymously auction off excess monitors, circuit boards, disk drives, or other items to any competing OEM that has a temporary shortage. This second OEM may, in turn, use the site to auction off its excess printers. The net result of this clearinghouse function is lower inventory and less component obsolescence across the entire system.

■ HOW DOES THE SCOPE DECISION APPLY TO YOUR BUSINESS?

As you think about the optimal scope of activities that you should control, begin by identifying the activities that *must* be performed to satisfy the value proposition. Are those being handled effectively? Are you doing things that other entities could perform with greater efficiency and at lower cost?

You do *not* want to surrender the customer touch points. If you already control them, are you exploiting their full potential?

Questions of scope lie at the heart of value net design and apply to enterprises large and small. Many companies should consider the value of a *choiceboard*. A choiceboard is particularly adept at supporting value propositions that feature customization. It is also powerful in industries that have not traditionally offered structured or fulfillment-linked choices to customers. And it is a great tool for any company that sells from an extensive product catalog, especially for industrial products with multiple sourcing and production options.

Opportunities for *delivery service* differentiation also exist for companies in many industries. Here are a few examples:

> ➤ Products that require delivery within very precise time windows (e.g., building materials, food products, auto components)

➤ Situations in which direct delivery from the manufacturer could eclipse current fulfillment or retail
activities (e.g., automobiles, building materials, garments, appliances, fuel)

➤ Complex products with intensive installation requirements (e.g., computer and telecommunications hardware, other industrial equipment)

Value net–wide *production* synchronization becomes
more critical under the following conditions:

➤ Production facilities and suppliers span several geog-
raphies.

➤ Stages in the production process are outsourced to
multiple vendors.

➤ Product demand is highly volatile and the market
window is narrow.

➤ Change orders are frequent and difficult to accommodate.

Opportunities for *outsourcing* are especially relevant in
industries characterized as follows:

➤ Many capable and reliable suppliers

➤ Globally dispersed suppliers that can function
seamlessly and efficiently through sophisticated
logistics and communications links

➤ Activities that can be performed more effectively on
behalf of a portfolio of buyers than for a single company

➤ Suppliers and service providers ready to do business
via e-commerce

As the outsourcing wave continues to sweep through
more industries, opportunity is created both for companies
that wish to concentrate on the "sizzle" of new products and

brand management and for those whose operational prowess suggests they can provide the "steak." Whole industries are ripe for the emergence of total solutions–oriented providers to handle the full gamut of manufacturing, customer support, logistics, and sourcing.

With regard to *collaboration,* the opportunity is greatest in those businesses that are characterized by antagonistic relationships. A company that switches to a collaborative view of its scope can gain strategic advantage in this setting. Look for collaboration opportunities where these conditions prevail:

➤ The supply base is consolidating (e.g., automobiles, computers, steel, petroleum).

➤ Businesses have become commoditized (e.g., utilities, building materials, home PCs, paper, steel).

Many companies can benefit from revisiting their scope. A fresh perspective is essential in building a value net. Biogen is one company that jump-started its operations by taking an innovative approach to its scope and building a value net.

■ AGGRESSIVELY MANAGED PARTNERING: THE RIGHT ℞ FOR BIOGEN

Scope decisions are especially critical for a young company that must invent itself and its role as it grows through innovation. We have chosen the case of Biogen, Inc., to illustrate those decisions. Biogen and its executives faced urgent questions about "where to play" as they evolved from an R&D laboratory to an operating company.

In 1994, Massachusetts-based Biogen was approaching a breakthrough on a new drug with blockbuster potential.

Getting the new drug to market quickly would be imperative if the small company were to reap the full benefit of its
discovery. In the pharmaceutical business, where the earn-
ing power of a product can be quickly eclipsed by a new and
superior formulation, any delay in moving a newly approved drug to end customers can result in the loss of many
millions of dollars.

For Biogen, with limited manufacturing and distribution capabilities, the question was, "Which is the best and
fastest route to the market?" It could license its discovery
to a major industry player—the usual practice for small
drug developers—or it could retain control of manufacturing and distribution. How the company addressed this
critical question provides important insights into the
problem of scope in a value net business design.

➤ History and Strategy

Biogen, the world's oldest independent biotechnology
company, was founded in 1978 in Geneva, Switzerland, by
a group of European and U.S. biologists. At the time, it represented a new kind of pharmaceutical company, one dedicated to harnessing the power of human genes to improve
human health.

The company's business model in the early years, as
one senior Biogen executive recalled, was "based upon
great science, getting an interesting compound, and licensing it to a big pharmaceutical company."[14] But cash
was being eaten up by research expenses as well as travel
and administrative costs linked to the company's dual
headquarters in Cambridge, Massachusetts, and Switzerland. A Wall Street analyst described Biogen's early years:
"Wally Gilbert [Biogen's cofounder] planted the seed, and
it grew into a handsome radish ... [but] this handsome
radish was bleeding $100,000 a day. . . . Instead of giving
stockholders a return on investment, the radish gave them
serious indigestion. . . . There was more red ink in East
Cambridge than MIT students. Finished products were virtually nonexistent."[15]

➤ **AVONEX®**

In 1982, the company made an important discovery: Interferon beta 1-a. Interferons, as produced naturally in the human body, are proteins that inhibit cell division and help the immune system fight off viruses. While interferons hold promise against many diseases, Biogen targeted the development of its Interferon beta 1-a against multiple sclerosis (MS), a progressive disease with no known cure that attacks the central nervous system, afflicting 1 million people worldwide and almost 350,000 in the United States. The first drug approved to treat MS was Betaseron, or Interferon beta 1-b, an interferon with a different molecular structure and manufacturing process than Biogen's Interferon beta 1-a. Betaseron, produced by Chiron and marketed by Berlex Laboratories, was approved in July 1993 as a therapy to prevent relapses (not to slow the progression of the disease) for patients with the relapsing/remitting form of MS. Betaseron, which was suitable for about 100,000 U.S. patients, required subcutaneous injections every other day at a cost of approximately $1,000 a month.

A year after official approval of Betaseron, Biogen received a positive response to its Phase III testing of its product. The drug (later named AVONEX®) was found to slow the progression of physical disability *and* to reduce the number of relapses. John Palmer, who had a background in marketing, business development, and operations, was Biogen's director of operations, responsible for the development and execution of a supply chain strategy for the launch of the new drug. He recalled for us the excitement and promise of that moment:

> *We opened the envelope with the Phase III results and said, "Oh my God!" It was that promising. We knew we had something—an important drug to manufacture and distribute.*[16]

But Biogen at that time was a company with revenues of only $140 million, modest profits, and limited supply chain capabilities. Palmer continued:

We were an R&D boutique with excellent research and science but little else. We had a licensing department and only a rudimentary regulatory function. AVONEX® gave us the opportunity—and the challenge—to become a real operating drug company.

➤ Biogen Builds a Value Net

With positive Phase III results in hand, the company felt it had fulfilled one-half of its motto, "Delivering on the promise of biotechnology." It had found the *promise.* Now it had to *deliver* . . . literally. Once it received final approval, Biogen had to find a way to get the promising drug to patients quickly and to build a system for efficient distribution over the long haul. Its executives saw three options for its scope of activities:

➤ Partner with a major drug company ("Big Pharma") for its supply chain capabilities.

➤ Build a complete supply chain in-house.

➤ Outsource some or all of the manufacturing and delivery activities.

The first choice—licensing to a major pharmaceutical house—was rejected. The economic possibilities of AVONEX® were simply too big and too promising for Biogen to give up control. It was a breakthrough drug with breakthrough potential for the company. Biogen executives feared that a partnership with Big Pharma for its supply chain capabilities would entail also giving up a piece of the action and would impose the schedules, timetables, processes, and culture of the big company on the much smaller Biogen. As Palmer noted, "We would have been a gnat on an elephant to them."

Another possibility was for Biogen to build a complete supply chain of its own, but the company lacked the money and time to support that option. It was dead set against betting borrowed sums against full regulatory approval that might be delayed. "Our philosophy and our practice," says John Palmer, "has always been, 'Spend no dime before its time,' and we weren't about to change that."

Thus, Biogen's best option was a selective collaborative approach, one that led to building a value net. As the company considered specific alternatives, it looked to its main rival in the MS market for a useful lesson—and a warning.

➤ An Instructive Example

Although Berlex initially enjoyed a 100 percent market share with Betaseron, Biogen executives viewed its problems in distributing that drug to patients as lessons in what *not* to do. Betaseron had been approved just a year after its application was filed—much faster than anticipated. As a result, Berlex was not ready for manufacturing and distribution and needed several months after regulatory approval to bring the drug to market. Even then it failed to satisfy demand. One magazine described this failure of the supply chain:

> Betaseron's speedy approval in July [1993] caught both its marketer, Berlex Laboratories, the American unit of Schering A.G., and its manufacturer Chiron . . . off guard. Right now, Chiron can make only enough for 20,000 sufferers (one-fifth of those eligible) but hopes to catch up with demand by 1995.[17]

To make matters worse, a lottery system was devised to determine which patients would receive the limited quantities of the drug. Doctors were asked to send in the names of qualified patients, and a blind drawing came up with the names of the lucky recipients. Patients and physicians were angered by this rationing of what should have been a godsend to so many. The lucky patients whose names were picked had still another barrier to cross in obtaining the drug. Patients had to present a special "Betaseron card" to a pharmacist who was enrolled in a special network. The pharmacist would then request the drug. That request was transmitted to Berlex, which then shipped a month's supply of Betaseron to the pharmacy. Two or three days later, the patient could pick up the drug.[18]

The Biogen team headed by Palmer viewed this system as fundamentally flawed:

> [Their] approach ... was a one-size-fits-all system, with a principal goal of optimizing the business for the company ... not the patient. Product packaging required multiple prescriptions, and patients had to incrementally buy needles and syringes. Distribution was via a single, direct company-to-pharmacist/or-doctor arrangement and limited to essentially cash sale terms. Moreover, policy decisions being made by a German parent organization further distanced them from the patient community.

Biogen executives felt that the Berlex approach aggravated everyone. They wanted to avoid the same mistake. Berlex, in essence, told the patient: "Have it only our way." In contrast, one Biogen team member notes, "We were determined to be like Burger King and say, 'Have it your way.'" They wanted the patient to be able to get a complete product package through whichever channel was most convenient (pharmacy, physician, mail-order, etc.).

➤ Biogen's Approach

As Biogen began to consider the value net partners it would need, it also evaluated its internal resources for handling the four steps of a drug's production and distribution:

1. Manufacturing the drug in bulk
2. Formulation (in the case of AVONEX®, freeze-drying the substance and keeping it at cold temperatures)

3. Packaging and labeling (including the package insert)
4. Distribution to retailers, doctors, and patients

Because commercial bulk production would be similar to clinical production, although on a much larger scale, company officials felt they could handle bulk manufacturing in their Cambridge facility. A decision was made to contract out everything but the bulk manufacturing and the responsibility for aggressive management of the entire value net. So Biogen began looking for companies that excelled at what they did, that were big enough to offer flexibility and skills, yet small enough to consider Biogen an important customer.

The Value Net Team Takes Shape

Biogen set tough standards, applying "best-of-Big-Pharma" criteria for execution and quality. Additionally, it insisted on a goal of "no stockouts." Team member Robert Hamm, now the firm's operations vice president, recalls, "We wanted everyone to realize that the worst thing that could happen was a stockout."[19] A stockout would be bad from a customer perspective, but it would also be detrimental from a profit viewpoint because the cost of carrying inventory (based on cost of goods) was tiny relative to the cost of a lost sale. Biogen likewise insisted on no delays in the drug launch timeline due to operational issues.

Determined to handpick the best available partners, Biogen made the following selections:

➤ *Formulation:* Ben-Venue Laboratories, a contract manufacturer near Cleveland that had served several large pharmaceutical companies.

➤ *Packaging and labeling:* Packaging Coordinators Inc. (PCI), a small but innovative and flexible development house near Philadelphia.

➤ *Storing and distribution:* Amgen's new distribution center in Louisville, near the airport and UPS facilities, offered excess refrigerated capacity and a quality approach compatible with that of Biogen.

Transportation was a critical part of the supply chain, and arrangements had to be made for trucking from site to site. AVONEX® needed refrigeration throughout its manufacture and required cold temperatures once formulated. Temperature in transit had to be monitored and recorded hourly. Equally strict FDA regulation and validation procedures governed every step of the supply chain and manufacturing activity.

Biogen worked closely and intensely with its partners, overseeing how things got done. "We are a high-maintenance customer," explained a member of the Biogen team. Biogen was firm in its belief that the key to success was in outsourcing activities, but not the responsibility for managing them.

The Patient Link

With its customer-centric approach, Biogen extended the scope of its value net to include customer support. Biogen's fledgling marketing department helped organize focus groups from the medical community and included potential patients in them. The company then worked to incorporate what it learned into its packaging and distribution plans. The emphasis continued to be on the patient and on not precluding any possible ways of getting AVONEX® to the patient.

Home intramuscular injections were a new form of therapy, and Biogen wanted to make sure this approach worked. The company offered training and home visits for instruction or injection. Staying customer-focused was a priority, and Biogen went to great lengths to ensure customer convenience. For example, in contrast to Berlex, it decided to package all needed supplies (diluent, syringes, alcohol wipes, bandages, etc.) in one convenient unit requiring a single prescription. Doing so meant that Biogen had additional challenges with the FDA regarding each component, but patient convenience was optimized.

Biogen did not stop there, however. In a break with usual pharmaceutical practices, it set up its own customer service organization and staffed it with well-trained, enthusiastic, and empathetic people. Traditionally, a patient's only contact with a drug company had been through a doctor or other medical person and usually dealt only with adverse reactions. Palmer and Hamm explain how Biogen's approach encouraged patient interaction:

> *The more direct contact the better. . . . We wanted to offer help with injections, reimbursements, answer questions, whatever the patient wanted, all from one 800 number. Even if the call was transferred, there was a single point of contact, and all handoffs were warm, person-to-person transfers. Our goal was to establish a bond with our ultimate customers.*

Biogen also set up several distribution options to help patients manage the expense: pickup at a local drugstore, distribution through their doctor's offices, and direct home delivery. In each case, the insurance company was billed directly; the patient did not have to pay and then file for reimbursement.

The 35-Hour Launch

Even as it was selecting its partners and preparing to make and market AVONEX®, Biogen worked its way through the regulatory approval process. By March of 1996, it had a letter from the FDA saying the drug was "approvable," but no actual approval had been granted. Biogen had also filed for European approval and was simultaneously trying to prepare for these even more complex situations, involving multiple countries, languages, and regulatory bodies. Jim Mullen, then vice president of operations (now president and COO), reminisced about this waiting time and uncertainty: "You never know when the final approval is going to come, when you will get the letter or the fax, so you have to be completely ready. The whole thing was a physical and marketing ballet that had to be coordinated."[20]

As the company orchestrated this ballet, it worked to excite its value net partners by setting a launch goal. Amgen claimed to have launched a drug within 48 hours of FDA approval. The Biogen team was determined to beat that record, and John Palmer stressed the importance of setting that goal. "If we hadn't made such a big deal of the launch, we wouldn't have gotten the support of our supply chain team. The goal of the fastest launch in history was a way to get our supply chain partners excited. They jumped on the bandwagon and had fun."

As Biogen prepared for the fastest launch ever, it developed alternative scenarios, some with plans detailed down to 15-minute blocks of time. Team members wore beepers, rented hotel rooms, reserved rental cars, and lined up airplane reservations. They had four complete contingency plans. They waited, ready, for the word to come. Finally, on Friday, May 17, 1996, at 11 A.M., the FDA's approval of AVONEX® was faxed to Biogen's regulatory department.

The planning paid off. The first shipments of AVONEX® reached pharmacy shelves 35 hours after approval, and the drug was ready for dispensing by Monday morning. As one reporter observed:

> The launch of AVONEX® has been viewed by financial analysts as an example of a well-orchestrated, well-planned introduction that rivals products launched by powerful pharmaceutical companies. AVONEX® was in place within two days of launch. The first shipment of AVONEX® occurred 33 [sic] hours after approval. Area managers contacted more than 2,000 U.S. neurologists within the first two weeks after

AVONEX® approval. The speed of availability was possible because Biogen was ready.[21]

The launch transformed the company. Says Jim Mullen, "The launch was a statement to ourselves and to the world that Biogen was a real drug company. It established our credibility and gave us confidence."

➤ Results

AVONEX® became the U.S. market share leader within six months of launch, displacing Betaseron and subsequently garnering over 60 percent of new prescriptions. AVONEX® was successfully launched in a number of European countries as well the year after its U.S. debut. Because of the numerous languages, regulatory bodies, cultures, and pricing mechanisms involved, the company was essentially producing 20 SKUs rather than one. Biogen succeeded there, too, and AVONEX® has become the drug of choice on both continents.

AVONEX® earned the "highest satisfaction" accolade by the patient community several years in a row. In 1998, Biogen received the National Technology Award. The patient hot line likewise has been a major success and continues to receive over 1,000 calls per day years after the launch. After four years of operations, there have been no stockouts, no serious consumer service issues, no product recalls. Biogen was given the "Supplier of the Year" award by Cardinal Health (the second largest U.S. drug wholesaler) in both 1997 and 1998—a compliment to the company's sustained high level of operational performance. Erin Smith, a buyer at Cardinal for Biogen's AVONEX® drug, told us: "Biogen is a great company to work with; it's truly a hassle-free vendor. It has lead times of two to three days compared to a one-week average for most drug companies."[22] This positive sentiment is echoed at other major drug wholesalers. Greg Stellato, inventory manager at McKesson HBOC, praised Biogen's 100 percent order fulfillment rate, saying: "We have never had any problems with shortages or delays in filling orders. They are really easy to work with."[23]

A new Biogen bulk drug manufacturing facility in North Carolina was eventually added to meet growing demand, but otherwise the original supplier partners remain the same. While the volume of drug production has increased over five times from 1996 to 1999, Jim Mullen notes how the value net has accommodated that growth:

> *The supply chain as we set it up gave us flexibility. It also exploded the myth that we needed all this time to bring the new product to market and meet demand. We did it fast, and the way we did it let us off-load and balance the risk. We avoided having to make capital investments or get internal approval for everything; we did not have to forecast accurately because of the leeway our supply chain gave us.*

Biogen's outsourcing of key operational elements allowed it to achieve a competitive cost structure despite its limited experience and small scale. It also helped the company to keep fixed assets low, even when production volume increased dramatically. The capital investment needed was modest relative to the size of the business and was timed to minimize the investment risk behind product performance—not ahead of it. Financial results bear this out, as indicated by comparisons of Biogen with the top 10 pharmaceutical companies (Astrazeneca, Glaxo WellCome, Eli Lilly, Merck, Pfizer, Novo-Nordisk, Pharmacia & Upjohn, Roche Holdings, Schering-Plough, SmithKline) in Figure 4.3.

Like Betaseron, AVONEX® is an expensive drug, costing $1,000 for a shoebox-size package of four weeks' supply, and rising sales had an immediate effect on Biogen's financial performance. Revenues and profitability rose sharply after the successful launch (Figure 4.4).

Growth continues, and Biogen's market value has reflected that growth, increasing by over 600 percent between mid-1996 and December 1999.

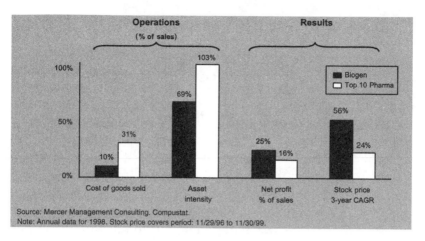

Figure 4.3 Comparison of Biogen's financial results.

➤ Conclusion and Lessons

Biogen executives cite several lessons from the launch that may be relevant to other companies as they consider the scope of their own operations. Specifically, these executives believe that the success of AVONEX® was built on these preconditions:

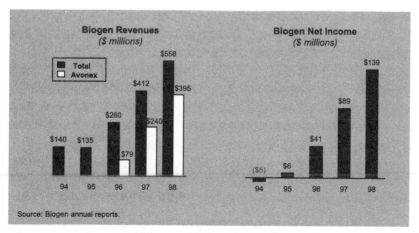

Figure 4.4 Biogen revenues and net income.

➤ *Deciding where to play.* Biogen could not have succeeded by doing everything itself. Also, its market value growth might have been far less had it relinquished operational control. The right choice of scope was critical.

➤ *Finding partners with sufficient capabilities to support the value net.* The existence of such companies in the pharmaceutical industry allowed a new entrant to contract out for the capacity needed for a major product launch with less direct capital investment and less risk.

➤ *Choosing partners large enough to accommodate significant increases in production and orders, yet small enough so that maintaining the relationship is very important to them as well.* This agility or flexibility helps ensure that the value net arrangements can last.

➤ *Making sure that the collaboration is truly hands-on partnering.* Close operational involvement was critical for Biogen; it colocated staff on partner premises, offered training and supervision, and learned about partners' businesses.

These lessons harken back to characteristics we have associated with value nets:

➤ *Customer-aligned.* The supply chain was aligned to meet customer needs for multiple delivery channels and extensive after-sales support.

➤ *Collaborative.* Biogen worked closely with a group of partners to make and deliver AVONEX®.

➤ *Agile.* The design flexes as demand increases and responds to change without significant additional investment by Biogen.

➤ *Scalable.* Biogen achieved a smooth launch in Europe the year after its debut in the United States; the product is shipped to more than 30 countries altogether, mainly in northern Europe, where MS is most prevalent.

➤ *Fast.* Speed is demonstrated not only in terms of the initial launch time but also in terms of continuous availability in the face of rising demand.

➤ *Increasingly digital.* Biogen is implementing new IT systems to coordinate and integrate with those of its partners.

Biogen made critical scope decisions in bringing AVONEX® to market. Aggressive outsourcing and skilled management of its value net was the right prescription for Biogen.

■ NOTES

1. Frank Britt. Interview with author, June 23, 1999.
2. Mahmoud Ladjevardi. Interview with Denise Auclair (Mercer Management Consulting), August 19, 1999.
3. Leigh Gallegher, "The Virtual Startup," *Forbes,* August 9, 1999, 78.
4. Doug Suna. Interview with author, November 11, 1999.
5. M. J. Rowan, *Prudential Securities Analyst Report,* September 23, 1999, 5.
6. Hugh Aitken, VP-Operations, Sun Microsystems–Europe. Interview with Kamenna Rindova (Mercer Management Consulting), August 16, 1999.
7. Kyle McNamara. Interview with author, December 6, 1999.
8. Victor Fung. Interview with Kirk Kramer (Mercer Management Consulting), August 16, 1999.
9. Joan Magretta, "Fast, Global, and Entrepreneurial: Supply Chain Management, Hong Kong Style," *Harvard Business Review,* September 1, 1998, 105.
10. Joanna Slater, "One-Stop Shopping," *Far Eastern Economic Review,* July 22, 1999, 14.
11. Donna Parolini, head of International Business Development, quoted by Paul Eisenstein, "Is Chrysler about to Disappear?" *Investor's Business Daily,* May 7, 1998, A1.

12. Mazy Sehrgosha. Interviews with author, May 1, 1998, and November 11, 1999.
13. David Sisson. Interview with author, November 10, 1999.
14. John Palmer. Interview with author, July 9, 1999.
15. William Brandel, "Business of the Year: How Biogen's Jim Vincent Got Biotech to Turn a Profit," *New England Business,* January 1991, 17.
16. John Palmer. Interview with author, July 9, 1999.
17. Ricardo Sookdeo, "Oh Baby! What a Year for Products," *Fortune,* December 27, 1993, 94.
18. Cynthia Starr, "Berlex, PCS Launch Novel Distribution Plan for MS Drug," *Drug Topics,* October 11, 1993, 12.
19. Robert Hamm. Interview with author, July 9, 1999.
20. James Mullen. Interview with author, July 9, 1999.
21. "Biogen Breaks Through: A Company Profile," *Med Ad News,* December 1997, 29.
22. Erin Smith. Interview with Kathryn Yung (Mercer Management Consulting), November 15, 1999.
23. Greg Stellato. Interview with Kathryn Yung (Mercer Management Consulting), November 15, 1999.

Chapter

Profit Capture: Casting the Net

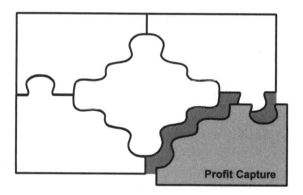

Profit Capture

A company can grow if it has a powerful and appealing value proposition. But growth benefits a company only when it has a mechanism for capturing profits from the value it creates for its customers. A value net uses elements of its operating design to generate and capture superior profits.

The idea that the design of operations and the supply chain impact profitability is not new. The reengineering work done in many supply chains in the late 1980s and early 1990s was precisely intended to identify and eliminate pockets of profit-sapping inefficiency. Supply chain software installations in the late 1990s promised still more integrated solutions, but both types of initiatives have generally been limited to optimizing within the constraints of existing business models. These efforts have produced limited results: a 5 percent reduction in procurement costs or a 10 percent reduction in inventory levels. A value net is not constrained by an old business design. Instead, it takes a fresh look at the mission and configures operations in ways that optimize value creation for customers and profits for the company. A value net achieves superior profits in the following ways:

1. By generating *profitable revenues* from enhanced operating capabilities
   a. Super service
   b. Money in solutions
2. By radically improving a company's *cost and asset* positions

Profitable revenue generation is driven by an ability to provide super service and convenient solutions. On the cost and asset side, value net designs drive profits through order-of-magnitude reductions in inventory, extremely efficient operating processes, and an ability to grow rapidly with limited cash for working capital or fixed asset investments.

■ PROFITABLE REVENUES

Traditionally, companies have relied on new products and aggressive marketing to drive the top line. Supply chain activities have not typically been viewed as contributors to the revenue stream. However, when superior service levels create utility for customers, they can increase revenues through either premium prices or higher sales volume. While this is intuitively clear, it is often hard to prove. The revenue and profit benefits of a superior service wrap are buried in overall pricing and revenue figures, making their documentation difficult. Yet they are no less real than the profits attributable to new or better products.

➤ Profits from Super Service

Cemex provides a sterling example of a company's ability to charge a premium for superior supply chain performance. In this case, the company sells a commodity product—cement—and delivers it within a 20-minute time window 98 percent of the time compared to a three-hour window and 34 percent reliability for its Mexican competitors. The reward for this nimbleness is Cemex's ability to charge a 2 to 10 percent premium in most markets. Premium pricing for superior service has a direct impact on Cemex's profit margin, which is 50 percent higher than that of its five top international competitors.

Other companies have used value nets to increase profitable volume instead of raising margins. Progressive Insurance, with its on-the-spot auto accident claims resolution, for example, aims to increase volume at a low margin in order *not* to attract excessive competition. Companies like Progressive and Spanish apparel manufacturer Zara use their speed-to-scene capabilities to please customers and differentiate themselves. This allows them to maintain faster (yet still profitable) growth in their respective markets. Progressive's revenues grew 24 percent per year from 1993 to 1998 versus 5 percent for the U.S. auto insurance industry as a whole. Zara has grown (profitably) at a 30 percent annual rate from 1996 to 1998, faster than rivals Cortefiel (14 percent), Adolfo Dominguez (24 percent), and Hennes & Mauritz (24 percent) during the same period.

An operating design that ensures rapid and reliable delivery is not just a customer pleaser. It also minimizes lost sales. As Nike's Paul Saunders told us, "Delivery is huge for the retail customer. They want the product there at the right time. Most of Nike's retail customers are mall-based, meaning that competitors are in the same space. If consumers want a particular product and it's not there, they will go to a competitor's product."[1]

A key factor in Biogen's rapid growth, as discussed in Chapter 4, has been its ability to scale up production at a pace capable of meeting rising demand. In contrast to its competitor's lottery system, which frustrated customers and missed thousands of potential sales (at roughly $1,000 apiece per month), Biogen has never missed a sale through a stockout. Timely delivery allowed Biogen to grow at 60 percent per year from 1995 to 1998 and has placed it among the handful of profitable U.S. biotech firms. Its profit margin surpasses those enjoyed by the 10 top pharmaceutical companies (25 percent versus 16 percent).

Rapid and reliable delivery plays an equally critical role in the fashion industry, where customer tastes can change in the blink of an eye. Fashion apparel retailers know that what's hot today may be passé next week and will end up on the clearance racks at 50 percent off. The key to profits in the "rag trade" is to make products available when and where they are hottest.

Nicholas LaHowchic is president of Limited Distribution Services (LDS), the distribution arm of fashion retailer The Limited. He handles a supply chain for nearly $10 billion worth of goods distributed through The Limited's 10 main brands, and he knows that getting trendy new products into stores quickly is a must. He explains, "Brand-new fashion products are like ripe fruit—as soon as you have them, that's the best price you're ever going to get for them."[2] To maximize profits, The Limited has developed an operating design that prioritizes time, service, and cost of delivery, in that order. LaHowchic explains: "Time is of the essence. We constantly chase the margin timeline. A 30 percent markdown will wipe out any kind of logistics savings I could have on the other end."

Because the money is on the sell side, not on the buy side, the strategic role of the LDS supply chain is to help to sell products, not cut costs. With this as its goal, LDS works in concert with the merchandising group in making deployment and redeployment decisions. The two teams meet one night a week for a rigorous information scrub. By 10 P.M., the conference room walls are lined with data on what's selling, what isn't, and where. Product redeployment plans are developed, and LDS has the job of shifting products to where they will move fastest—the quicker the better! LDS can get the right products to the right stores and change the floor layout of virtually every one of its U.S. stores within 72 hours.

The Limited's supply chain capability has played an important role in the company's financial performance. During the 1990s, The Limited outpaced its industry in sales growth while maintaining a reasonable profit margin. Its 28 percent average return on equity during that period was five times the industry average of 5 percent.

➤ Money in Solutions

Providing a more complete solution for customers is another source of revenues and profits that is enabled by a value net. Busy families are willing to pay a $30 monthly fee for the convenience of home grocery delivery. Demand for other personal-convenience services, such as lawn and garden care, pet walkers, and house cleaners, is exploding. Membership in the U.S. Personal Chefs Association has expanded from 15 in 1992 to 2,800 in 1999.

Convenient solutions opportunities are even more pronounced in business-to-business commerce. GE Medical, for example, has responded to customer demand for broader solutions by expanding from its product base to a business model designed to address a larger portion of its customers' service needs, moving to a higher-margin revenue base in the process. GE Medical asked, "What creates utility for our customers?" and realized that its customers were buying running time on their expensive medical equipment, not 6- by 4-foot boxes. Acting on this insight, GE Medical developed service solutions aimed at maximizing equipment running time for customers, allowing them to focus on quality patient care. To achieve its goal, it began to maintain and repair *all* equipment used by customers (not just its own machines, but those manufactured by competitors as well)—a radical proposition at the time.

GE Medical's decision to move to solutions required substantial supply chain alterations:

➤ Exacting standards had to be developed for all replacement parts and components to ensure compatibility with the equipment of other manufacturers, and these components had to be of equal or better quality than those replaced.

➤ Technical support and replacement parts had to be made available to global customers around the clock. A global parts network and a system of rapid delivery were established for this purpose.

The shift from products to solutions created profitable growth for GE Medical. In 1998, services grew 11 percent, representing almost half of the organization's revenues, and they were projected to continue growing at a rate of 15 percent annually in the near term. At the same time, the unit's 1998 operating margin was 50 percent higher than that of the corporation as a whole.[3]

GE Medical is not unique; a growing share of business spending is shifting to high-margin solutions services, many enabled by customer-focused and -responsive value nets. When companies develop service expertise through their supply chain capabilities, those capabilities can directly support client needs and become a new source of revenue and profits. Companies such as Becton Dickinson, W.W. Grainger, Saturn, and Cemex have parlayed their supply chain expertise in materials management, inventory management, or transportation services into profitable consulting services.

Caterpillar, the world's largest construction equipment manufacturer, is a leading example of a company that has turned its internal operating capabilities into a successful business. In the late 1980s, Caterpillar realized that its global parts delivery and inventory management capabilities had evolved to a point where they could be leveraged for revenue and profit generation. With that in mind, it formed a globally integrated third-party logistics provider (3PL), Caterpillar Logistics Services, Inc. This subsidiary developed a comprehensive logistics service offering for companies, guaranteeing the speedy, accurate delivery of service and replacement parts to customers anywhere in the world.

From its parent's standpoint, Cat Logistics serves several important functions. It provides the company with an entrée into the rapidly growing 3PL market, leverages existing capabilities to earn new revenues, and provides a cushion against the natural cycles of Caterpillar's core business.

From its initial service parts business, Cat Logistics has expanded its offerings into a broad spectrum of logistics services for more than 30 clients in diverse industries. These services include materials and inventory management, warehousing and transportation management, and use of proprietary global information systems to integrate data flows across a client's entire supply chain. Bill Springer, president of Cat Logistics, explains: "Our vision is to be the leading integrated provider of logistics services around the world. Integration is the key to what we offer; that is where we add value." Integration results in lower distribution costs, improved service rates, reduced inventory, and higher turnover for clients. From an initial base in automotive and industrial equipment service parts, Cat Logistics now works with clients in 17 countries and in industries ranging from aerospace to consumer goods and computers.

Jim Baldwin, Caterpillar's vice president for parts and service support, emphasizes the benefits that Cat Logistics provides to its parent: "Cat Logistics has been a great success for its customers and its parent. We knew we had strong supply chain management capabilities. Now the logistics marketplace has confirmed it. The business has grown substantially, and we appreciate the less cyclical nature of Cat Logistics' revenues as they help dampen the fluctuations in the capital equipment market."

Cat Logistics' ability to leverage its supply chain capabilities has produced profitable results for Caterpillar Inc., in line with contract logistics industry expectations. While growing at a rate of 18 percent annually, Cat Logistics has helped many companies achieve significant cost reduction, greater asset turnover, and improved customer service—a win-win situation for all concerned.

Speed, service, solutions. Each is valued by consumers and businesses, and each can drive profitable new revenues for an enterprise. The key to making it happen is for executives to view operations as a strategic capability that can boost the top line. The innovators we have cited have made that shift.

■ COSTS AND ASSETS

Cost reduction and asset optimization are among the perennial concerns of logistics and supply managers. To them, every link in the supply chain represents an opportunity for reducing costs and increasing yields. And many are very effective in hunting them down. Though each cost reduction may be small, they can add up to big savings. But, as with all incremental improvements to an existing system, the law of diminishing returns makes each new cost reduction smaller and more elusive. At some point, the only way to make meaningful improvements is to replace the old system with a new one. Value net design is that new system, and it can *radically* change a company's cost and asset structures. In this section we address three ways in which value nets release hidden profits: (1) melting inventory stockpiles, (2) achieving operations effectiveness through digitization, and (3) growing without cash.

➤ Melting Inventory Stockpiles

Traditional supply chains pile up inventory (safety and cycle stocks) at every step of the production and fulfillment process. The reasons are well known: unreliable demand forecasts, poor communications, poor visibility of holdings and shipments, and unreliable deliveries from upstream suppliers. The U.S. auto industry may lead the pack in this regard; an estimated $50 *billion* in finished goods inventory—typically a 60-day supply—sits on dealer lots or is in transit to them on any given day.[4] Even in the electronics industry, where inventory depreciates at a stomach-wrenching 1 percent per week, an estimated $21 billion in excess inventory sits in warehouses on a typical day.[5] These unproductive assets drain cash and profits.

Value nets achieve order-of-magnitude reductions in inventory holdings by replacing physical stocks with accurate information, reducing complexity, standardizing components, consolidating stocks, working with partners to ensure greater reliability, and building to order.

Information

Accurate information about customer demand is the first requirement for inventory reduction. Accurate, real-time information about parts and materials availability is the second. Once you know what customers want, when they want it, and when suppliers will deliver the goods, the need for safety stocks evaporates.

Customer choiceboards are powerful tools for capturing actual demand. Knowledge of real end-user demand can reduce or eliminate inventory requirements throughout the entire system, but only when each element of the system has access to the information. Fortunately, digital technologies and collaborative information sharing make this possible. Companies are giving their suppliers access to actual order or point-of-sales data and are allowing them to track supply and demand in real time. Many of the supply chain management software packages currently on the market support this information visibility, replacing months-old, inaccurate forecasts and reducing the need for buffer stocks at all levels.

Iomega, a $1.7 billion manufacturer of data storage systems, has demonstrated the benefits gained when companies create direct information linkages in the supply chain. Iomega implemented several i2 Technologies software packages—Demand Planner, Factory Planner, and Supply Chain Planner—to create efficient information flow throughout its net. The new system slashed Iomega's inventory holdings by $155 million, a 50 percent overall reduction.

Information sharing can be particularly powerful (and challenging) for a network spanning many entities in many countries. When Hewlett-Packard's distribution operations office in Singapore implemented a new automatic replenishment tool to manage inventory for 17 resellers in six Asia-Pacific nations, it discovered that it had to work closely with its partners to get them to share information that was customarily viewed as proprietary. This initiative called on resellers to collaborate with HP by collecting and sharing sell-through data. In return, HP gave its partners priority and commitment on their deliveries. According to HP's Michael Chuang, information sharing created a win-win situation. And the results were impressive. Resellers' inventory was slashed from six weeks to two weeks of supply, on average, while maintaining zero stockouts.[6]

Good information is the key to keeping inventory levels manageable, especially in global operations that involve many partners (customers and suppliers), long distances, and customs crossings.

Reduced Complexity

The second important factor in shrinking inventory stockpiles is reduced product complexity. Complexity reduction embraces the notion that 90 percent of customer demand is often fulfilled with 10 percent of a company's total product line. The remaining 90 percent creates complexity, takes up space and cash in the form of inventory holdings, and adds no value to the vast majority of customers. Complexity reduction is beneficial for mass production and traditional supply chain operations, but it is *absolutely essential* for a value net design, which must efficiently and rapidly sort through any set of combinations made available to a customer.

Boeing provides an instructive example of the complexity problem. Consider the inventories and process complexity required to manufacture a modern commercial aircraft, which is essentially built to order. Customers can create combinations from 6 million individual components. Boeing offers 109 different shades of white and 37 distinct designs for cockpit clipboards alone! This level of complexity requires an extensive array of parts, expensive inventories, and/or lengthy lead times. It also confuses customers. Now aware of these disadvantages, Boeing has begun to address complexity in its supply chain.

The benefits of complexity reduction are often substantial, as IBM found out in its personal computer business. In the early 1990s, IBM PC Company, like many others, tried to increase market presence by offering a growing number of products as predefined models. SKUs grew fivefold from 1993 to 1996. Unfortunately, as models proliferated, market share shrank. IBM recognized the need to reduce complexity. Its analysis revealed four key issues: (1) it offered twice as many models as leading competitors; (2) 90 percent of its sales were generated by 10 percent of its models; (3) channel and sales teams were unable to discern the selling-point differences between models; and (4) forecasting was performed model by model, creating inaccuracy and causing inventory to accumulate.

In early 1996, the IBM PC Company embarked on a complexity reduction effort and, in approximately nine months (by year-end 1996), eliminated 90 percent of its models. Forecast accuracy improved and market share began to rebound almost immediately, rising from 7.2 percent to 8.5 percent within the year.[7] Complexity reduction combined with pull-based management allowed the company to raise its inventory turns on high-spend parts by 60 percent and to slash its overall inventory levels by 50 percent. The company gave its customers the choices they wanted while vastly improving the agility and cost efficiency of its own operations.

Standard Components

The third inventory-reducing element of many value net designs is a reliance on standard components. Standardization allows many OEMs to use the same components, smoothing out the production curves of upstream suppliers; this reduces the cost of components and inventories systemwide.

The importance of standard components is highlighted by the experience of Monorail, a PC maker. Monorail entered the personal computer market as an OEM with the idea of creating a distinctive Monorail image. Part of that image was a unique black keyboard with salmon-colored keys. As the only OEM using the black-and-salmon combination, however, Monorail experienced higher costs and difficulties in sustaining just-in-time supply. It quickly abandoned its unique keyboard image in favor of lower costs and more reliable delivery. Subsequently, Monorail PCs were built entirely from standard components.

Consolidating Stocks

Reconfiguring distribution networks to consolidate stocking locations is another powerful way to reduce inventories as well as to simplify customers' experience and reduce fixed costs. Transportation and digital technology advances are responsible for much of the distribution simplification that has occurred in the United States. Mergers have also driven change. For example, the former General Foods, Kraft Inc., and Oscar Mayer were consolidated and reorganized in 1995 as Kraft Foods, a $17 billion manufacturer of food and beverages. Kraft redesigned its U.S. distribution system around plant-direct-to-customer shipping, supplemented by seven fast-flow, regional mixing centers that commingle all Kraft SKUs by temperature class. Some 20 warehouses were closed or converted in the rollout of the seven new facilities. "Customers can now mix all Kraft products in a single order," says Stephen Tibey, former vice president of operations services at Kraft Foods. Kraft's costs are reduced by eliminating inventory, reducing the redistribution of products from one facility to another, and dropping offsite overflow storage.[8]

In Europe, network consolidation is largely driven by a desire to shift to a pan-European solution. One company that has successfully implemented Europe-wide distribution is CIBA Vision, the contact lens–making unit of Swiss pharmaceutical giant Novartis. Over an 18-month period (1994–1995), CIBA Vision was able to replace the national inventories of 14 European group companies with a single Eurologistics facility at the Grosswallstadt, Germany, plant. Results have been impressive: overall inventory reduction of 50 percent *and* service level increases from 85 percent systemwide to over 97 percent. More than 50,000 opticians across Europe are now served within 24 hours. SKU availability has increased dramatically for smaller countries (e.g., Denmark and Ireland), which previously drew on limited product stocks. Roland Carlen, CIBA Vision's head of international operations, is pleased with the outcome: "We kept everything simple for our country sales teams and our customers," he says. "We've been able to dramatically reduce assets and distribution costs. At the same time, we are providing more customized and faster service."[9]

Managing Supply Reliability

Another reason companies have traditionally hoarded inventories is to protect themselves against unreliable deliveries from their upstream suppliers. Imagine that you are a widget maker scheduled to begin production of your popular Model A widget on October 15. Your supplier has promised to deliver all necessary components to your dock on October 14. You know from experience, however, that this supplier's promises are worth very little. You've been burned too many times! To protect your production schedule, you keep a seven-day stock of Model A components on hand at all times. That way, you can begin production on schedule, even if the supplier is late with its shipment.

Like the widget maker, many companies (and many units within those companies) hold excess inventory for no other reason than to ensure their own smooth operations. The collective impact of this behavior is billions of dollars of idle assets. Value net design tools that improve supplier reliability include creating a network of shared information, locating supplier staff on-site, and/or developing joint operational teams. These tools help attain systemwide visibility of final demand, supply requirements, and shipment tracking.

Pioneered by Japanese automakers, the idea of working closely with suppliers to manage supply reliability has now been embraced by personal computer manufacturers as well. PC manufacturers are situating supplier hubs within minutes of their assembly facilities, colocating staff at supplier sites (and vice versa), and aggressively working with suppliers to improve the efficiency of information and material flows. Opportunities for this type of collaboration abound, but remain largely unexploited in many industries.

Building to Order

The combination of good information, complexity reduction, standardized components, consolidated stocks, and collaborative supplier relationships are nowhere better exemplified than in the build-to-order business models of companies like Dell, Gateway, and (more recently) Apple.

We explore the power of the Gateway design at the end of this chapter, but essentially, these companies keep no more than a few days' supply of parts inventory and no finished goods inventory. The question often arises: Have powerful PC makers simply pushed their parts inventory onto their suppliers? A look at the levels for contract manufacturers such as SCI Systems and Jabil Circuits indicates that they have not. Between 1995 and mid-1999, their inventory levels have in fact *declined* by 55 percent. Other suppliers' inventories have been shrinking as well. Intel's inventory levels dropped 30 percent during the same period, and a company executive affirms that "there is no question that inventory is being taken out of the entire system."[10] Finished goods are manufactured only when an actual customer order arrives. Components are industry standard and readily available; their variations are tightly managed to minimize complexity. Order information is immediately visible to suppliers, and demand forecasts are updated daily.

Inventory improvements for these companies over the past five years have been truly remarkable (see Figure 5.1). We estimate that Dell, Gateway, and Apple as a group have avoided over $2 billion in inventory holdings through value net practices.[11] The cost of financing that level of in-

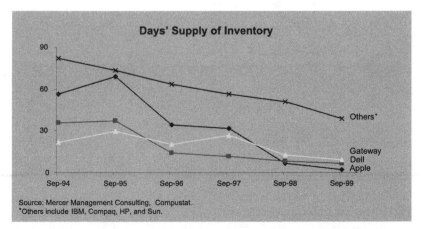

Source: Mercer Management Consulting, Compustat.
*Others include IBM, Compaq, HP, and Sun.

Figure 5.1 Days' supply of inventory for key PC manufacturers.

ventory would be colossal, yet inventory cost savings are not the only benefit when inventory is reduced. As Tim Cook, Apple's senior vice president of worldwide operations, explained: "Less inventory is not really the key. Less obsolescence is what has improved our margins."[12] In high-tech industries, where product innovation is absolutely critical, the ability to flush the pipeline of obsolescent inventory and focus on the newest, hottest products translates into superior financial performance. "It is hard to quantify the gain from reduced obsolescence," notes Cook, "[but] you can look at every financial measure of the company—and the results speak for themselves."

➤ Achieving Operations Effectiveness through Digitization

Digital technology forms the essential backbone of the value net. It penetrates each and every aspect of company operations. We will discuss the key elements of a digital strategy in Chapter 7, but to appreciate the potential impact of digitization on profitability, consider the experience of Weyerhaeuser's door-building facility in Marshfield, Wisconsin. In 1995, that facility was in bad shape. As Weyerhaeuser vice president Jerry Mannigel explained to us, "The business had been struggling for the past decade to be financially profitable."[13] And Mannigel told a business reporter, "It was a 'dead dog' of a door plant weighted down by bloated costs, flagging sales, and bad morale."[14] Weyerhaeuser considered closing the plant, but opted in late 1995 for a program of modernization at the heart of which was a homegrown digital technology called DoorBuilder. "DoorBuilder has impacted every aspect of our business," says Mannigel. It links all employees to critical information, such as factory-floor operations, performance, and supplier inventory.

Redesign of the Marshfield operation included the development of a digital customer interface—a choice-board—that produced dramatic improvements in the ordering process. "It used to take three to four weeks just to process the information to create an order," recalls Mannigel. "Today it takes 15 minutes!" Weyerhaeuser computers now sit on the desks of customers, who can place orders directly on the Marshfield facility's web site. The choiceboard is ideally suited to the plant's custom-built operation, which is capable of producing any of 2 million possible door configurations. As Mannigel told us, "To get the combination correct, it used to take three or four weeks and many calls and faxes back and forth with the customer. Doors have to meet local, city, and state building codes. Historically, a human being had to go line item by line item to catch conflicts. Now that's all done on the computer. The rule-based digital system immediately detects conflicts and offers a solution."

The digital ordering process improved the customer experience and cut costs for Weyerhaeuser. According to Mannigel, "[Digitization] has helped us with the costs associated with information rehandling. Historically, when we received an order, we handed it from one individual to the next. It would go from paper to computer and back to paper. We'd handle it a minimum of seven different times. Every time we rehandle it there is the opportunity for error. Now, it is inputted at the source and never rehandled. We've eliminated the error, and we've been able to reduce overhead because of that."

In the old system, orders in the form of handwritten notes and printed pages were stapled to doors as they moved through production. These often fell off, creating confusion, inaccuracy, and costly rework. Together with all the process improvements, DoorBuilder has drastically reduced such inefficiencies and has contributed to cutting order turnaround times in half.

An added profit-enhancing function of DoorBuilder is its ability to calculate the value (profitability) of each customer to Weyerhaeuser in real time. By looking at a customer's creditworthiness, volume ordered over a period of time, and the cost of every option selected, the system helps Weyerhaeuser personnel identify and concentrate on the best customers and turn away unprofitable customers—an unthinkable proposition under the previous system. Using this new capability, the plant has reduced the number of distributors it works with from 500 to under 200. But while the number of customers has decreased, order volumes have doubled, topping 800,000 units in 1998.

The significant reduction in lead times and the increases in on-time and complete shipments made possible by DoorBuilder has allowed Weyerhaeuser to stake out a more profitable position in the marketplace. "We no longer need to be the low-price [bidder]," said Mannigel. "Now we can sell the concept of service as a value—having the shortest lead time and [the best] service. We now ship our orders 100 percent on time and complete. And we get a premium. We go in higher than everyone else and still get the job."

Weyerhaeuser's investment in DoorBuilder, which was three times higher than original projections, has paid off. Today, its "dead dog" door plant has returned to profitability, and its revenues are growing at 10 to 15 percent annually. On-time deliveries have swelled from 60 to 70 percent in 1995 to 97 percent, and return on assets has exploded from negative territory to 25 to 27 percent. The plant's ERP system, the digitized customer interface, and computer-controlled production processes have revolutionized operations. But Mannigel cautions, "[People] often miss the point and give all the credit to the technology. It's the business processes as well. It's a 50-50 combination."

The Weyerhaeuser example is not unique. Similar digital revolutions are under way or waiting to happen at many companies and in many industries. Our research uncovered examples in industries ranging from high-tech to office furniture (Miller SQA) and cement (Cemex). Digital technology can and will rewrite the operating codes of many companies.

➤ Growing without Cash

One of the time-honored principles of finance is that companies need large amounts of working capital to operate and grow. The faster they grow, the more cash they need for working capital and fixed asset investments. Finding that cash is one of the growing company's perennial problems.

Value net companies offer a unique solution to the cash and capital problem. To solve their demands for cash—for both working capital and fixed assets—value net business designs look to partners for leverage. Some will leverage supplier assets, scale, and experience to reduce their own need for working capital and fixed assets. Others will leverage their customers. Let's examine each briefly.

Leveraging Suppliers

Partner leverage allows small companies to grow rapidly and decisively with little cash of their own. To the extent that they can outsource manufacturing, distribution and logistics, and other asset-intensive activities to partners, they can make the most of their partners' scale, experience, and financial resources. Several companies we present in this book have used the growth-through-outsourcing strategy very successfully:

➤ Biogen used extensive outsourcing to achieve commercial scale almost overnight. It has grown five times over its original projections without the need for significant capital investments.

➤ SOHO, the virtual company examined in Chapter 4, has also grown without having to make significant initial or ongoing capital investments. This essentially variable-cost growth model gives virtual companies the ability to grow and change in step with the market, with minimal cash constraints and no sunk costs.

➤ Sun Microsystems likewise emphasizes its leveraged model as a key ingredient in its market growth strategy. Mel Friedman explains: "In a fast-growing environment, you often get stuck by the need for cash to grow your operations. . . . If you are growing rapidly, you are laying out the cash before accounts receivable can get the money. You have to buy the material, convert the material, build the product, all of which burn cash dramatically. When you outsource, you don't have to burn the cash, even if you are paying a little extra. . . . Sun, from its earliest days, has had what we call a 'leveraged model.' "

Leveraging Customers

Companies like Amazon, Dell, and Gateway have been able to minimize or eliminate working capital requirements by reversing the accounts payable–accounts receivable cycle; they are paid by customers *before* they have to pay their suppliers. As a result, Amazon operated with negative working capital in its initial years. Customers paid at the time of order, and Amazon held onto their cash for several days before paying book publishers, which held most of the inventory. Every dollar of sales at Amazon generated $0.06 in capital in 1997, compared to $0.40 of capital consumed for every dollar of store sales at Barnes & Noble at that time.[15]

Another way to look at the growth constraint problem is the cash conversion cycle. The *cash conversion cycle* is the length of time between a company's payments for raw materials (accounts payable, net of inventories in-house) and its receipt of money from customers for the final product (accounts receivable). A look at Dell's liquidity (end of January 1999) shows an enviable picture, particularly the very low inventory position:

Liquidity Elements	Days
Days of sales in accounts receivable (DAR)	36
Days' inventory (DI)	6
Days in accounts payable (DAP)	54
Cash conversion cycle (DAR + DI − DAP)	**−12**
Source: Dell Computer Corporation *Annual Report,* 1999.	

In other words, customers made cash available to Dell 12 days before Dell had to pay for its components. A 12-day advance on $18 billion of annual revenue is a nontrivial benefit in terms of float and capital costs.

■ HOW CAN YOUR BUSINESS EFFECTIVELY CAPTURE PROFITS?

Value net design can produce superior profitability in many industries. But which of the methods described in this chapter would be best for your company? Should you go for revenue expansion, cost reduction, or both?

Generating new top-line revenues is the profit booster least commonly associated with the supply chain, yet opportunities to do so arise whenever product delivery, installation, operation, maintenance, or disposal require significant time and effort.

> ➤ Do your customers have to struggle to properly install or maintain your products and those of your competitors? If they do, they may be willing to pay an expert (you) to do it for them.

➤ Is the cost of downtime extremely high for your customers? If it is, they might welcome rapid on-site service for the equipment you sell them.

➤ When a customer buys new equipment from you (a computer, piece of machinery, etc.), what happens to the old equipment? Does the customer have to pay someone to remove it? Is a disposal permit required? Solving the customer's disposal problem might be a revenue-enhancing part of your business.

➤ What is the accepted on-time and complete order fill rate in your industry? If it is in the 60 to 80 percent range, the opportunity to achieve differentiation through better service can be significant.

In each of these situations, you may find that your customer's costs of installing, maintaining, or disposing of its assets are much higher than yours—in which case you have the basis for a business that will benefit both you and your customer.

On the cost/asset side of the equation, opportunities to achieve dramatic inventory reductions are available in any industry characterized by high unit values, rapid obsolescence, perishability, or severe price competition. As the leading PC manufacturers have shown, value net design makes it entirely possible to operate effectively with amazingly thin inventories. The keys to slashing inventory levels are complexity reduction, component standardization, stock consolidation, and supplier reliability—all supported by an effective information system that, ideally, includes a choiceboard and makes order and inventory data available to all.

The next place to look for cost reductions is in your fixed asset base. Are you doing things that supply partners could do just as well, if not better, and at a lower cost than you? If the answer is yes, outsourcing these activities will allow you to *eliminate* the fixed assets and inventories that support them. Slimmed-down companies are faster, more flexible, and able to grow with less capital.

Gateway presents an excellent example of a company that has leveraged its value net design for profitable growth.

■ THE GATEWAY DESIGN FOR PROFIT CAPTURE

Few corporations illustrate the profit capture potential of a value net better than Gateway, Inc. Many of the ideas presented in this chapter—digital choiceboards, outsourcing, inventory reduction, complexity reduction, and component standardization—are found at work in this company.

The PC industry has a history of odd beginnings. The first Apple was created in a garage owned by Steve Jobs's parents. The IBM PC was built by a skunk-works team operating out of rented office space in Boca Raton, Florida. Michael Dell got his start by selling PCs out of a college dorm room at the University of Texas. Add Gateway to the list of unusual birthplaces. Gateway was started in 1985 in an Iowa farmhouse by entrepreneur Tim Waitt and his business partner, Mike Hammond, with the aim of producing and marketing personal computers to the consumer market. Both men had experience in selling hardware peripherals and software to PC owners through advertisements in computer-related publications.

Gateway began operations during the formative years of the PC business, when most buyers were first-time users who needed lots of advice and hand-holding, both in making purchase decisions and in using their new machines. The PC had just become a regular fixture in the white-collar world, and the home market remained largely untapped. But things were changing fast. By 1987, Waitt recognized another opportunity among more technically sophisticated users who knew enough about PCs to enable them to comfortably order a machine without touching or trying it out first. Under Waitt's direction, Gateway assembled customer-configured, IBM-compatible systems. Its supply chain and sales channels were designed for fast, built-to-order assembly and direct shipment to the customer.

Success came quickly. In December 1993, Gateway 2000 (now Gateway, Inc.) became a publicly traded company. By the end of fiscal 1998, Gateway reported revenues of $7.5 billion, making it a leader in the $170 billion global market for desktop and laptop PCs. For the third quarter of 1999, Dataquest ranked Gateway fifth worldwide in total shipments of PCs (desktops and portables).

➤ The Gateway Business Model

In many ways, Gateway's direct-sales, build-to-order business model resembles that of Dell, but there are important differences, starting with the choice of target customers. Gateway's primary focus is on consumers and small businesses, which account for two-thirds of the company's customer base (Figure 5.2). Rival Dell, on the other hand, derives 80 percent of its revenues from corporate accounts.

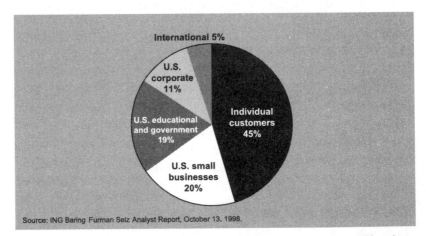

Figure 5.2 Gateway's customer mix by revenue contribution, 1998.[16]

Gateway recognized several important facts about its target customer segments:

➤ The majority of first-time buyers (consumers) want to touch and see the computer prior to the purchase.

➤ Approximately 30 percent of computer buyers are unlikely to use the phone or Internet to make a purchase.

➤ Only 55 percent of the population is expected to be online by 2003, and only a fraction of that will actually make purchases online.

➤ Only 40 percent of small businesses are being served by competitors such as Compaq, Hewlett-Packard, IBM, or Dell. Most of these small businesses are left to meet their needs through local dealers and resellers.

Gateway's CEO Theodore Waitt summarized the situation in 1998: "Only 25 percent of the consumer and small business market bought PC hardware over the telephone or the Internet, and we don't see that getting over 50 percent anytime soon."[17] Given the limited penetration potential of the pure Internet channel and the greater need of target customers to touch and feel the product and to discuss their needs with computer sales professionals, Gateway introduced a "call, click, or come in" approach to interacting with its customers.

Gateway's customer interface now consists of a three-channel choiceboard. Customers can configure their PCs and interact with the company through a direct Internet connection, a phone call, or a visit to a local Gateway Country® store. The Internet provides a digital medium for customers to express their preferences and for the company to manage the sales process. The phone and the stores are more traditional, but still serve critical customer functions. The stores, in particular, represent a unique approach in the PC market. They are inventory-free showrooms. Between 1996 and 1999, Gateway opened more than 200 such stores in Europe and in the United States, a number that is projected to grow to 300 or 400 stores by the year 2002.

While many balk at bricks-and-mortar facilities in an Internet age, Gateway reasons that its stores give new buyers an opportunity to test-drive their PCs, get advice, and meet a knowledgeable Gateway face. They provide a convenient location for pickup, repairs, and returns, and they facilitate urgent or impulse purchases. Business Solutions Centers within the stores allow business owners to discuss options with sales reps and design the solutions they need. At the same time, the stores reinforce the company's brand and the customers' trust. They provide space for Gateway's popular (revenue-generating) software training courses. Last but not least, these inventory-free stores are generally profitable within a year of their opening and have an average return on capital of 45 percent. Stock analysts agree: "Gateway Country stores have played a major role in the increase of non-system revenues because they have created a unique opportunity to upsell. The opportunity for one-on-one contact with customers . . . is far more effective than the phone or Web in capturing a buyer's dollars beyond the PC."[18]

All three channels serve the choiceboard function—allowing and assisting customers to configure their choices from CPU, peripheral, component, and software options, which means that 600,000 unique machines are available to prospective buyers. Once a customer order hits the company's information system, the specifications are transmitted to one of the company's assembly facilities and to each facility's supplier hub, known as centers for production replenishment. Gateway works with many suppliers, but just 10 of them account for 80 percent of the company's annual $5 to $6 billion in direct materials purchases. Since it first initiated its concept of supplier hubs in 1997, most key suppliers store raw component inventories close to Gateway's assembly plants, four of which are currently sited in the United States, with others in Ireland and Malaysia. Supplier hubs enable shorter lead times. As described by one company official, "There are a lot of similarities between the technology industry today and the automobile industry a decade ago in terms of their supplier hubs being tailored for JIT [just-in-time] delivery."[19]

The machine specified by the customer is built to order from a set of standard components and loaded with customer-specified software. Generally, an order spends less than one day inside a Gateway plant. Physical activities include assembly (2.5 hours or less), queuing, boxing, and labeling. Simultaneously, the financial release is obtained. Approximately 10 percent of all customers ask for changes to their order at some point in the fulfillment process; these are generally accommodated without creating undue shipment delays. Finished goods are shipped daily. There is no warehousing of these products.

Shipping and delivery are handled by UPS. Shipments of supplier-provided peripherals such as printers and monitors never pass through Gateway's hands, but are merged in transit to complete the customer order. All elements are targeted for delivery within five business days of order receipt. Currently, UPS and Gateway hit that target 99.5 percent of the time. The siting of the three U.S. assembly plants was determined with two- to three-day ground freight delivery in mind. Specifically, the eastern United States is served by a plant in Hampton, Virginia, the west by a plant in Salt Lake City, Utah, and the central portion of the country by a plant in North Sioux City, South Dakota.[20] These locations meet the delivery requirements for all cities in the continental United States.

Follow-up technical support is provided by several Gateway phone centers located around the country. The company's emphasis on individuals and small businesses make that support more people-intensive than it is for rivals.

This business model has been remarkably successful for Gateway, supporting revenue growth at a compound annual rate (CAGR) of 68 percent between 1994 and 1998.

Profits grew apace, rising at a 38 percent CAGR during the same period, and the stock price grew at a CAGR of 68 percent between 1994 and 1999. Customers have registered their approval of Gateway's products and its operating model in at least one other significant way: customer loyalty. Ziff-Davis named Gateway as the 1998 brand leader in customer loyalty, as measured by the percentage of PC users who repurchased the same brand (75 percent of Gateway customers who bought new computer systems in 1997 were repeat buyers, putting Gateway in the brand loyalty winner's circle).

The five puzzle pieces of Gateway's business design exemplify value net design principles:

➤ *Value proposition.* Gateway is very specific about its customer choice. Its channel strategy reflects clear alignment with the needs of the target customer segments (primarily individuals and small businesses). It offers these customers built-to-order, state-of-the-art Wintel machines at competitive prices. It gives them access to knowledgeable sales assistance and makes ordering and delivery fast and efficient. Gateway's service and delivery quality are setting the standards in the industry. The company supports each purchase with life-of-the-machine technical support, which is costly but appears to have paid off in terms of customer loyalty. More recently, Gateway's value proposition has expanded rapidly from a product focus to a total solutions/service focus. The company introduced the Your:)Ware^{SM} program in 1998 to provide financing, trade-ins, Internet access, and other service options valued by target customers. This personal-touch, service-intensive value proposition is carefully attuned to the needs of selected customer segments.

➤ *Scope.* In true value net spirit, Gateway's scope of activities starts with an active, three-media choiceboard, which captures the real customer demand information needed to drive the rest of the business. The company retains control of all the things it views as absolutely necessary for delivering on its value proposition and the things that it performs better than anyone else: all points of customer contact (for both ordering and after-sale support), assembly, and the role of supply network orchestration. Everything else is outsourced.

➤ *Strategic control.* We have defined *strategic control* as the ability to protect profits over time from encroachment by competitors. As we will see, Gateway pays great attention to building long-term customer relationships. Gateway has taken measures to make the customer's experience easy and convenient and to give customers a reason to come back. This has created a high degree of customer loyalty, the most effective antidote to encroachment.

➤ *Execution.* As an effective value net manager, Gateway uses smart information flow design to hold its supply network together and to make everything work fast and without failures.

Profit capture is the fifth piece of value net design. As the focus of this chapter, it merits deeper analysis.

➤ Design for Profit Capture

Gateway provides a useful example of how profit capture can be designed into the value net business model. By offering customized products and customized solutions wrapped in extensive customer service and rapid, reliable delivery, it has turned a trickle of revenues into a torrent. The effective application of value net principles allows Gateway to operate with a lean and efficient cost and asset structure, ensuring that many of the revenue dollars make it to the bottom line, thus creating profits for the corporation and value for its shareholders.

➤ Driving the Top Line

Gateway's profitable revenue growth has been driven by two factors. First, Gateway was among the first computer companies to offer *configured-to-order, customized products,* delivered rapidly at or below the price of mass-produced PCs. Not surprisingly, PC companies that were able to customize grew three times faster than their traditional competitors, and Gateway rode the crest of this wave with its nimble, build-to-order business design. Second, Gateway has continued to expand its revenues by offering *complete solutions* for PC buyers. From add-on sales of computer peripherals and software to services such as financing and store-based training courses, Gateway leverages the customer touch points to provide total solutions for its clients and, in the process, drive profitability.

Add-on sales help increase the company's revenue stream. Most people who set out to purchase a basic PC for $1,400 quickly find themselves adding upgrades that inflate the final bill to over $2,000. Gateway customers are no different. Buy a new desktop machine from Gateway and you will quickly find yourself building a whole system that includes a printer, a built-in or external data storage device, the latest version of Quicken and other software, and perhaps a scanner.

The latest broadening of Gateway's offer provides an even more "complete solution" for customers. Value-adding services under its Your:)Ware program, introduced in 1998, include customized hardware and software options, financing, Internet access, and trade-ins of old equipment. Gateway was the first PC maker to offer access to the Internet through its own Internet service provider (ISP), gateway.net. It expanded that service in late 1999 through a partnership with America Online. As of June 1999, 60 percent of Gateway's customers were participating in the Your:)Ware program.

Financing, product life-cycle management (trade-ins), and having all the troublesome configurations, codes, and account numbers built in for immediate Internet operations are advantages that save time and headaches for inexperienced users, as well as being beneficial for the company. The impact of company-sponsored financing alone on revenues is remarkable, accounting for slightly more than $1 billion of the company's $7.5 billion in 1998 revenues. Financing also increases Gateway's gross margin from roughly $200 to $420 per machine![21]

Finally, the company has leveraged its Gateway Country store assets to offer innovative, value-adding, and revenue-generating services—training courses and professional assistance with system design and setup for small business customers and consumers, who are trying to solve problems for which they typically lack resources. Trained employees at the company's network of Gateway Business Solution Centers (located in the Gateway Country stores) analyze current computer networks or provide build-to-order solutions. Beginning, intermediate, and advanced training in applications software is also available.

The combination of Gateway's build-to-order capabilities and solutions approach has supported a rising tide of revenues from new and repeat purchasers. Gateway's profitable sales have nearly tripled in five years, rising from $2.7 billion in 1994 to $7.5 billion in 1998.

➤ Getting to the Bottom Line

On the cost and asset side, Gateway's efficient operations exemplify several key strategies for driving higher profitability and shareholder returns. Specifically, the company has adeptly minimized inventories (and the associated carrying costs), maximized operational and asset efficiency, and leveraged customers to fund its growth with lower cash requirements.

Minimal Inventories

Gateway's inventory levels are razor thin—five to ten days. To achieve this level of performance, Gateway uses most of the techniques discussed earlier in the chapter. Its manufacturing is designed to respond only to real customer demand. *Accurate information* about customer preferences is captured via a web-based, phone-based, or in-store *choiceboard*. And because machines are built to order, there is no finished goods inventory to store, insure, and finance.

Gateway leverages its choiceboard capability to guide customers toward parts and components that are in better in-stock positions at a given time. Company officials confirm that proactive management of the customer choice allows Gateway to minimize the total parts inventory it needs to hold. Gateway is also mindful of keeping *low complexity* in its system. Although the total number of possible product combinations exceeds 600,000, the number of individual component SKUs is carefully selected and controlled. All components are *industry standard,* ensuring that the company can replenish stocks reliably without having to keep large buffer inventories.

Last but not least, Gateway *works closely with suppliers* to ensure rapid and reliable replenishment. IT systems allow the necessary visibility of customer orders and inventory stocks in the net. Although these systems are not the seamless, integrated ideal for which every manager hopes, they do get the job done, according to Gateway executives.

The Gateway manufacturing system is not immune to stockouts. Periodically, a stockout occurs for one or another of the 200-plus components that go into one of its PCs, either because Gateway's forecast was too low or due to supplier error. To avoid losing a sale or having to extend the delivery date to the customer, Gateway will generally encourage the customer to upgrade the out-of-stock component to one that is in stock. If the customer is not interested in upgrading, the company will often make the substitution at no cost, because the client always comes first. In one case, for example, an Asian supplier failed to deliver the promised shipment of 15-inch monitors on time. Demand was strong, so Gateway upgraded the affected customers to 17-inch monitors at no additional cost and charged the supplier for the difference.

The combination of working with actual demand, keeping complexity low, using standard components, collaborating with suppliers, and getting Gateway's salespeople to simultaneously optimize customer need with inventory levels in the value net has allowed Gateway to operate with enviably low inventory levels. In the rapid-obsolescence, high-tech PC market, this has contributed significantly to overall company profitability. Gateway, for example, enjoys lower inventory carrying costs and lower asset intensity than many traditional PC manufacturers. At the same time, it avoids the potentially major cost of price protection— which can represent as much as 8 to 10 percent of revenue— that traditional PC manufacturers offer their retail partners.

Operational and Asset Efficiency

Two key aspects of Gateway's business design lead to higher than average operational and asset efficiency and profitability: strategic outsourcing and collapsing the value chain (Figure 5.3).

Gateway is not a virtual company by any stretch of the imagination. It maintains several large division and corporate headquarters, an IT development center, a data processing facility, several assembly plants, a payroll of 11,000 employees, and a growing network of Gateway Country stores. Yet strategic outsourcing is an important element of its design. Gateway outsources major modules to contract manufacturers and logistics to UPS.

At the same time, the company has collapsed the value chain by eliminating layers of retailing and warehousing. By selling direct, it avoids the retail margins that traditional PC manufacturers have to support. It also allows

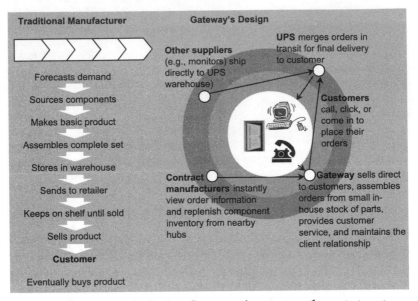

Traditional Manufacturer

Forecasts demand

Sources components

Makes basic product

Assembles complete set

Stores in warehouse

Sends to retailer

Keeps on shelf until sold

Sells product

Customer

Eventually buys product

Gateway's Design

Other suppliers (e.g., monitors) ship directly to UPS warehouse)

UPS merges orders in transit for final delivery to customer

Customers call, click, or come in to place their orders

Contract manufacturers instantly view order information and replenish component inventory from nearby hubs

Gateway sells direct to customers, assembles orders from small in-house stock of parts, provides customer service, and maintains the client relationship

Figure 5.3 Gateway's design for superior cost and asset structure.

suppliers to view real-time sales information, which speeds up replenishment and enables processes such as merge-in-transit. Monitors coming from Asia, for example, never enter a Gateway warehouse. They move directly from ship to UPS truck, where the full order is assembled for seamless delivery to the customer. This eliminates unnecessary handling and the time and costs associated with it. It also minimizes the inventory and assets required for Gateway's operation.

As a result, Gateway's asset utilization is extremely high; it lags rival Dell by a token percentage and is head and shoulders ahead of the industry as a whole. *Asset intensity,* the dollar value of assets needed to generate a dollar of revenue, is only one-fifth that of major competitors (Figure 5.4). Gateway uses only 11 cents to generate every dollar of sales, compared to an average of 51 cents used by the competition.[22] Gateway also enjoys an impressive average return on invested capital of 38 percent.

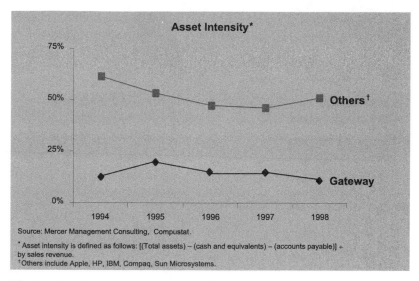

Figure 5.4 Gateway's comparative asset intensity.

The combined effect of revenue-generating solutions, low inventories, and high operational and asset efficiency has provided a healthy profit margin and an enviable return on assets (Figure 5.5). Gateway, for example, enjoyed a 12 percent return on assets in 1998 versus 5 percent for other major PC manufacturers.

➤ Cash Requirements

Gateway's model of selling direct and building to order and its system of collecting payment from the customer at the beginning of the process allow it to operate with a *negative* cash conversion cycle. When the typical customer orders a Gateway computer, he or she generally pays with a credit card, giving the company almost immediate cash once the product ships. Gateway, in turn, does not pay its suppliers until after their parts are used in the computer assembly for which the customer is paying. Thus, days payable exceed days receivable. And because the days of inventory are quite low, the speed at which cash is earned

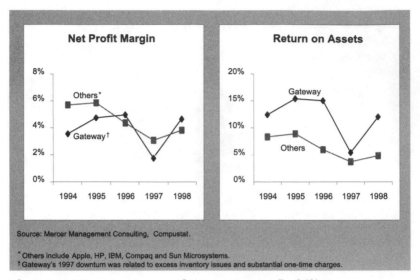

Source: Mercer Management Consulting, Compustat.

* Others include Apple, HP, IBM, Compaq and Sun Microsystems.
† Gateway's 1997 downturn was related to excess inventory issues and substantial one-time charges.

Figure 5.5 Two measures of Gateway's profitability.

can exceed the speed at which it is spent, giving Gateway almost a week of free financing. Here are the results, using data from Gateway's 1998 financial statements:

Liquidity Elements	Days
Days of sales in accounts receivable (DAR)	22
Days' inventory (DI)	9 (turns: 40)
Days in accounts payable (DAP)	36
Cash conversion cycle (DAR + DI − DAP)	**−5**

Negative cash conversion has been a feature of Gateway's operations since the company's start-up phase (except for a brief period of lapsed discipline). According to company lore, this "cashless" approach was a consequence of the fact that the founder had no funds. In those early days, Ted Waitt would simultaneously accept an order and the payment for it via a customer's credit card. He'd then order the required parts, which would arrive a few days later on a COD basis. By then, Waitt would have the cash to pay for the parts, which he would assemble and quickly ship out to the customer. This cycle would be repeated over and over, effectively leveraging customer capital to fund the company's impressive growth.

➤ Key Lessons

Gateway has built a remarkable moneymaking machine, and its growing market valuation (Figure 5.6) reflects its power. Ted Waitt and his team have created $20 billion of shareholder wealth between 1994 and 1999. This success is based on a powerful business design. At the customer level, it has created an appealing offer:

➤ Excellent PC systems based on the latest technology

➤ Opportunities for individual buyers to understand what's available and configure products that fit their unique computing needs

➤ Convenient payment terms (including trade-ins of used equipment)

➤ Remarkably fast delivery

➤ An unmatched level of postsale technical support

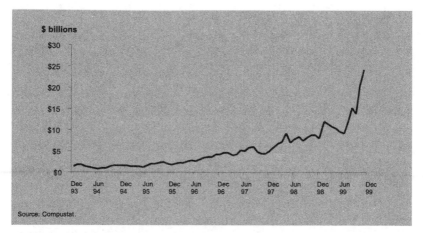

Figure 5.6 Gateway market value.

This is the face of Gateway that customers see, and they apparently like what they see. Gateway's sales have been growing steadily. Behind that public face is a remarkably effective operation that makes good on the company's offer and produces a healthy profit. That operation fits our definition of a value net in every respect. It is customer-aligned, fast, digital, agile, and collaborative.

What can we learn from this company? Are any of its practices transferable to companies outside the consumer electronics industry?

We believe that Gateway holds important lessons for many companies, regardless of industry. Its profitability depends on two closely related things: (1) a powerful offer that customers value and (2) a value delivery mechanism that is both effective and efficient. Effectiveness satisfies customers. Efficiency contributes to profitability. Gateway does both of these things exceptionally well.

It also makes the most of several mechanisms that increase top-line revenues and reduce operating costs:

> ➤ Use of an Internet-based choiceboard to accurately capture and transmit customer preferences to the supply chain
> ➤ Asset minimization through strategic outsourcing
> ➤ Razor-thin inventories made possible by good information, reduced complexity, reliance on standard components, and close collaboration with suppliers to ensure supply reliability

Look at your own business. Are your customers impressed by what you have to offer and how you offer it? Are they impressed to the point that they will reward you by either paying a premium price or referring others to your company? If you answered no to either of these questions, what are the opportunities to change?

Now consider the operational capability that your customers are less likely to see. Is your business design a natural consequence of the customers you're targeting and the offer you've extended to them (i.e., is it customer-aligned)? To what extent does it possess the other value net characteristics (i.e., is it fast, digital, agile, and collaborative)?

Finally, have you made the most of opportunities to increase revenues and to reduce costs through the methods described in this chapter? If not, take a lesson from Gateway's book and get started today.

■ NOTES

1. Paul Sanders. Interview with Denise Auclair (Mercer Management Consulting), August 10, 1999.
2. Nicholas LaHowchic. Interview with Les Artman (Mercer Management Consulting), July 20, 1999.
3. Richard C. Nelson, *ING Baring Research Analyst Report,* June 10, 1999, 38, 60.
4. Lee Sage, *Winning the Innovation Race* (New York: John Wiley & Sons, Inc., 2000), in production.
5. Diane Trommer, "Site Offers 'Risk-Free' Auctions," *Electronic Buyer's News,* July 5, 1999, 70.
6. Michael Chuang. Private communication, October 28, 1999.
7. George D. Elling. *Lehman Brothers Research Analyst Report,* May 8, 1997, 3.
8. Stephen Tibey. Interview with author, January 12, 2000.
9. Roland Carlen. Interview with author, June 15, 1999.
10. Michael Waithe. Interview with author, October 28, 1999.
11. Based on 1998 sales volumes at 1994 inventory intensity levels.
12. Tim Cook. Interview with author, September 29, 1999.
13. Jerry Mannigel. Interview with Kamenna Rindova (Mercer Management Consulting), October 22, 1999.
14. Stepanek, Marcia, "How the Internet Opened the Door to Profits," *Business Week,* July 26, 1999, EB 32.
15. *Capital* in this case is defined as asset intensity (total assets minus cash and equivalents minus accounts payable divided by sales).
16. Robert Cihra, *ING Baring Furman Selz Analyst Report,* October 13, 1998, 20.

17. Roger O. Crockett, "Gateway Loses the Folksy Shtick," *Business Week,* July 6, 1998, 80.
18. Charles R. Wolf, *Warburg Dillon Read Analyst Report,* July 24, 1999, 3.
19. Group of Gateway executives. Interview with authors, July 13, 1999.
20. Assembly of servers is done at the company's Irvine, California, plant.
21. Robert Cihra, *op. cit,* 29.
22. Asset intensity is both a good measure of a value net (fast, agile, collaborative are all qualities that might lead to low asset intensity) and one of the five key metrics we use to look at the strength of any business design. The five metrics are *return on sales* (profit margin), *growth of profits over time, asset efficiency* (same as asset intensity), *strategic control index* (like the rankings we show in Chapter 6), and *market-value-to-sales ratio.*

Chapter

Strategic Control: Staying in the Game

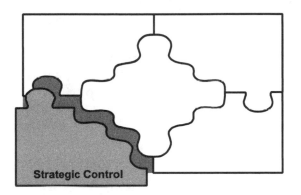

Strategic Control

While profit capture (the topic of Chapter 5) focused on how companies make money, this chapter looks at strategic control, the element of business design that protects profits over time.

Value nets achieve strategic control through one or more of the following mechanisms:

➤ A value net *brand* that provides differentiation in the eyes of customers

➤ A *hook* that holds customers in a satisfying relationship

> ➤ A set of solid *provider relationships* with supply part-
> ners

> ➤ An *innovative design* that puts a company's service far
> ahead

> ➤ A *low price* that competitors find tough to match

These mechanisms protect profits by strengthening
customer and supplier loyalty while fencing out competitors. Some, such as *brand* and *hook,* create a high degree of
customer loyalty and provide longer-lasting protection of
the profit stream. Others, such as *innovation* and *low price,*
offer a shorter-term advantage and are easier to copy. The
degree of strategic control conferred by a value net can be
arrayed along a high-to-low-control continuum (see Figure 6.1).

Not one of the companies listed in Figure 6.1, not even
those that fall into the high-control category, is immune to
imitation. Not one has patent or copyright protection of
its mechanism of strategic control. A hook can be copied;
an innovation can be replicated; low price can be
matched. Thus, strategic control, like every other element
of business design, must continuously change and adapt
to current market conditions. Keeping this injunction in
mind, let's examine the role of supply chain capabilities
in creating the different control mechanisms we have
identified.

Degree of Control	Control Point	Examples
High	Value net brand	Cisco, Cemex, Miller SQA, Gateway
	Customer hooks	Streamline, UPS, Amazon
	Provider relationships	Li & Fung, Biogen
Medium	Design innovation	Gateway, Miller SQA, Weyerhaeuser, Progressive
Low	Low price	Monorail, eMachines

Figure 6.1 Degree of strategic control conferred by value nets.

■ VALUE NET BRAND

Value net brand is analogous to the more familiar concept of product brand. In both cases, a company that owns a successful brand enjoys a high degree of customer awareness, trust, and loyalty. Over time, it can spend less on customer acquisition, experience fewer customer defections, and charge a premium price relative to competing, unbranded options. In some cases, a product brand accounts for 100 percent of the sustained profitability of the brand holder.[1] Product brand power can be immense. Think about what makes Coke, Tide, Advil, and Sony special. In 1996, for example, *Financial World* estimated Coke's brand to be worth $43 billion and McDonald's to be worth $19 billion.

Whereas a product brand is built on product attributes, a value net brand is built on consistently superior service, on total solutions, or on the ability to deliver a customized product. Exceptional speed, reliability, convenience, and other service aspects can provide the strong differentiation that every company wants to maintain in the eyes of its customers. When these service qualities become routinely associated with a company's name, that company enjoys brand power.

Value net brand is as powerful as product brand, but it is not nearly as prevalent. A few PC makers have built value net brands. According to industry analysts, for example, Gateway and Apple are the PC industry brands with the highest customer awareness. Apple's brand has long been associated with the user-friendliness and the unique functionality of its computers. It is a product-based brand. In contrast, Gateway's computers have few major unique product characteristics, but they are built exactly to customer specifications and arrive exactly as promised in just a few days. These service qualities set them apart and, we would argue, invest Gateway with a *value net*-based brand that distinguishes it and gives it a measure of strategic control. Supply chain excellence and the ability to deliver a consistently high level of service have rewarded Gateway with substantial market share, high customer loyalty, and a premium stock valuation. For example, 75 percent of Gateway purchasers in 1997 were repeat buyers, and Gateway enjoyed a price-to-earnings ratio of 53 versus 46 for IBM, Compaq, and Hewlett-Packard, on average, at the end of November 1999.

The power of a value net brand is even more striking in the case of a commodity product like cement. Cemex, whose ability to deliver cement like pizza—in 20 minutes, guaranteed[2]—has customers signing up even though Cemex's prices exceed those of competitors in many markets. The guarantee offered by Cemex is unique in its industry and is part of the company's value net brand image. Cemex's consistently fast and time-definite delivery has earned accolades from the business community and has helped the company enjoy the highest market value–to-sales ratio among its five major global competitors.[3]

At the end of this chapter, we will examine in detail how another company, Miller SQA, has built a value net brand in the office furniture industry.

■ CUSTOMER HOOKS

Designing a business with built-in customer hooks is another powerful way to maintain customer loyalty. At their best, these hooks lock in value for both customers and company. Hooks typically create high switching costs for customers as a direct by-product of the unique service provided. Staying with the company as a customer becomes easier and less costly than quitting. Traditional hooks are created through sales and marketing campaigns like these:

➤ MCI's Friends and Family program
➤ Thirty-day free trials for magazines and other products in which failure to cancel (i.e., failure to switch) results in continued service and billing

➤ Music, book, and coffee club memberships that send new selections every month unless specifically instructed not to

➤ Frequent flier programs

Value net hooks can be established by leveraging customer information to design unique services or by building in switching costs.

Value nets are adept at gathering in-depth customer information through choiceboards or other customer touch points. That information is used to build deeper relationships and to keep customers hooked into company services. Consider Ritz Carlton Hotels. Its information system captures more and more data about individual customers and their preferences with each visit. After the first visit, customers do not have to tell a registration clerk their address, company affiliation, or credit card number. They do not have to waste time answering routine questions such as, "Do you prefer a smoking or nonsmoking room?" Whether a repeat customer is checking into a hotel in Barcelona, Berlin, Boston, or Dubai, Ritz Carlton already has the relevant information and uses it to speed guest registration and to make the traveler's visit more satisfying. Many travelers will choose Ritz Carlton hotels on future trips simply to avoid the hassle of educating a competing hotel on what it must do to provide the same personalized service.

Hooks can also be built effectively through the supply chain design. Streamline.com, whose business design we examined in Chapter 3, provides a good example. Its delivery design creates a hook, which entails a high initial cost for the company and depends on several months of continued service to provide a payback. Specifically, Streamline invests in The Box (its garage storage unit) and in the installation of a special garage door lock. The customer, too, makes an investment—trust and access to his or her private space. To get unhooked from this arrangement, the customer must schedule someone to come to the home and remove The Box and the special door lock; this involves personal effort and inconvenience. The company's automatic replenishment program—Don't Run Out—also provides a hook. A subscriber must make a special effort to *not* make a purchase. It is easier for customers to continue receiving routine items through Streamline's scheduled weekly delivery than to pull the plug on the automatic replenishment routine. The result is that Streamline enjoys high customer loyalty rates and more than twice as many repeat orders as its largest competitor. Streamline's hooks support customer retention, provided that the company signs up a customer before the competition.

United Parcel Service (UPS) uses a process hook to keep business customers loyal. Its electronic shipment tracking, for example, gets customers hooked into its proprietary tracking software. The electronic tracking creates value for customers, but it also makes it costly for them to switch providers, because doing so requires changing software systems and retraining employees in their use.

UPS has yet another hook for customers: It allows them to set up value-adding operations in its warehouses. For example, Hewlett-Packard completes final assembly and Gateway does computer repairs on UPS premises. If these companies dropped UPS in favor of competing logistics providers, they would have to redesign portions of their larger operations, making the switch more costly.

Creative value net design can therefore provide important mechanisms to keep customers coming back.

■ PROVIDER RELATIONSHIPS

Strong relationships with suppliers and service providers impart strategic control to the extent that those relationships cannot readily be copied. Biogen, for example, may be able to protect its position as an agile producer in part by virtue of the fact that rivals cannot easily copy its value net of supplier partners. New, clean-slate entrants to Biogen's market would at least find it a time-consuming and demanding challenge to piece together the right value net relationships.

Relationships give staying power to another company we examined: Hong Kong's Li & Fung. With 7,500 suppliers in Asia, Europe, and South America, Li & Fung works hard to forge relationships of mutual benefit and trust that ultimately provide strategic advantage. To build those relationships, Li & Fung has been willing to put some of its own efficiency on the line. Victor Fung explains:

> *The volume we give each supplier will fluctuate, but ideally [will be] between 30 percent and 70 percent of a supplier's capacity. So there's always some business going on and an ongoing relationship. You've got to keep feeding people, you can't switch on and off. . . . It takes a lot for us to close an office, because it would not be very good for our long-term reputation. We are always there to show that there's longevity in the relationship.*[4]

That philosophy, according to Victor Fung, has paid off. When Li & Fung needs to tap the production capacity of a supplier partner, that partner recognizes its part of the bargain:

> *A lot of [our success] is based upon having dealt with people and having long relationships and a certain amount of trust. When our people call up and say an order's coming, block that capacity—don't give it away—that's useful, because every time we've said that, we've honored our word for the last 50 years.*

New competitors would be hard-pressed to replicate the network of relationships that Li & Fung now commands on behalf of the Western consumer goods companies that are its key customers. Li & Fung's relationships create a formidable barrier to entry for newcomers.

Some value net relationships confer strategic control by virtue of trust that takes time to build and is hard to replicate in the short and medium term. Others build strategic control by locking in exclusive or preferred access to key players in a given market. This is a key strategy for e-commerce companies. Fingerhut, a premier fulfillment company with package management expertise, over 3 million square feet of warehouse space, and the capacity to process 60 million packages annually, saw the burgeoning potential of e-commerce. It realized that it could capitalize on the growing market only if it had flexible and scalable order-processing capability. So in late September 1999, Fingerhut's Business Services Division allied with OrderTrust, a Lowell, Massachusetts–based company with best-in-class order-processing technology. OrderTrust digitally connects e-tailers with suppliers, fulfillment houses, and drop-shippers, ensuring that massive volumes of orders are handled accurately and efficiently. Fingerhut's relationship with OrderTrust will allow it to develop complete "e-fulfillment" solutions for a broad range of clients, which will present a significant barrier for potential rivals.

■ INNOVATIVE DESIGN

Being first to market with a new product or technology is a proven strategy for growth and differentiation. Innovation in value net design also confers first-mover advantages. The first company to offer exceptional service levels or customized products at the same prices as mass-produced competing products is able to differentiate itself and gain strategic control for as long as it takes competitors to catch up. The good news for trailblazers is that an innovative operating design can be more difficult to replicate than a product or technology innovation. We rate this as "medium-degree" strategic control. It also serves as the launching pad for brand status.

Dell and Gateway are the most obvious examples of value nets with innovative operating designs. Their build-to-order, direct-sales models were extremely innovative when first introduced. Both operate efficiently with minimal inventory and negative cash conversion cycles, setting performance standards that rivals are still struggling to meet. They have now achieved brand control. But competitors are pursuing them. Apple has adopted major aspects of their highly efficient operating model. "We now offer configure to order worldwide at our [online] Apple Store," says Apple's Tim Cook. "Dell was the first to do it and has made it extremely popular."[5] Others are sure to follow. The only way to maintain this type of control is to keep innovating.

Where will it end? Innovation continues to transform the business designs of computer manufacturers. Gateway, for example, is changing its profile from that of a computer company that offers Internet service to that of an Internet service provider that also sells computers. It is in effect converting its computer manufacturing and delivery capability into a stepping-stone toward developing a broader and deeper customer relationship. Its late-October 1999 deal with America Online (AOL) confirms Gateway's new direction. AOL will invest $800 million in Gateway and bundle its web service into Gateway PCs. The two companies are also creating a co-branded software store. The net result is brand reinforcement through innovation.

■ LOW PRICE

Companies that can deliver products to customers at dramatically lower prices than competitors have distinct competitive advantages, all else being equal. Low price alone, however, is a relatively weak source of strategic control. Why? Because low price, driven by low costs, is a difficult strategy for any business to defend over time. One manufacturer may drive low prices through high-volume buying. A start-up may slash the overhead structure. A third company may leverage the scale economies of partners by orchestrating its supplier network.

The PC industry once again provides an instructive example. A high degree of component standardization and rapid technology innovation has resulted in the commoditization of personal computers. In this environment, a number of companies have tried to create strategic control by becoming the lowest-cost player. In 1995, for example, former Compaq executive Doug Johns created a new, nimble, low-cost competitor, virtual PC maker Monorail. Johns explains, "We developed a company with the notion that there's nothing wrong with a mature market if you have a cost structure for a mature market."[6] Johns believed that established PC manufacturers would find it impossible to off-load enough assets and overhead to be able to compete with Monorail's virtual cost structure. The company had only 25 employees; it sold through resellers; and it outsourced nearly everything—production and assembly to contract manufacturers, delivery to FedEx, customer service to Sykes Enterprises, and finance and accounts receivable to SunTrust Bank. Even R&D was largely eliminated from the books.

Johns explains, "[We are a] humble packager of other people's technology. . . . We have the world's largest R&D departments: Intel's and Microsoft's. They can spend 8 or 10 percent of their revenue on R&D. For us, whatever comes out, if the customer wants it, we'll package it." This lean structure translated into $2.4 million in revenues per Monorail employee by early 1999, compared with $540,000 for Compaq, $300,000 for IBM, and $890,000 for Dell.[7] According to company executives, minimal overhead alone gave Monorail a 10 to 20 percent cost advantage. By mid-1999 it placed fifth in retail sales in the United States. Despite its cost advantage, Monorail ceased production in late

1999, due to financing shortfalls. (It has since signed a deal to make and sell PCs for a Fortune 100 company.)

By all accounts, Monorail's structurally lower-cost business design should have provided strategic control through lower prices. But in 1998, the business press trumpeted the arrival of another newcomer, eMachines, Inc. A joint venture of two Korean manufacturers, eMachines stormed the market with $399 to $599 PCs. From September 1998 (its inception) to August 1999, eMachines grabbed 11 percent of the U.S. retail market. In less than a year, this low-cost business design had become the third most popular PC maker selling through U.S. retail channels. But did eMachines enjoy any greater strategic control than Monorail? How low does the price have to go to ensure some degree of strategic control?

Free-PC, Inc., has provided the answer to the last of these questions: *zero*. Free-PC has developed a business design that *gives away* PCs in exchange for advertisement viewing time. Customers agree to have their PCs hooked to the Internet for a period of time each month and to have a portion of their screens dedicated to advertisements. In exchange, they receive the hardware for free. The company gets paid by advertisers. Between June (inception) and November 1999, the company gave away 30,000 computers in response to overwhelming demand from consumers. At the end of November 1999, Free-PC announced it was being acquired by eMachines, which would use Free-PC's software to place advertising on users' screens. The moral of this tangled tale is the vulnerability of the low-cost/low-price approach in establishing strategic control.

We aren't, of course, against low prices. Value nets generally deliver both remarkable service *and* cost savings, as we've noted. But in our view, the cost advantage (enabling lower price) is more ephemeral than the service edge. Furniture maker Miller SQA, for example, developed its vision of breakthrough service after observing the pitfalls of price-based competition. "In the late eighties, the office furniture industry was becoming commoditized," Bill Bundy, SQA's vice president of operations, told us. "Competitors were killing each other on price to win big projects."[8] And while "affordable" became an integral and important part of SQA's value proposition, it was only part of a broader offering of superior speed and reliability, as we will see.

■ HOW DOES STRATEGIC CONTROL APPLY TO YOUR BUSINESS?

What is the measure of strategic control your business exercises over its revenues and profits? If it's low, think about how a value net design might help you.

Are the service levels in your industry notoriously poor? How good is the "on-time and complete" delivery rate? How long is the cycle time or time to market? Is that as good as it gets? Industries where service levels are undifferentiated provide a great opportunity to gain a first-mover advantage in getting to the customer faster and more conveniently. Traditional, unglamorous industries are particularly ripe for *innovative designs* that can make one company stand out from the pack.

While a brand takes time to build and is not an overnight strategy, an innovative design that can build and support a *value net brand* is the critical first step. Poor service and a mismatch between what customers need and what providers are offering are the preconditions for the creation of a value net brand. What are your customers telling you they need? When they finally asked the questions, many of the companies we studied heard the same theme from their customers: "The products are just fine, but the service is terrible."

What keeps your current customers coming back? What does it take for them to switch providers? Are they *hooked?* Could you offer a trade-in program? Could you run your equipment at their site? What are you learning from your customer relationships that can make their experience with you worth more than what they'd get from another provider?

Finally, are *supplier relationships* giving you an edge in the marketplace? How do your competitors work with suppliers? What could you do differently that would make you the favorite customer of your suppliers? What are the nonprice elements of the relationship? Do they drive value for your customers as well? Investing in deep relationships with carefully selected providers creates a value net that is hard to beat.

These are just a few of the questions you need to ask about your business and the issue of strategic control. The following case reveals how one company began by asking the right questions and then went on to implement a successful value net design.

■ OFFICE FURNITURE AS YOU LIKE IT FROM SQA

In this case, we examine a relatively new enterprise within a large, established company. This unit has succeeded in capturing profits and market share in a competitive industry. SQA's recipe for success is speed and reliability—a value proposition that appeals to its customers—and a value net capable of supporting it. The question for us in this chapter is: What mechanisms does SQA use to protect its stream of profits?

Herman Miller, Inc., is a major manufacturer of office, healthcare, and residential furniture and a provider of furniture management services. Headquartered in Zeeland, Michigan, the company has annual revenues of $1.7 billion and is one of a handful of vendors—along with Steelcase, Haworth, and Knoll—that corporations regularly turn to when they furnish new or renovated office space. Among its laurels, Herman Miller is credited with designing the world's first open-plan office furniture system, which revolutionized the office environment. Today, many businesses around the globe use open-plan offices, and many fill them with Herman Miller furniture systems.

The typical ordering process for large corporate customers of office furniture and cubicle systems is lengthy and involves substantial hand-holding, customer education, and committee-based decision making. Most of these big customers, however, aren't in a rush; they are moving into new or renovated space that will not be ready for occupancy for anywhere from six months to two years. During that time, cross-departmental teams work at committee speed to define how people will work together in the new space, to determine what their needs will be for furniture and local storage units, and to study the product offerings of competing vendors. Vendors go to great lengths to secure these orders and to please customers. In many cases, they develop two-dimensional plans and physical mock-ups, or they may fly customer teams to showrooms where the latest in office layouts and options for color, fabrics, style, and modularity are on display. The range of choices can be mind-boggling— multiple standard and custom colors (including 40 different shades of white finishes), several hundred fabric choices, and so forth. Once a deal is made and the customer has selected from a blizzard of options, production begins and stretches for up to six to eight weeks. Change requests are difficult to accommodate, and add time and cost. While most business continues in this mode for Herman Miller and its key rivals, workplace changes have created an opportunity for a new approach to selling, building, and delivering office furniture.

➤ The Concept Is Born

Big corporations remain big, but the real growth in the economy, at least in the United States, has been among small and medium-size companies. The percentage of the U.S. workforce employed by Fortune 500 companies has plummeted since the early 1960s. Meanwhile, the ranks of self-employed people working full- or part-time from home offices, and companies of fewer than 50 employees, have exploded, creating a new class of customers for office furniture. These new customers aren't interested in major outlays for office furniture. They don't have "employee furniture committees" to study thousands of options. They do not value hundreds of style, fabric, and color choices. And they will not wait two months for delivery. They want affordable, functional furniture that is available on short notice.

Herman Miller recognized these customers as a new and important market with unique requirements that its existing business and its supply chain were not designed to serve well. It attempted to serve them through Phoenix Designs, a trade-in/refurbishment office furniture company it started in the late 1980s. Seeing this strategy as a half measure that would not realize the market's full potential, Herman Miller rolled out a new capability, an innovative value net design: SQA (simple, quick, affordable).

The new unit, launched in 1995, was the brainchild of then head of Phoenix Designs Bix Norman. Norman's experience in sales and marketing had taught him that the product differentiation game in office furniture was getting stale, resulting in slow growth and thin margins. Yet, according to Norman, Herman Miller continued to emphasize product differentiation—furniture products designed to make the office more efficient. But so did everyone else. "A product's a product," Norman told us. "It isn't about product, it's about simplicity and how fast you can get it. . . . If you looked at our industry from a customer's viewpoint of what it was like to buy and get office furniture, you'd find that it was just a big, huge pain."[9]

Norman and his associates decided to build on Herman Miller's competencies in furniture design, quality, and product performance, but to differentiate SQA in terms of speedy and reliable delivery. They studied the requirements of small businesses and developed a number of new furniture products for them. These products were simple, with a fraction of the complexity found in the parent company's product lines, and were designed with cost-effective, quality materials and rapid assembly in mind. At the same time, SQA designed a value net with the speed and flexibility to produce and deliver mass-customized orders in record time. Any operating functions that suppliers could do faster, more reliably, and at lower cost were outsourced. Figure 6.2 highlights key differences between traditional contract office furniture makers and SQA.

SQA fashioned its supply chain into a network for creating sustainable profit growth. Several aspects of that design have helped it protect those profits from encroachment. But before we get to these, let's briefly examine key aspects of SQA's design.

	Traditional contract furniture makers	SQA
Product	Higher-end, higher-priced products	Affordable functionality
Choice	High level of product choice: ❑ Hundreds of different fabrics ❑ Many color choices, including custom colors ❑ Dozens of product families, with high variation within each	A simple set of choices (e.g., five base colors) customized within three product categories: ❑ Seating ❑ Freestanding furniture ❑ Office systems
Speed	Six- to eight-week order-to-shipment cycle time	Less than one week from order to shipment
Reliability	Low rate of on-time shipment	99.6 percent on-time shipment
Responsiveness	Order changes difficult and expensive to make	Changes easy to make

Figure 6.2 A new model.

➤ Business Design

SQA began with a key prerequisite for success: It selected a promising customer segment and developed a product/ service that was highly valued by that segment. In this case, the targeted customers, at least initially, were home offices and small businesses of from 5 to 50 employees. Described by the company as "efficiency buyers," these represented 20 percent of the market for office furniture (anticipated to expand to 50 percent in the future). SQA's offer to this customer group was straightforward:

➤ A reliable delivery date.

➤ Build-to-order assembly.

➤ Speed—from customer contact to delivery and setup.

➤ Simplicity—product and feature choices not valued by the customer segment are eliminated; the selection and ordering process is also simplified.

➤ Affordability—a superefficient supply network delivers high value at a reasonable total cost.

➤ Achieving Speed and Reliability

SQA's offer to customers was a tall order, and not one that could be handled through the operational infrastructure of the parent company. Herman Miller was an efficient manufacturing enterprise. It had been practicing build-to-order customization for years and had deep competencies in furniture design. But speed and exceptionally reliable delivery—the foundations on which SQA aimed to differentiate itself—were not among its best practices. Nor were they best practices for other major furniture makers. SQA would have to break new ground.

To master speed and reliability, the company stood back from the problem and examined the entire set of activities involved in securing and fulfilling an order. Those activities extended from the salesperson's first contact with a customer, through the order fulfillment and shipment process, to the point at which new furniture is delivered and installed on the customer's premises. It broke that activity set into three parts:

1. *Customer contact to order entry.* This part often consumes up to three months for traditional furniture makers. A dealer's salesperson makes contact with a potential customer, becomes acquainted with the customer's needs, and both then join in a long and detailed discussion of employee work processes, furniture features, and options. Furniture configurations are rendered in either two-dimensional or computer-aided design (CAD) formats, neither of which produces an offering price or error-free bill of materials. Prices and bills of materials must be created separately and changed with each reconfiguration requested by the customer. At best, only an estimated delivery date can be offered.

2. *Order entry to shipment.* Traditional furniture making must translate every order into a bill of materials, then schedule the manufacturing and shipment that will get the job done. According to Bill Bundy, SQA's vice president of operations, this part of the value-creation process represents only about 20 percent of the total time in the end-to-end process, yet it is where traditional furniture makers focus their improvement efforts.

3. *Shipment to installation.* Most shipments are made to dealer warehouses, where they must be stored and handled at significant cost prior to reshipment and installation at the customer's site. Direct shipments from the manufacturer to the installation site are clearly preferable, but unreliable delivery dates have led dealers to err on the side of caution, accepting delivery into inventory well in advance of the installation dates promised to customers.

SQA attacked each part of the value-creating process with the goal of reducing time and enhancing the reliability of its customer delivery dates.

Z-Axis Software

SQA's main weapon in slashing time from the first part of the activity chain was its proprietary software. Developed by Herman Miller with a considerable investment, Z-Axis is a rule-based product configuration tool—a choiceboard—that allows a customer to see a furniture choice or a complete office arrangement in three dimensions and from any angle. It is the critical element of a set of applications known inside the company as the "1:1" suite (because it is utilized in one-to-one buyer-salesperson situations).

Z-Axis software makes it possible to design, specify, price, and place an order from a dealer salesperson's laptop computer brought to the customer's site. Changes in panel heights, furniture models, fabric selections, and other variables can be viewed immediately, and their impacts on total package price are automatically calculated and displayed for the customer. This software alone is credited with reducing the ordering process from several months to a few days in most cases. As one dealer told us, "The Z-Axis technology is wonderful both for the client and for the dealer."[10]

Z-Axis is more than an aid to selling SQA products. Once the customer accepts a package and commits to an order, Z-Axis automatically renders all customer choices into an accurate bill of materials that is transmitted electronically to a server accessed every 15 minutes during the working day by SQA's two manufacturing sites, Holland, Michigan, and Rocklin, California. The manufacturing facilities access the orders and port them automatically to their enterprise resource planning (ERP) and expert scheduling systems. Within two hours, the customer receives an order confirmation and delivery date. Each step in the process automatically generates a status update e-mail to the dealer. "This is a seven days a week, 24 hours a day system," says

Bundy. "It's not unusual to find that our orders have grown by half a million dollars overnight."

The Manufacturing Middle

Every order that hits the SQA system is picked up and moved along with the help of computerized systems:

➤ ERP software specifies materials, schedules production, and issues shipping dates. Over 50 percent of all orders are scheduled with no manual intervention whatsoever.[11]

➤ Manufacturing execution software sequences jobs to facilitate synchronized, one-order-at-a-time assembly. According to Bundy, one-order-at-a-time assembly is critical to both speed and fixed asset utilization. "[It] reduces the time required to consolidate an order for shipment," he says. "It also improves space utilization because less consolidation space is required when order-completion velocity improves. For some manufacturers, order-completion time can exceed one week."[12]

➤ SupplyNet, a proprietary information system, improves the visibility and speed of material flows within the company's network of suppliers. Every participant can see the same real-time information. Customer demand, safety stocks, promised shipment dates, and supplier-owned inventory are just a few of the essential pieces of information made available by SupplyNet to partners via the Internet. Real customer demand is updated four times each day. "Theoretically, we could update demand in real time," says Bundy, "but our suppliers tell us that four times per day is enough for them today." This accurate and timely information is credited with reducing systemwide inventories by close to 30 percent, lowering suppliers' costs, SQA's costs, and costs to end customers.

Another key to SQA's manufacturing effectiveness is its Production Metering Center (PMC), a facility operated by Menlo Logistics within a few miles of the company's assembly plant in Holland, Michigan. The PMC is a flow-through, just-in-time holding area for supplier-owned inventory. It frees up space at the assembly plant, yet keeps materials and components in position to facilitate just-in-time delivery. Before the PMC was built, almost one-third of SQA's production floor space, and an equal percentage of supplier manufacturing space, was encumbered by materials inventory. These areas are now free for value-adding work.

For the most part, inventory sited at the PMC stays on the books of suppliers until it is delivered to the SQA assembly plant. Except for items triggered by a just-in-time system, materials move from the PMC to the assembly facility at two-hour intervals.

The Final Leg

Getting finished furniture and office systems from manufacturers' shipping docks to end customers has historically been a time-consuming and costly segment of the total value-creating process. Given the industry's unreliable record on finished goods deliveries, dealers have developed a practice of requesting delivery well in advance of the installation dates they promise to end customers. Orders that *do* arrive on time are stored in dealer warehouses, where they await scheduled installation dates at customer sites. SQA and its dealers are working together to eliminate this time-consuming step through direct deliveries to end users. The goal is to have the delivery truck and the dealer's installation team arrive at the customer's site on the promised delivery date. Even now, SQA's dealers are pleased with the delivery process: "I've never been let down by SQA," one dealer told us. She reports full confidence in SQA's promised delivery dates—always within two weeks and sometimes as fast as two days—and can place those dates on her calendar.[13]

Results

SQA's results, summarized in Figure 6.3, make a good case for a value proposition based on speed and reliable delivery, and they illustrate the economic power of a well-designed value net.

Sales	❑ $250 million in 1998
	❑ 15 to 20 percent of total Herman Miller sales
Profit margin	❑ Higher than parent company (not reported separately)
Compound annual growth rate of sales	❑ 25 percent as opposed to 7 percent for the industry (1991 to 1998)
On-time shipments	❑ 99.6 percent (1998); 60 percent of days experience 100 percent on-time shipment; record of 45 consecutive days of 100 percent on-time shipmen
Inventory turns (finished goods)	❑ 200 turns per year
On-hand inventory	❑ 1 to 2 days at the PMC; 10 days at the SQA warehouse
Accounts receivable	❑ 20-22 days versus 50 days for the industry
Internet direct sales	❑ In June 1999, $100,000 per week
Order-to-delivery time	❑ 2 days to 2 weeks
Dealer feedback	❑ "Easiest manufacturer to do business with"
	❑ "Ranks first in quick and complete delivery, on-time delivery, and service"

Figure 6.3 SQA performance summary, 1998.

SQA has been an important new venture for its parent, Herman Miller. It has created a major new stream of revenues and a secure beachhead in a new and rapidly growing market segment. Perhaps as important, SQA has been a valuable learning experience for the company as a whole. Concepts of speed, collaboration, complexity reduction, and the use of information technology are being introduced to product lines in the parent organization.

SQA and Strategic Control

Office furniture manufacturing is a highly competitive business with many capable players. Steelcase, Haworth, and Knoll are formidable competitors, and they are not sitting still as markets change and new technologies roil their industry. Steelcase and Knoll have both demonstrated the ability to ship an order in two weeks if pressed to do so. This raises an important question: How will SQA protect its profit stream from these and other competitors in the years ahead? Let's answer that question in terms of the mechanisms of strategic control described earlier in this chapter. SQA exhibits three of those mechanisms:

➤ *Innovation in business design.* SQA has benefited from first-mover advantage with its rapid and reliable delivery. Innovation has been one of the powerful control mechanisms enjoyed by SQA. Its Z-Axis technology, its information systems, and its supplier relationships have begun to set the standard for the industry. So SQA retains the lead. Can these capabilities be replicated? Of course. But as the first player on the learning curve, SQA aims to keep its lead through continual innovation.

➤ *Supply chain brand.* SQA's outstanding service levels have set it apart. Dealer accolades indicate that "simple, quick, and affordable" has become a significant point of differentiation for the company. "No one in the business is faster or more reliable,"[14] one dealer told us. Its descriptive name has been invested with the value of a service brand.

➤ *Customer hook.* The company foresees a time when the facilities' managers of larger customers will have Z-Axis software on their desktop computers, giving them the ability to run their own configurations and submit orders as they expand or replace outmoded furniture and office systems. Mastery of this easy-to-use yet robust software tool will make many customers reluctant to change vendors, just as package-tracking software helps build loyalty for UPS.

SQA has no patent on its value net design. Nor does it appear to control a single thing that the other major-league office furniture vendors or start-up companies could not imitate. Although its Z-Axis software is proprietary and state of the art, competitors' software can only get better, thus challenging SQA's lead in the years ahead. ERP and scheduling software is available to everyone. Even the concept of the Production Monitoring Center can be replicated in another setting.

Each strand in the SQA network of information systems and supply partner relationships is potentially replicable. The strongest assurance of continuing strategic control for SQA may ultimately be its determination to stay ahead of the curve. Former president of Miller SQA Bix Norman estimates that "to put the necessary infrastructure in place would take four to five years." SQA does not intend to relax behind that barrier to entry, but plans to solidify its control of the small business segment through improvements to all systems and through more direct relationships with suppliers, dealers, and customers. "We're going to leapfrog ourselves before the competition does it," Norman told us.

According to Bill Bundy, "We know that competitors are looking at us, trying to figure out how we do what we do." They are also developing quick-ship programs for special orders, though the speed and reliability of these programs trails SQA's performance. "They are trying to do pieces of it," Bundy observes. The big difference may come down to how these companies view the office furniture business. Says Bundy,

> *They look at [office furniture] as a product business. We view product as important, but have decided that the real business we're in is service around the product. We have chosen to focus on completing the order, not the products. I don't see them doing that. We build 85 percent of our orders right here in this plant. They build part of an order in one plant and the remaining parts in several different places. Think of the logistical challenge they have of bringing the office together on time.*

SQA's strategic control rests in the design, development, and interrelationship of its many parts, in the value net it has created, and in continuing innovation of that design that allows it to maintain a five-year lead against the competition.

Lessons Learned

Miller SQA's experience provides valuable lessons for any company seeking to create a lasting advantage from its value net. Three points are crucial:

➤ *Strategic control begins with a sound understanding of customer needs.* The first step toward differentiation lies in identifying unmet customer needs. This forms the basis for a value proposition that sets the company apart, creating a perceived edge in the eyes of buyers that, if it can be sustained over time, yields strategic control.

➤ *Delivering convenience and reliability is a powerful innovation.* The value proposition is only as strong as a company's ability to deliver on its promise. A complete rethinking of the ordering, fulfillment, and delivery system ensures the desired performance. Consistent execution of this differentiated service develops the value net brand in the marketplace.

➤ *Unique, digitally enabled customer touches build loyalty.* A good customer hook must be based on unique convenience or other services, as perceived by the customer. The front-end selection and ordering process offers scope for unique linkages, as with SQA's Z-Axis software. The delivery process also provides rich opportunities. Establishing unique connections into the customer's own operations offers a valuable measure of strategic control.

Strategic control is earned, not bought. Miller SQA shows the way. Is your company ready to embark on a similar journey?

■ NOTES

1. Adrian Slywotzky and David Morrison, *The Profit Zone* (New York: Times Books, 1998), 63.
2. The current guarantee provides 5 percent off, but Cemex is considering a move to an "on time or free" guarantee. Source: Thomas Petzinger, Jr. "This promise is set in concrete," www.cemex.com/articles/petzinger.asp; Henry Tricks, "Deliveries in Pizza-Style," *Financial Times,* November 30, 1998, 7.
3. On an EBITDA basis (see note 7 in Chapter 3).
4. Victor Fung. Interview with Kirk Kramer (Mercer Management Consulting), August 16, 1999.
5. Tim Cook. Interview with author, September 29, 1999.
6. Doug Johns. Interview with Jack Dougan (Mercer Management Consulting), June 8, 1999.
7. Marketguide.com, October 10, 1999.
8. Bill Bundy. Interview with Jack Dougan and Eric Vratimos (Mercer Management Consulting), June 22, 1999.
9. Bix Norman. Interview with Jack Dougan and Eric Vratimos (Mercer Management Consulting), June 22, 1999.

10. Andrea Hopkins, Sales Executive, American Office Equipment Company, Rockville, MD. Interview with Denise Auclair (Mercer Management Consulting), August 3, 1999.
11. William Bundy, "Leveraging Technology for Speed and Reliability," *Supply Chain Management Review,* spring, 1999, 64.
12. Ibid., 65.
13. Andrea Hopkins, Sales Executive, American Office Equipment Company, Rockville, MD. Interview with Denise Auclair (Mercer Management Consulting), August 3, 1999.
14. Frank Soleski, Sales Executive, Office Pavilion K (F2), Inc., Washington, D.C. Interview with Denise Auclair (Mercer Management Consulting), August 3, 1999.

Chapter

Design for Execution: Realizing the Net

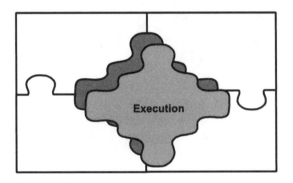

Execution is the fifth element of value net business design. It translates business design into fast, reliable, and flexible value-creating activities. Execution links all other design decisions—decisions about the *value proposition,* where the company will play in the *scope* of value net activities, its mechanisms of *profit capture,* and how it will strategically *control* its position in the market. Logically, those decisions matter only to the extent that a company can execute them well. That is why designing for superior execution is so critical. For example, a grocery delivery business that promises customers the convenience of reliable on-time delivery will fall on its face if its deliveries are late or if it fails to show up with the right items. Execute poorly and you're out.

Each of the successful value net companies we have examined in this book is excellent at execution, and each is excellent by design. Gateway. SQA. Weyerhaeuser. Cemex. Biogen. Li & Fung. Streamline. Zara. These companies aim to get it right the first time every time. They plan, they act fast, and they learn on the fly. When we went looking for the mechanisms of their execution excellence, we found two simple characteristics: a breakthrough culture and a shift from "atoms to bits."[1]

In our definition, a *breakthrough culture* encompasses leadership vision, grassroots entrepreneurship, a clear set of goals, and the right people skills for the job. By a *shift from atoms to bits,* we mean the transition to a digital culture of information and connectedness. These companies have built information systems that allow intelligent choices by customers, both within company operations and with external partners.

■ CREATING A BREAKTHROUGH CULTURE

When we began our initial research for this book, one of the things we planned to do was to look for organizational features that correlated with execution excellence in value net operations. A number of the value net companies we studied, however, were quick to tell us that we were looking in the wrong direction. "*Organization* is a much overrated and overused word," Apple's Tim Cook told us. "What makes a supply chain successful is taking the boxes away and working horizontally, not vertically."[2] Zara's human resources director, José María Gonzalez, echoed a similar sentiment, stating that his company had *no* organizational structure in the traditional sense. "Any model that we could propose would be immediately obsolete,"[3] he said. So value nets are not about any particular organizational structure. Nor do they require a senior vice president of "value net operations." For managers and employees weary of company-wide restructurings, this is good news. What is needed instead is a culture with the following characteristics:

- ➤ Leadership vision
- ➤ An entrepreneurial team
- ➤ Simple and clear goals
- ➤ New skills

Invest to embed these characteristics in your organization and you will have laid the foundation for execution excellence.

➤ Leadership Vision

In the business world, all big changes require vision and commitment at the top. Corporate change does not percolate up from the bottom. Leadership at the top is what really matters. GE's Jack Welch, IBM's Lou Gerstner, Disney's Michael Eisner, and the late Roberto Goizueta of Coca-Cola have each demonstrated how a strong leader committed to change can move a huge organization in new, more productive directions.

Visionary leadership is a requirement for any established company that wants to reshape itself as a value net. The CEO has to "get it." The executive team has to get it. They must have a clear vision of the benefits of this new type of business design. Here is how Bill Bundy described the role of SQA's first president, Bix Norman:

> *Bix had the fundamental belief that office furniture had become an absolute pain in the [neck] for customers. The industry was not reliable, the industry was not responsive, all the way from lead times to order entry to shipping. You even got lousy customer service when you made a phone call. So Bix decided, "I think if we wrap good furniture with great service, we can win." And he started by building reliability*

into manufacturing. Today, we're averaging five-day lead times and 99.6 percent on-time shipments.

Bix Norman "got it." He saw the potential of supply chain design to drive a powerful new business. That vision became the cornerstone for Miller SQA's value net.

Once the leadership has embraced the vision, the next big challenge in creating a breakthrough culture is getting other people on board.

➤ An Entrepreneurial Team

The biggest barrier to change in any organization is the existing establishment—the bureaucracy, the protected turfs, the politics, "the way we do things around here." Bix Norman was emphatic in his conviction that traditional companies could not change decisively within the confines of their existing structures. In his view, they were weighted down with too much baggage. "It's impossible," he told us. "There are so many internal constituencies that gravity holds them back. . . . You'd spend all your time fending off the incumbents. It requires a brain transplant."[4]

Norman overcame the barriers to change by going around them—that is, by creating Miller SQA as a fairly independent unit within the parent company. Many entrepreneurs opt for breaking out with an independent company. The transformations at Apple, on the other hand, took place within the existing company structure.

Whether change happens within the existing organization or via a new one, every successful case of change we encountered involved a tightly knit entrepreneurial team that took responsibility for every aspect of the makeover. Tim Cook describes Apple's change in terms of a team effort: "We have an executive team—one person from engineering, one from marketing, one from operations, one from finance, and an attorney—and we talk every Monday about the state of the company." At Biogen, a small team was given the task of bringing AVONEX® to market and converting Biogen from a biotech firm into a full operating company. That team, headed by Jim Mullen, John Palmer, and Bob Hamm, was given a high degree of freedom to carry out its vision. Hamm elaborated on this philosophy:

> *A key success factor [for Biogen] involved freedom— giving people the freedom to do what needed to be done. Some people couldn't hack that amount of responsibility, but others thrived. A key to rapid execution is to plan up front and then leave the people alone to do it. Get the right people and turn 'em loose. That's what worked here, and I think it can work elsewhere.*[5]

Biogen emphasized a team-oriented approach and a spirit of entrepreneurship at all levels. Employees were encouraged to follow these principles:

> ➤ *Tell the truth.* Communicate openly, honestly, and frequently all along the supply chain; solutions can come from anyone.
> ➤ *Build teams.* Create a sense of belonging to Biogen's success among all participants, internal and external.
> ➤ *Resist layers, trust people.* Stay close enough to contractors' operations to know what's going on, but rely on them to get the job done.

A team-oriented culture and sense of shared responsibility is absolutely critical for value net responsiveness. At Biogen, for example, marketing and operations worked extremely closely and effectively. They were able to talk one-on-one. There were no large departments, no big committees. Small multicompany teams worked together on manufacturing and delivery problems and came up with joint solutions. Openness was encouraged, and opposing ideas were sought and discussed. Any idea was viewed as good until proven otherwise.

The fact that Biogen was building much of its organization from scratch was both a blessing and a challenge. On the positive side, its leaders were free to build the culture they wanted. On the challenge side, explains John Palmer, "Coordination across different functions was difficult, as new procedures had to be developed everywhere, new people hired, departments built into homogeneous teams and, importantly, infused with the same risk-taking profile as the rest of the company in order to support, not hinder, the creative process."

Diffusing an entrepreneurial spirit to all levels of the organization and to outside partners is a challenge for any company that aspires to a value net business design. Goals and incentives help make it happen.

➤ Simple and Clear Goals

A striking feature of the companies we studied is the extent to which simple, clear goals permeate employee ranks from top to bottom. At SQA, for example, the importance of speed and reliability is deeply ingrained in the culture of the company and its nearly 500 employees. Rewards, excitement, and esprit de corps are all organized around "hitting the bull's eye." Hitting the bull's eye at SQA means shipping 100 percent complete and error-free orders on time—something that customers view as extremely important. The choice of performance measure—perfect on-time orders—is highly significant because it aligns the interests of SQA employees with those of customers and tracks exactly with SQA's business proposition. It is also simple, easily grasped by all staff, and provides immediate performance feedback. This simple goal contrasts with commonly used, well-meaning, but abstract measures.

On-time shipments are measured three times each day at SQA, and the definition of *on time* is severe. If even one part is missing from an order, the entire shipment is counted as a *total miss*. If a truck is scheduled to load and depart by 11 A.M. but does not leave the loading dock until noon, it, too, goes on the books as a *total miss*.

The importance of hitting the bull's eye is driven home to SQA employees in many ways. A sign indicating the previous day's on-time performance is prominently displayed at each entrance to the plant. Every employee sees it. Bill Bundy makes sure that floor employees appreciate its importance and take it seriously. "Every day I draw an employee name at random and then go looking for him. When I find that person, I ask two questions: 'How many days in a row have we had 100 percent on-time shipments?' and 'What is our record for consecutive days of 100 percent on-time shipments?' (The answer is 45!) If he or she answers those two questions correctly, I hand over a $100 bill. The person can take the money or take one extra day of vacation. We play this game every day."

Five- and ten-day strings of perfect shipments are likewise celebrated in creative ways, but with progressively bigger awards, such as a free three-year lease on a new automobile. "They're reminded every day about the importance of on-time shipments," says Bundy, whose enthusiasm for concocting new and exciting ways to celebrate on-time success is unrestrained. "It's a blast!"

A similarly relentless focus was echoed by Apple's Tim Cook: "We set out to beat Dell [on inventory]. . . . And it goes down all the way to our production employees who have inventory targets like they have volume and quality targets. . . . The most important thing [we did] internally was to tell everyone what the target is. People will do amazing things if they have a target. We have this down to every factory worker. Every worker knows how much inventory is allowed. . . . It's Leadership 101—tell people what you want and then reward them for doing it."

Jerry Mannigel at Weyerhaeuser also emphasized the importance of communication in getting people committed to goals:

[Getting people on board] took an intensive level of communication. It's a traditional manufacturing facility, blue-collar, unionized, and it was fairly adversarial between the management and the union. But we had to say, either we all win or we all lose. . . . We began an intensive business education process with the entire workforce. Now, every supervisor has to spend one hour a week minimum in communication meetings with all his or her employees. Then, each quarter, I shut the plant down for a day, and we go offsite to have a four-hour informational meeting with each shift (there are three shifts). We do a full hour of questions and answers.[6]

According to Mannigel, the most powerful voice, at least during the transition period, was the customer's:

We videotaped [350] customer interviews, and we brought the videotapes back and played them for the workforce. Customers described the problems created when their orders didn't arrive on time or complete from their perspective. On time and complete became the rallying cry. We now know every day how we're doing against that target. An internal system of TV monitors shows us how we're doing every day. There are monitors in every lunchroom and on the work floor. It's on everyone's screen saver; there are 325 computers here on the production floor alone. Every department knows how it's doing and how it stacks up.

The lessons about goals that we distilled from our field research with these and other value net companies are twofold:

1. State the goal in simple, clear, and quantifiable terms; then go all out for it. Get everybody on the same bandwagon and reward people for achieving the goal.

2. Don't settle for incremental improvement when you set goals for a value net. Value nets are about perfect orders delivered in two to three days, not weeks; product launches in days, not months; and inventory supplies counted in hours, not days or months. These results require nonincremental goals.

What are the appropriate measures to set for value net performance? The old measures were expenditure-to-revenue ratios, unit cost, and product availability. The new ones can be the traditional ones taken to breakthrough levels—inventories measured in hours, for example. More likely, the right measures are new ones: alignment with the value proposition (Streamline), speed of ramp-up (Biogen), or the ability to manage the network of suppliers and partners effectively.

➤ New Skills

The final key ingredient of the cultural revolution is arming the right people with the right skills. Value nets are so collaboration- and coordination-intensive that most companies need new policies, new processes, and people who can effectively manage these relationships. The stakes are high. A value net company may outsource hundreds of millions of dollars worth of production and services, and this requires corresponding management expertise.

Functional expertise, transaction processing, and fire fighting—dominant supply chain skills in the traditional organization—must yield to strategic thinking, project planning, and relationship management. The "right" talent is represented by people who can build relationships and thrive in dynamic, open, team-oriented environments. Value nets require people who understand complexity and who can work with many constituents (e.g., customers' customers and suppliers' suppliers). Operations managers at all levels must be equipped with the strategic, analytical, and people skills normally associated with general management.

Unfortunately, effective training programs for value net executives are few. The new roles require training that's not typically included in standard logistics or operations programs. UPS, for example, is working with MIT, the University of Louisville, and Northwestern University to create customized programs that aim to develop the project and relationship management skills it needs in an evolving marketplace. MBA programs face a major opportunity to launch interdisciplinary programs in this new field.

■ MOVING FROM ATOMS TO BITS

Value nets rely on good information to achieve speed, reliability, and efficiency. They substitute digital information (bits)—with low variable costs and almost no space requirements—for hard assets (atoms).

Digital information greases the skids of every one of the companies profiled in these chapters. Information links them with their customers and supply partners, and it improves everything that happens. Customers know *right now* what these companies have to offer, at what costs, and when their purchases will be available. Suppliers are in the same information loop. The impact of information on inventories has already been explained: Most of it goes away.

Every value net activity contains opportunities for time- and cost-saving *digitization:* taking a customized order, creating a bill of materials, lining up components and assembly capacity, checking order status, making shipping arrangements, billing, and providing customer service. These opportunities range along a continuum from simple connectivity and transaction automation to fully integrated, data-based decision making. The higher the degree of bit intensity in this continuum, the greater the required investment and the greater the potential benefits (see Figure 7.1).

To understand the role of digitization in a value net, let's examine its application at the two extremes: simple connectivity and transaction automation versus complex decision making based on information integration.

➤ Connectivity and Automation

Establishing internal and external links and automating transactions is an important first step in building the "digital nervous system"[7] of a value net. It may include digitizing communications with customers, with suppliers, on the shop floor, and across a global office network.

Digitizing Communication with Customers

At a minimum, companies put up web pages to provide richer information to customers. The digital medium makes it possible to automate the ordering and invoicing process and to transfer some of the transaction workload

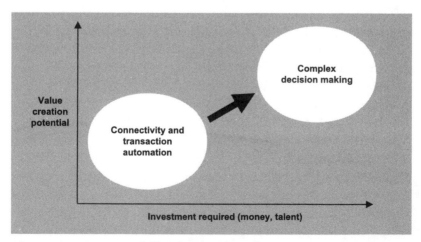

Figure 7.1 Degree of digitization in value nets.

to the customer. These connections can be leveraged to increase the number and quality of customer touch points (e.g., order-shipping notification, order-tracking capability, customer service) and to reduce operating expenses associated with activities such as customer service, which are much less costly when done digitally.

Direct digital connection between a company and the end customer does *not* necessarily mean disintermediation of traditional sales channels. Dell and Gateway eliminated layers of dealers and retailers when they established direct interfaces with customers, but many other companies are using digital interfaces to support existing channel partners in providing superior customer service. The term *clicks and mortar* describes one facet of this support system. Ford's new Internet-based alliance with Microsoft's Carpoint illustrates the clicks-and-mortar approach. As Ming Yeh of Ford told us, "The Internet will allow manufacturers to reach customers quicker and better and will allow customers to specify what they want. I don't think [online buying] will bypass dealerships whatsoever."[8] Yeh believes the direct link to Ford's manufacturing availability will streamline customers' ordering experiences and lead to higher satisfaction without disturbing traditional channel relationships. Miller SQA's model, which combines the efficiency of digital ordering with the personal service of a dealer, provides a useful example.

Vauxhall, the General Motors brand in the United Kingdom, has scored a worldwide first in connecting with consumers over the Internet. On November 1, 1999, it became the first automaker to sell cars directly to customers on its own web site (www.vauxhall.co.uk). And it does so in a way that fully involves dealers. Vauxhall's achievement is based, first of all, on excellent manufacturer-dealer relations. According to Alan Grimshaw, managing director of Grimshaws, a large Vauxhall dealership in Manchester: "In the U.K., Vauxhall and its dealers work very, very closely on every project, and dealers were involved in this dot-com project right from its inception."[9] Martin Brindley, Vauxhall Motors' order fulfillment and sales analysis director, confirms this sentiment from the manufacturer's perspective: "It was a no-brainer, really, to work closely with the retailers and make sure the retailer's role was clear in the dot-com process."[10] This is one factor that allowed the initiative to be launched in a mere eight weeks.

Second, in this experiment to see how Internet car buying might work, Vauxhall built a set of cars to stock, representing a relatively narrow range of choices (e.g., two colors, limited accessories). So Vauxhall's coup does not reflect a Dell-like build-to-order capability. However, Vauxhall's back-end fulfillment operation is designed to support the Internet front end and customer convenience. This was facilitated by the fact that Vauxhall had previously consolidated U.K. dealer inventories into five vehicle storage centers around the country. Once the customer makes his or her selection and clicks on Yes to buy, a set of activities is set in motion. The nearest dealer arranges to visit the customer and to offer a test-drive in a vehicle similar to the one ordered. The dealer also completes the documentation and provides a valuation for the customer's trade-in vehicle. Within seven days, the new car is delivered to the customer at his or her residence or other convenient location. The consumer never has to visit a dealer or leave the comfort of home.

In Vauxhall's hybrid clicks-and-mortar solution, convenience and speed are delivered to customers via a digital connection. As Alan Grimshaw told us,

> *People who are using the web expect things immediately if not sooner. But I don't think speed is the be-all and end-all. People want a reliable [delivery] date they can bank on. They will wait for the exact car they want provided we give them a reliable date and we keep them informed. Convenience is something everyone is looking for. The Internet is just helping people buy time.*

Hybrid solutions like Vauxhall's will undoubtedly grow more sophisticated and migrate to other industries in the months ahead. Digital technology—*combined* with collaborative channel relationships that deliver the personal touch—is a promising way to realize the value proposition. It's not bricks versus the Internet, but rather a combination of both that's most likely to work in the new economy.

Digitizing Communication with Suppliers

To achieve the speed, accuracy, and reliability of a value net, it is absolutely essential for supplier interactions to move beyond phone and fax to the Internet, *intra*nets, and *extra*nets. These provide secure environments in which companies and their suppliers can exchange information and maintain real-time communication. They have created a degree of connectivity and transaction automation unimagined just a few years ago. Digital supplier interfaces and a culture of information sharing substantially reduce transaction and inventory costs, and they improve accuracy and service reliability.

Volkswagen was one of the early auto industry adopters of digital links for inbound logistics (i.e., the movement of production parts from tier one suppliers to the assembly plant). Eighty percent of VW's auto production for its domestic German market is built to order. This is great for customers, but it results in considerable variability in inbound parts flows. As an antidote, VW has installed computers aboard inbound GPS-equipped trucks. It issues a digital parts release to its lead logistics provider (trucking coordinator), who transmits the pickup sheet to the supplier, receives electronic confirmation, dispatches the truck, and alerts the plant. According to Dr. Hermann Krog, VW's corporate executive director of group logistics, "The truck driver is doing a qualified job of materials pickup and an advanced material-receiving function as well. The plant is using its newfound visibility into inbound logistics on an exception basis. So, if the plant is waiting for a particular component, [plant personnel] can type [the component number] into the computer and find out that the part is on a particular truck and that it will arrive at [a particular time]."[11] This online logistics planning capability has given a great boost to VW's build-to-order manufacturing.

The first wave of automated supplier links washed through the business community during the 1980s and 1990s in the form of electronic data interchange (EDI). EDI, however, was expensive, limited in reach, and required proprietary technologies. Only large corporations like Wal-Mart and Procter & Gamble could afford EDI and reap its benefits. Small companies, unable to justify the cost, were effectively locked out of the game.

The Internet has leveled the playing field of supplier connectivity. Consider Nintendo's experience. Nintendo introduced an EDI system and encouraged retailers to electronically transmit the serial numbers of Nintendo merchandise sold in their stores, the object being to reduce fraudulent returns. This approach was too expensive for small retailers. The registry program was redesigned in 1998 to work through the Internet, which is now accessible to all retailers regardless of size.[12]

The impact of the Internet on supplier-customer relationships is profound. Internet-based supplier markets, auctions, reverse auctions, and clearinghouses are changing how companies design their operations and their supply chains. For example, Chemdex, an Internet-based supplier for the life sciences industry, is reinventing that industry's entire procurement and sourcing process. In the past, when scientists needed chemicals and agents for life sciences research, they had to page through supplier catalogs (of which there were more than 2,500) and go through multiple layers of approvals to obtain them. Chemdex has created a one-stop-shopping solution with easy-to-use search engines and automated approval processes. It makes approximately 240,000 products available from almost 100 suppliers. In the process, it has created significant time and cost savings for all value chain constituents (Figure 7.2).

Similar Internet solutions are springing up in a variety of industries—Paperexchange.com, Producenet.com, and Metalsite.com, to name just a few. Many companies have set up electronic catalogs. Others have gone even further. Companies like FreeMarkets hold reverse auctions whereby a company defines what it needs and prequalified participants bid down the price. Others, such as FastParts, are clearing excess inventories for competitors through online auctions. Hewlett-Packard has established its own site, TradingUp.com, to sell excess parts to brokers and to obtain components suddenly in short supply. "We held our first auction on July 20, 1999, and we expect to be running at about $10 million a month by February 2000," Don Schmickrath, HP's general manager for the product processes organization, told us.[13] These ventures are capitalizing on the digital revolution and reducing supply chain costs for their users.

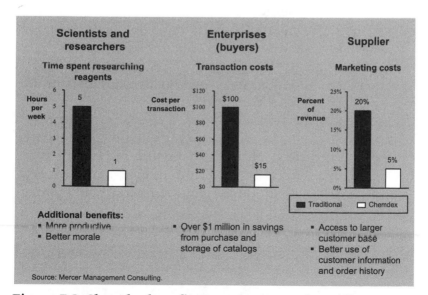

Figure 7.2 Chemdex benefits to customers and suppliers.

Digitizing Internal Communications

Converting internal processes from atoms to bits can take days, weeks, or even months out of production schedules and have a profound impact on costs, workforce morale, and management decision making. Consider the impact of the simple e-mail on complex production processes. Jim McGuire, a Boeing technologist, explains:

> *Let's say someone in Dallas needs to know if he has a defective solder joint. He can't simply mail the piece of hardware to me, because it belongs to the government, or to an air carrier, and requires detailed tracking. In the past, I probably would have packed a bag, taken a red-eye flight to Dallas, spent ten minutes looking at the board, and taken the next flight back to Seattle. Now the guy can e-mail me a picture of the solder joint, I can draw all over it, and send the annotated picture back over e-mail. The whole process takes 20 to 30 minutes.*[14]

At Weyerhaeuser's door manufacturing facility, digital technology has reduced information handling and cut the cost of routine tasks. According to Jerry Mannigel: "DoorBuilder [the digital ERP system] has reduced the number of sales reps and reduced the number of order writers who transcribe orders and put them in the computer system. We've definitely had overhead reductions."

Digital interfaces and transaction automation are important first steps in building value nets. They provide the medium for real-time, instantaneous information exchange. They eliminate human error and improve cost efficiency. The greater impact of digitization, however, comes when companies combine instant information with analytical tools to improve complex decisions.

➤ Digital Decision Making

Digital decision support is one of the most notable characteristics of value nets. Rule-based decisions must be made instantly and accurately to continually reoptimize daily operations. At the same time, digitization provides an integrated basis for human decisions on longer-term, strategic dimensions such as customer selection, network design, and supplier performance review.

Hugh Aitken, vice president of European operations for Sun Microsystems, is constructing a digital value net around an Oracle ERP system. As Aitken explained to us,

> *The new initiative is called BTSC: Break Through Supply Chain. I can't tell you today what the supply chain will be in five to ten years, but the BTSC should set us up to be ready for whatever comes along. This initiative is a move toward flexibility, modularity, and scalability. The modularity is in the IT infrastructure. There are some 27 pieces to the initiative, but basically it will be heavily IT-based. The bread-and-butter of any supply chain is information. So the BTSC is being built on information and speed.*[15]

E-tailers face some of the same scalability issues found at Sun. Many Internet-based merchants focus their initial efforts on their web sites. They begin by offering a limited number of products that are sourced from a single supplier. The information flows are simple. A small volume of orders is transmitted to a single fulfillment house and its national warehouse.

Successful e-tailers typically expand their product offerings, often rapidly. Every tripling of SKUs creates 5 to 10 percent more sales over the same web site. This is because the same customers will spend slightly more per order and will actually place more orders if they encounter a broader offering on the site. But adding more SKUs means

adding more suppliers. "Therein lies the rub," according to
Jim Daniell, president and CEO of OrderTrust, the Lowell,
Massachusetts–based digital order processing network.
Daniell explains,

> *People who use a small fulfillment house typically can
> do a good job for a modest number of SKUs. As you in-
> crease the number of SKUs, you increase the likelihood
> you're going to need multiple suppliers, multiple ful-
> fillers, and multiple drop-shippers. Then you start run-
> ning into the buzz saw of complexity. To do a
> high-quality job, you need to handle multiple shipper
> partners, real-time credit card verification, and real-
> time inventory checking, with good transaction-level
> information flowing back to your system.*[16]

Information flow design becomes critical. A well-
engineered order fulfillment network can introduce intelligent decisions into the order flow. For example, the
system can route an order directly to one of many fulfillment operations. When notification is received that an
item has shipped, it can dispatch an e-mail to the customer confirming the shipment. If an item is back-
ordered, the customer can be automatically contacted to
see if he or she would like to cancel. And when the transaction is completed, the network can automatically issue
a settlement request to the bank. FooFoo.com, a new e-tailer
offering upscale merchandise to upwardly mobile professionals, is a case in point. Phil Hawken, director of commerce, confirms why FooFoo.com uses a third-party order
processing network: "As a small business just starting out,
we do not want inventory. That means we need to pass orders to suppliers in real time."[17] OrderTrust receives all of
FooFoo's customer orders and passes them on to suppliers,
line item by line item. It handles the credit card processing functions. And it connects suppliers to the network.
"The only thing left [for us] to do," says Hawken, "is to
make deals with the suppliers. And OrderTrust helps make

those introductions. . . . They handle the supply chain so that we can focus on our business." The ease of digitally connecting through their partner to 15 different suppliers has given FooFoo.com the scalability it needs.

How will the Internet support the business-to-business supply chain in future years? Possibly by incorporating new "intelligent agents" into a wide range of business processes. Visions of the future emerging from technology hothouses like MIT's Media Lab are replete with communicative machinery. Jim Daniell explains:

> We'll see bid boards, customer service, and customer care handled over the network . . . automated replenishment where you have no consumer interaction. People think about consumers going online, but they haven't talked about what happens when more and more machines can automatically sense when they are low on supply. For example, the office copier lets the supplier know, "Hey, I'm running low on toner, I'm running low on paper." And the supplier to the business is automatically receiving these requests and showing up with the supplies.

This may sound far-fetched today. But do not discount the likelihood of this level of digital integration in the not-too-distant future.

In this fast-paced, digital, interdependent, and interconnected world of value nets, operational decisions become more complex and can instantly impact customers and network participants in ways not always easily predictable. New analytical tools and optimization software are emerging to help managers make quicker and better decisions. Companies like Sun Microsystems and Apple Computer are combining the powerful information-gathering and access capabilities of their ERP systems with intelligent planning and scheduling optimization and simulation tools to make better decisions regarding demand, supply, fulfillment plans, and daily operations.

These digital decision-making technologies offer tremendous potential for value nets and their customers. Customers can instantaneously be promised reliable delivery dates, and the value net's use of resources is orchestrated and optimized to deliver flawlessly on that promise. Demand for even faster decisions across the value net, combined with rapid and universal access to information, will necessarily lead to the convergence of planning and executional capabilities.

■ HOW DOES EXECUTION APPLY TO YOUR BUSINESS?

The world is full of companies with great strategies, but the number of companies that *execute* their strategies consistently well is much fewer. In the burgeoning field of e-commerce in particular, we see lots of exciting new online companies with offers that are bound to appeal to consumers and business customers. As the world is fast learning, however, *there is many a slip twixt the cup and the lip.* Few of these companies have figured out how to deliver flawlessly on their appealing offers. It's a striking paradox that Internet shoppers can place orders instantly but have to wait days or weeks to get the goods. Some online customers never receive their orders, or they receive the wrong items. All of which underscores the fact that there is more to a successful e-business than an appealing offer and a flashy web page, something more than the little man behind the curtain in the Land of Oz. Somewhere behind the customer interface, you must have a fast, carefully crafted value net that can execute transactions with clockwork precision.

Our prescriptions for execution excellence are a *breakthrough culture* and effective application of *digital technology*. Bring these together and your execution capabilities will take a quantum leap forward.

Ask yourself the following questions to determine where your company stands in terms of design for execution.

Breakthrough Culture

➤ Do we have the vision and the leadership needed to transform the old supply chain into a value net business design?

➤ Are our corporate goals aligned with our customers' preferences?

➤ Do our employees have simple, clear goals for execution? Are they aware of these goals, and do they take them seriously? Are our rank-and-file employees' goals aligned with corporate goals through rational incentive systems?

➤ Are we approaching execution improvements through small incremental steps only, or are we prepared to go for order-of-magnitude changes?

Digital Technology

➤ How fast do we communicate with customers and suppliers? Do we use regular mail and phones, or do we rely on digital connections? Are we sharing information?

➤ Are there opportunities to increase speed and accuracy, as well as to save costs, through information systems and computer-aided decision making?

➤ How does information flow? Where does it stop? What is the optimal information flow design?

➤ How and by whom are operational decisions made? Does digital technology provide active support?

This book has provided several examples of masterful execution—Gateway, Sun, SQA, Weyerhaeuser, and others. Chances are that these leaders are not members of your industry. But what if they were? What cultural and operational changes would it take for you to be able to compete with them in speed, accuracy, and cost? Let's look at the case of Cisco Systems, a powerful story of value net execution based on a breakthrough culture and information integration.

■ EXECUTION EXCELLENCE AT CISCO SYSTEMS

In this case, we examine how Cisco Systems Inc. has perfected value net execution and has transformed itself into a true Internet-enabled business. Our focus here is on the roles that digital and cultural elements play in making the Cisco value net hum. Cisco's key to execution excellence is its insight that successful deployment of Internet technology requires substantial changes to the existing business design—driven by customer requirements. Its dedication to that insight has resulted in greater customer satisfaction and outstanding bottom-line results. The question is: What does it take to ensure perfect execution in creating a value net?

Cisco is a $12 billion company with 23,000 employees worldwide and one of the major success stories of the Internet age. It has grown at an astounding pace, and its products have enabled much of today's Internet protocol-based infrastructure. The most obvious reflection of its success is its stock price, which grew a thousandfold between February 1990 and November 1999. Continuous product innovation, and Cisco's value net design, were key elements of that growth.

Cisco was founded in late 1984 by Sandy Lerner and Len Bosack, two computer scientists affiliated with Stanford University. Lerner and Bosack invented the technology that makes it possible to access or transfer information independent of computer system type. That technology laid the foundation for today's Internet. The company currently designs and sells the components required to build and manage Internet technology-based networks: routers and switches, remote dial-up access servers, network management software, and related items. These leading-edge products have given Cisco the number one market share position in 16 of the 20 key markets in which it competes, and the number two position in the remaining four. Cisco now sells its solutions in more than 100 countries and competes with companies like Lucent Technologies, Nortel, 3Com, Siemens, and Alcatel.

In early 1994, Cisco managers recognized a problem that other manufacturers might envy: They could not increase production capacity fast enough to meet anticipated demand. They also realized that they would have to hire more people than they could reasonably hope to find and recruit. And they recognized that the company was not meeting its customers' fulfillment preferences. "Our lead times were all over the map," recalls Ram ChandraSekaran, senior manager of Internet strategies. "They ranged from six to eight weeks—even ten weeks in many cases. The same was true for on-time shipments."[18] Customers were asking for higher reliability of promised delivery dates and for shorter lead times.

Faced with projections of rapidly growing demand and challenging customer preferences, Cisco recognized the need for a totally different business model, one that would (1) allow it to scale its business to demand, independent of its plant and hiring constraints, and (2) assure customer satisfaction and profit margins. The case study that follows illustrates the changes Cisco made in meeting those ambitious goals. We begin with the value proposition to provide context for the targets Cisco set for itself and then discuss critical scope decisions. Our main focus is on the key execution elements that allowed Cisco's design to succeed. We conclude by outlining the tangible results this effort has produced and the key lessons for others seeking to implement a value net.

➤ The Value Proposition: Total Life-Cycle Experience

"Our leading-edge customers are deploying networks for the next century that deliver data, voice, and video capabilities over a single network," explains John Chambers, president and CEO.[19] Each customer network is fairly unique and deploys components that are substantially custom-configured.

Cisco's customers manage complex project schedules in getting their networks up and running and, as a consequence, require accurate lead-time commitments for the company's products. They also require short lead times; these enable them to delay orders until required installation dates become clear. Cisco aimed to exceed these preferences, believing that reliable delivery dates and short lead times alone would fail to generate customer satisfaction and repeat business. Cisco's stated value proposition, "Helping our customers become agile by implementing Internet business models that will position them for success in today's fast-paced business environment," required the ability to provide customers with an efficient and pleasant total life-cycle experience. That experience was defined as extending from initial contact with Cisco to fulfillment and after-order support, and it became the leadership vision for the value net design effort.

➤ Scope: Overview of Cisco's Value Net

Cisco had to find ways to grow its business despite severe labor constraints. Would it attempt to build internal capacity or outsource many tasks to suppliers? Where would the company play in the chain of value-adding activities? The answers to these questions were determined by the company's perception of its own capabilities and those of its suppliers. "We realized that our core competency was innovation, and introducing new products faster and with better-quality service than anybody else," says Chandra-

Sekaran. Taking an order life-cycle perspective, the company decided to own only its key customer touch points, sales and customer support, and outsource the vast majority of fulfillment operations to suppliers. As a result, about 80 percent of the company's product value is now created by suppliers. And about 60 percent of all units (40 to 45 percent of sales) are shipped directly by Cisco's suppliers to its customers. Items in those shipments are never touched by Cisco employees. Only orders for the most complex high-end products, which no single supplier can completely fulfill, are configured or integrated within Cisco facilities (Figure 7.3).

Particularly noteworthy is Cisco's approach to delegating even crucial activities to its partners. Quality control, for example, is performed by suppliers, but to Cisco standards. Cisco also works with component distributors to take advantage of their expertise and flexibility in routing shared components to contract manufacturers where high-demand products are being configured. Because external partners carry out most of the logistics, Cisco operates just three consolidation centers (two in the United States and

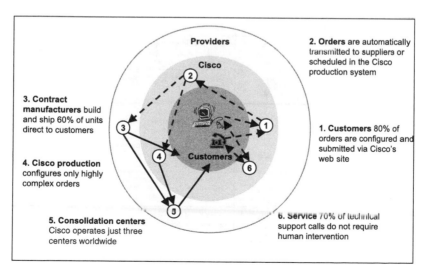

Figure 7.3 Cisco's value net.

one in Europe) where multiproduct orders are consolidated (Figure 7.4).

The larger goal of maximizing Cisco employees' focus on value-adding activities led to other critical decisions that impact the scope of direct company activities. A thorough analysis of the order life cycle from placement to after-sale support revealed a significant number of process steps that could be performed by others. For example, Cisco decided that customers could configure products themselves if given adequate and intelligent tools, thus freeing up salespeople to focus on solutions consulting. Technical support was another area that required management to consider how employees could best be utilized. Experience showed that 60 to 70 percent of calls coming through the technical support organization were inquiries about order status and standard technical problems. To focus Cisco staff on higher-value-adding activities, responses to low-level technical support inquiries were automated; technical support personnel were shifted to the more challenging problems encountered by customers.

Activity	Outsourcing	Automation	Comments
Configure	○	◐	• 83% of orders placed through the web site • Configurations are checked automatically for compatibility of selected product modules
Process order	○	●	• Order processing and materials management are fully automated
Build	◕	N/A	• 60% of units built by contract manufacturers • Cisco builds complex products where no single supplier has complete capabilities
Test	◕	N/A	• Cisco remotely controls passing of quality tests • Cisco retains ownership over shipment system that allows shipping only after all tests are passed
Deliver	◕	N/A	• Cisco operates 3 consolidation centers, 2 in the US and 1 in Europe, where orders are consolidated only if the customer requests this
Support	○	◕	• 60–70% of technical service inquiries solved through automated technical support system
Legend:	● Complete	○ None	

Figure 7.4 Outsourcing and automation in Cisco's value net.

An Army of Virtual Employees

"For every Cisco manufacturing employee, there are six virtual employees who use Cisco processes, are measured against Cisco metrics, and are located around the world," explains Pete Rukavina, director of Cisco's global supply chain management.[20] This heavy dependence on suppliers makes a high degree of partnership essential. As Cisco's ChandraSekaran explained to us,

> *We view quality and improvement as a process, knowing that it is going to change. We realize that in order to be successful in this competitive world, we have to have a complete, true partnership with our suppliers. So there is a lot of trust between our suppliers and us. We don't shift products from our suppliers to other suppliers at a whim. This motivates them to give us input into yield problems, quality problems, design for manufacturability, and design for serviceability, which improves the overall product and services we offer our customers.*

This level of collaboration has helped the company to slash six- to ten-week lead times down to one to three weeks and to achieve 98 percent on-time shipments. Outsourcing a large portion of manufacturing activities to suppliers also makes sense from a business design perspective, as ChandraSekaran further outlines:

> *Our suppliers have a very different business model. Their core competence is large-scale electronics manufacturing and they know best how to manage highly capital-intensive businesses. In order to access the best manufacturing technology, it makes sense to partner with them. We'd rather work with them to develop the best product from a manufacturing perspective while we focus on innovation, fast product launch, and taking care of our customers.*

Cisco also realized that in order to exercise control of value net activities it would need to make supplier processes consistent with its own. To that end, it created a single enterprise systems and processes scheme under which supplier employees are trained in Cisco processes and procedures. ChandraSekaran elaborates:

> *Take, for example, the employees at Solectron, one of our key suppliers. Even though they are on Solectron's payroll, they work on Cisco products, follow Cisco processes, and manufacture product as if it were made by Cisco's own employees. So material management, quality management, dynamic replenishment, and customer order configuration—all of the things that are necessary to support a digital order or configured order methodology—are done by our suppliers using Cisco-developed and -controlled processes and systems.*

Integrated Execution

Like all successful value net operations, Cisco's is built on a high degree of digitization and on a breakthrough culture that aims to satisfy customer needs. The two complement each other. For example, Cisco uses technology extensively, yet cautioned us to forget about technology until customer needs are well understood. When it began its value net initiative, Cisco discerned those needs through an advisory board of about 60 customers. And it continues to engage outsiders in weekly critiques of its e-commerce applications and web site features.[21]

Digitization

Six specific aspects of Cisco's value net design illustrate the extent to which its execution is facilitated by *digitization:* (1) front- and back-end integration, (2) customer integration, (3) autoconfiguration audit, (4) remote quality control, (5) automated technical support, and (6) demand planning and inventory management automation.

Front- and Back-End Integration

Cisco has been highly effective in using technology to connect partners and automate processes. Knitting together its front- and back-end operations is a key example, and online order taking is where it all begins. "All products are configurable on the web," says Ram ChandraSekaran. "Customers are able to generate configuration scenarios and get real-time price and delivery date quotes. This enables customers to fine-tune configurations according to their time and price constraints." In 1999, these digital orders represented more than 80 percent of all orders.

However, allowing customers to get real-time price and delivery date quotes requires links to a variety of information that is traditionally located in a company's back-end operations. It quickly became clear to Cisco that simply creating a web front end to existing processes would fail to achieve its customer satisfaction and value-creation objectives. "That was the biggest lesson learned in terms of the so-called webification of existing processes," explains ChandraSekaran. "Just putting a web site at the front end of your order fulfillment process is not going to give you the results you expect." The front-end customer interface and back-end supply capacity had to be brought together effectively, requiring Cisco to reconsider large parts of its organizational structure and processes. For Cisco, which was originally organized around functional silos, this required more than good intentions. Fortunately, the skillful application of information technology made it possible to knock down information barriers between silos. The company unified key databases on a single platform and selected single-vendor applications for order entry, financials, and manufacturing.

"We needed to eliminate the information barriers and consequently extended our IT systems to our top-tier suppliers," states ChandraSekaran. "These included contract manufacturers, distributors, and OEM suppliers." Cisco leased telecommunication lines to extend its network to its suppliers and partners, creating a true extended enterprise from an information technology perspective.

Customer Integration

In true value net fashion, Cisco realized that its self-configuration web site was not sufficiently convenient for its high-volume customers; it merely added a second layer to their existing procurement systems. The solution was to integrate customers' procurement systems with Cisco's order entry system using open Internet information transfer standards. "We have given them a true business-to-business systems integration such that they don't have to come to our web site," explains ChandraSekaran, "They actually configure and place orders on their own internal procurement system."

Autoconfiguration Audit

In addition to using technology to connect the actors in the ordering life cycle, Cisco has found exciting ways to use technology for decision making. Online product configuration, an attractive option for customers and a real time-saver for the company, is one example. Historically, 25 percent of orders received by the company contained a mistake. Fixing these mistakes required multiple exchanges of paper documentation and substantially prolonged the order fulfillment cycle. Cisco realized that software algorithms could be created to alert customers to configuration incompatibilities with legacy equipment and to propose alternatives. Building this kind of intelligence into the decision-making process has allowed Cisco to reach 99 percent order-accuracy levels, far beyond the level typically achieved by the direct sales force.

Remote Quality Control

Another example of digitally enhanced decision making is found in Cisco's approach to quality control. Whereas many OEMs are tempted to retain this activity in-house, Cisco uses information technology linkages with its suppliers to maintain its quality standards. As ChandraSekaran explains: "Every one of our direct shipment suppliers' assembly lines is directly integrated with Cisco's network. . . . Although Cisco does not touch a product, through remote monitoring we know everything about that product. Cisco's extended network is available at the assembly line of our supplier locations, and data is directly transacted on Cisco's operational systems and quality systems."

Before the digital shipment system prints a shipping label, it checks with other operations management systems to confirm that all quality tests have been completed and that the configuration is accurate. Only when these checks have been completed to the system's satisfaction can shipping labels be printed at the supplier's site.

Technical Support

Cisco also deploys digital decision making in the area of technical support, providing customers with self-service support on commonplace issues and ensuring that only complex problems are routed to real-time support personnel. "We pick areas where people have repetitive questions," says Peter Solvik, CIO of Cisco. "We catalog our knowledge about those areas and use artificial intelligence to dispense it."[22] Intelligent problem-solving algorithms lead a customer through a logical chain of questions to narrow down the issue and select the appropriate fixes, which can then be downloaded. Should customers bypass the algorithm, the system is intelligent enough to alert them if fixes are not compatible with their equipment. If the customer chooses to call a live person at this point, the tech support person can go to the URL and become immediately synced up with all the experience that customer has gone through. It then becomes a highly qualified tech support call. About 70 percent of technical support calls never require the intervention of a live person.

The Cisco technical support system is also used to rapidly disseminate knowledge about equipment problems and their fixes. So-called Email Bug Alerts disseminate knowledge about software problems within 24 hours from the time of their discovery. "This is a direct electronic link into the engineering organization of our company," explains Solvik.[23]

Cisco generates and integrates customer profiles, order profiles, and customer experience profiles with engineering changes affecting particular product configurations to offer automated technical support. This has generated tremendous savings for Cisco. Customers check the status of orders up to 300,000 times and perform 380,000 software downloads monthly. "Customers are getting information anytime they want it," says Chris Sinton, director of marketing for Cisco Connection Online, "without asking our customer service or salespeople for it. We believe that this has raised their productivity 15 percent."[24]

Demand Planning and Inventory
Management Automation

Service planning provides another example of digital decision support that has freed up staff for value-adding activities. Service planners are responsible for demand planning and inventory management. Before installing supply chain planning software, Cisco's service planners spent the majority of their time on data collection. "If you spend four days out of five gathering data, it doesn't leave you any time to analyze the information," explains Bill Weidert, a Cisco service operations manager.[25] "While we were able to plan and get inventory to our central warehouse, we weren't able to push it out to the hubs and depots as required." The supply chain planning software that Cisco implemented orchestrates six major hubs and 200 depots around the world, performing inventory analysis, demand forecasting, order generation, and materials allocation. According to Ferdinand Gonzalez, a senior service planner: "Our planners now spend zero time collecting data. . . . [They] now have time to . . . sit with the vendors to find out what issues may be occurring in the relationship."[26] Technology allows staff in what was historically considered a back-end operation to make a direct contribution to the overarching goal of customer satisfaction.

Breakthrough Culture

With respect to *breakthrough culture,* Cisco's value net design features two particularly noteworthy elements in understanding how cultural changes support value net execution: (1) customer satisfaction as a key goal and (2) refocusing the sales force on high-value activities. Although there are many more elements to Cisco's execution approach, these two stand out.

Customer Satisfaction as a Key Goal

Technology is critical to value net execution, but it must work in concert with cultural elements to produce excellent results. Cisco realized this in focusing all value net actors on customer-driven goals. It built customer satisfaction into the entire management system, for both employees and suppliers. "Whether it's a manufacturing organization, engineering product development organization, a sales organization, technical support, or order entry organization, one thing that drives a high percentage of the bonus is customer satisfaction," says Chandra-Sekaran. "Every Cisco employee is compensated based on customer satisfaction."

In making customer satisfaction a key performance measure, Cisco has made an integrated and consistent total life-cycle experience for the customer a key element of Cisco's corporate culture. This has contributed to improving customer satisfaction ratings from 3.4 to 4.2 on a 5-point scale of customer satisfaction (from 1997 to 1998).[27]

New Skills for Sales Force

Another aspect of a breakthrough culture is the new set of skills required as a result of automating processes. For example, Cisco's sales force used to spend a great deal of its time assisting customers with product configurations. Today, with more than 80 percent of orders being configured by customers through Cisco's web site, the sales force is learning a broader set of skills that revolves around customer solutions. "Our sales force is now helping people design their networks," explains ChandraSekaran. "This has moved our relationships with customers to a higher level, from selling products into more of a business relationship."

Critical to this role shift was the alignment of the sales incentives with the e-commerce effort. Because Cisco's salespeople were largely compensated through commissions, many feared that e-commerce would demolish their earnings. Cisco reduced this concern by granting commissions to salespeople independent of how an order is placed. "If a salesperson's named customer places the order over the Internet, he or she gets the commission whether he or she spends four hours with the customer or the customer spends one hour configuring it online," explains Sinton.[28] This motivated the sales force to fully support the e-commerce effort and improve Cisco's competitive position through solutions rather than through product-based customer relationships.

➤ The Value Net's Impact on Cisco's Financial Performance

The use of digital technology supported by cultural elements to deliver customer satisfaction and improve operational efficiency is the key theme that runs through our observations of Cisco's value net execution. From an operational perspective, Cisco has achieved tremendous savings by using this approach to value net execution. Carl Redfield, Cisco's senior vice president for manufacturing, has stated that the company's Internet-based business model has increased productivity and has saved approximately $500 million annually in business expenses.[29] The sources of those savings are as follows:

➤ *Low asset intensity.* Cisco generates revenue of $12 billion with only 500,000 square feet of its own manufacturing space.[30]

➤ *Lower inventory levels.* Unit inventory decreased 45 percent within three months of beginning to transmit real-time demand signals to suppliers.[31] Supply chain planning software has kept inventory flat on some 8,500 part numbers, despite surging volume growth.[32]

➤ *Lead-time reduction.* Six- to ten-week order cycle times have been reduced to one to three weeks.

➤ *Reduced order processing time.* Orders are placed and transmitted in 15 to 60 minutes, down from days or weeks, reducing order processing cost by $30 to $130 per order.[33, 34]

➤ *Higher productivity per employee.* Cisco's employees are highly productive, with $580,000 annual revenue per employee in 1999 (Figure 7.5) compared to an average of $230,000 for key competitors.[35]

➤ *Lower personnel levels.* Giving customers the ability to track orders via the web has reduced status inquiries by 300,000 per month, which has also reduced staffing needs.[36] Manufacturing head count has increased at a much lower rate than unit output over the last five years (Figure 7.5).

For Cisco, the value net has substantially raised revenues as well, through the customer-pleasing ordering and deliv-

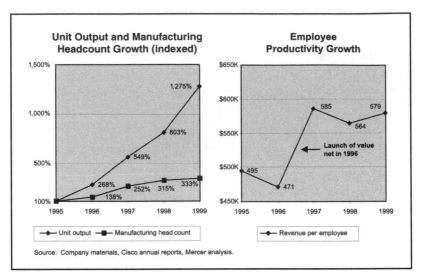

Figure 7.5 Productivity improvement.

ery experience. Higher revenues combined with lower costs have produced outstanding financial results (Figure 7.6).

Cisco's value net lead over its key competitors has given it three of the five strategic control elements discussed in Chapter 6: value net brand, customer hook, and provider relationships.

> ➤ *Brand.* Cisco is a recognized master of Internet commerce. Its success in building an Internet-enabled e-commerce organization has given the company tremendous credibility with customers, who are seeking to purchase the infrastructure components to build similar networks and systems. "Cisco . . . has walked the talk of how to use the Internet for all business operations," says ChandraSekaran. "We can go to our customers to show them how to run a business using the Internet as a medium."

> ➤ *Hook.* Intelligent configuration engines and digital links between the procurement systems of key cus-

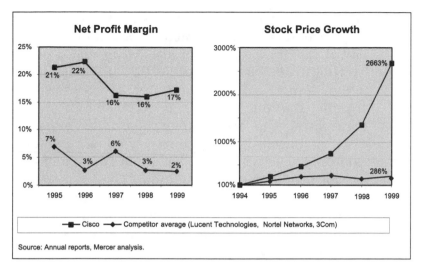

Figure 7.6 Comparative net profit margins and stock price growth.

tomers and Cisco's order management system create barriers to switching.

➤ *Relationships.* The close supplier relationships created through the Cisco value net are not easily replicable, constituting an element of strategic control.

➤ Lessons Learned

The Cisco case illustrates five important lessons that can guide value net implementation in any organization:

1. *Let customer preferences drive value net design.* Cisco used an advisory board of 60 customers to guide the design and continuous improvement of its value net. Weekly testing ensures that its digital interfaces with customers are as efficient as possible. Technology capabilities alone must not drive the move from atoms to bits. The road map for deploying technology in a value net needs to respond to changing customer expectations.

2. *Rethink the entire business design.* Cisco realized very early that a web site merely bolted to the front end of existing processes would be incapable of delivering on its value proposition. The division between front- and back-end operations must be eliminated through an integrated business design.

3. *Use technology to focus staff on value-added activities.* Cisco managers have aggressively sought out low-value-added activities and have substituted technology for people in executing them. The result is that staff can devote significantly more time to working with customers, enabling Cisco to maintain close relationships with customers that create satisfaction and loyalty.

4. *Adopt simple performance metrics.* Getting everyone in an organization aligned around execution is critical to value net success. Cisco has achieved this by making customer satisfaction the key measure in its performance management system. This motivates everyone to think from a customer's perspective.

5. *Think beyond the organization's existing boundaries.* Cisco's approach to pushing the envelope in integrating both suppliers and customers into its value net was key to achieving a high level of service. Opening up internal information systems to suppliers and giving supplier employees the same access rights to information as Cisco employees demonstrates the extent to which organizational boundaries must be removed to achieve execution excellence. However, more important than the physical extension of an enterprise is the approach to long-term partnership, which is based on mutual trust and collaborative improvement.

■ NOTES

1. Nicholas Negroponte, *Being Digital* (New York: Vintage Books, 1996), 11–17.

2. Tim Cook. Interview with author, September 29, 1999.

3. Jesús Maqueda, "Zara, la gran cadena textil creada por Amancio Ortega," *Gaceta de los Negocios,* August 5, 1997, 1.

4. Bix Norman. Interview with Jack Dougan and Eric Vratimos (Mercer Management Consulting), June 22, 1999.

5. Robert Hamm. Interview with author, July 9, 1999.

6. Jerry Mannigel. Interview with Kamenna Rindova (Mercer Management Consulting), October 22, 1999.

7. Bill Gates with Collins Hemingway, *Business @ The Speed of Thought: Using a Digital Nervous System* (New York: Warner Books, 1999), xvii.

8. Ming Yeh. Interview with Kamenna Rindova (Mercer Management Consulting), October 14, 1999.

9. Ibid.

10. Alan Grimshaw. Interview with author, December 7, 1999.

11. Dr. E. Hermann Krog. Interview with author, June 18, 1999.

12. "EDI: Internet Revolutionizes EDI," *Discount Store News,* May 24, 1999, 3.

13. Don Schmickrath. Interview with author, November 23, 1999.

14. www.speed-of-thought.com/getting/exploreboeing.html. March 29, 1999, 6.

15. Hugh Aitken. Interview with Kamenna Rindova (Mercer Management Consulting), August 16, 1999.

16. Jim Daniell. Interview with author, October 11, 1999.

17. Phil Hawken. Interview with Keanne Henry (Mercer Management Consulting), November 4, 1999.

18. Ram ChandraSekaran. Interviews with author, November 18 and November 30, 1999.

19. John T. Chambers, *1999 Annual Report,* Cisco Systems, Inc.

20. "Solutions Overview. Networking the Supply Chain for Competitive Advantages: An Overview of the Cisco Networked Supply Chain Management Solution," in Cisco Systems, Inc., company materials, 1999.

21. Bill Roberts, "E-commerce Poster Child Grows Up," *Datamation,* August 1998.

22. Eric Matson (1997): "What's Online at Cisco?" *FastCompany,* issue 7, February 1997, 36.

23. Ibid.

24. Matt Roush (1999), "Cisco Makes the Connection: IT Manu-

facturer Earns Top Spot in 1999. Netmarketing 200 with Portal-Like Redesign," *Business Marketing,* August 1, 1999, 23.

25. LPA Software, Inc., Cisco Systems, Inc., case study.

26. Ibid.

27. Cisco Systems, Inc., op. cit.

28. Bill Roberts, op. cit.

29. Rod Newing (1999), "Leaner, Meaner—And More Agile: Manufacturing Industry Was Using E-business Techniques Long Before the Phrase Was Invented," *Financial Times* (London), October 20, 1999, 2.

30. Philip Siekman (1999), "How a Tighter Supply Chain Extends the Enterprise," *Fortune,* vol. 140, no. 9, November 8, 1999, 272.

31. Cisco Systems, Inc., op. cit.

32. LPA Software, Inc., op. cit.

33. Institute for Technology and Enterprise, Polytechnic University (1988), *Cisco Systems. Electronic Commerce Success Story,* 1988.

34. "Cisco Systems Complete Nationwide Deployment of Ariba E-commerce Solution, *PR Newswire,* July 27, 1999.

35. "Cisco Reaches Out on the Net: On-line Tools Have Helped Create a Happy and Efficient Work Force," *The Globe and Mail,* June 15, 1999, metro C3.

36. Matt Roush, op. cit.

Chapter 8

Lessons from the Innovators

In fitting together the five puzzle pieces of business design, we have introduced many value net innovators. Value proposition, scope, profit capture, strategic control, and execution have each been illustrated through companies that have either invented or reinvented themselves using value net concepts. Each of these companies combines the puzzle pieces in unique ways. There are potentially hundreds, if not thousands, of different value net designs.

Despite their differences, the companies we studied offer a common set of practical lessons that any executive can use to score better with customers, transform his or her own organization, and unlock hidden profits. We've organized those lessons under five major headings: *new designs, customer focus, operating effectiveness, digitizing the value net,* and *management techniques.*

■ NEW DESIGNS

Value nets represent a vibrant new type of business design. They differ fundamentally from an efficient supply
chain or modern information technology because they
define a company's overall business strategy. Value net
designs are holistic in their interlinkage of customer
needs and fulfillment capabilities. The first set of lessons
learned from the innovators addresses this integrated, networked nature, which constitutes the broadest distinguishing characteristic of a value net. Four lessons are featured:
supply chain as business design, assembling the puzzle,
from sequential to networked, and hybrid clicks and
mortar.

➤ Supply Chain as Business Design

The basic premise and promise of value net design is
demonstrated by the innovators we have presented. Each
has mastered some (though rarely all) of the key value net
features: They are customer-aligned, collaborative and systemic, agile, fast-flow, and digital. They deliver convenience, reliability, speed, and customization—in varying
degrees and combinations—to the delight of their customers. And they are doing so with powerful integrated,
networked operations that provide value to customers and
shareholders alike.

The examples we cite confirm the emergence of value
nets as a new form of business design. Airliance Materials,
for instance, relies on agile, digital supply chain management to supply competing airlines with convenient, cost-
effective access to spare parts. Li & Fung's entire raison
d'être lies in managing a worldwide set of garment and
toy-making workshops that can respond with speed and
accuracy to leading retailers' demands. And Cemex's reliable delivery of cement has propelled it to leadership in its
industry.

In these and other cases, the operations-intensive nature of the differentiated product/service offering is key to market success. Whether it is Apple Computer's dramatic resurrection or Weyerhaeuser's door-building turnaround, these successes depend on customer-focused, agile, and digital value nets. And these models will become increasingly popular in many industries.

➤ Assembling the Puzzle

Preceding chapters have each focused on one of the five puzzle pieces of business design. This framework provides valuable guidance for the creative process. However, the pieces must be put together properly; the whole design must fit together seamlessly to release the greatest amount of economic energy.

A set of design options exists, for each piece of the puzzle, as we described in detail in Chapters 3 through 7 (Figure 8.1). Different options may align best with different customer segments. But matching up the options across the five major elements of design is critical to building an effective value net.

Cisco Systems, for example, recognized that it needed to rely on external providers (scope and profit capture decisions) and on digital technology (as an execution mechanism) in order to fulfill customers' needs for reliable lead times and convenient solutions (the value proposition). FooFoo.com, a young Internet merchandiser, chose an order network provider (scope) that offered digital management of the fulfillment process (execution) to meet the demand for convenient, reliable, and fast customer satisfaction. Zara, the Spanish garment maker, harnessed speed and agility from its supplier network (scope) and rapid inventory turnover (profit capture) to drive its reputation for fresh fashions (strategic control). Each innovator assembled the value net puzzle in a unique way to best serve its customers and shareholders.

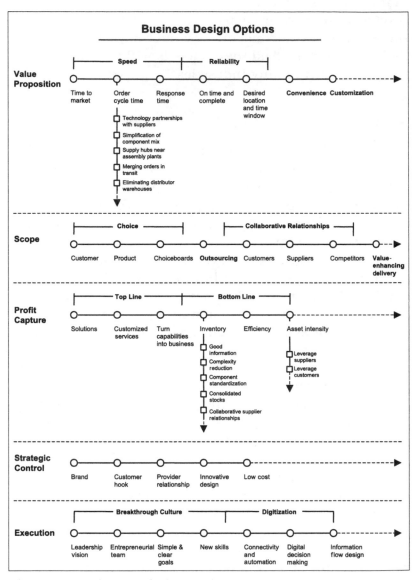

Figure 8.1 Value net design option summary.

➤ From Sequential to Networked

It takes a new type of supply chain to form the core of this new type of business design. The key conceptual shift is from a sequential, linear model to a networked, systemic approach. Value nets represent the biggest shift in the order-make-deliver process since the age of mass production began. Sequential processing of complex products takes so long and involves so many noncontrolled handoffs that speculative production to stock is the necessary result. Under the old system, customers are virtually guaranteed *not* to get the exact products and services they prefer.

The new model enables fast, reliable, convenient delivery through a networked solution. Cisco Systems, for example, ships 60 percent of its products directly from suppliers to customers. This eliminates the physical process and time typically required to move products from a supplier to an OEM. Gateway and Miller SQA have slashed cycle time by establishing rapid information transmission and streamlined physical flows across entire networks of customers, companies, and providers. Progressive Insurance has taken a similar approach in a pure service industry. It has broken the hold of entrenched, sequential auto claims processing and now brings settlement convenience directly to an accident scene. Cost estimates and repair arrangements can be delivered on the spot, saving valuable time for customers and the company alike.

A networked solution is the only way to deliver on customers' escalating demands for speed, reliability, and convenience. Ram ChandraSekaran at Cisco Systems refers to the "supplier ecosystem" created by eliminating the information barriers as key to Cisco's direct fulfillment model. This network, in turn, has allowed Cisco to provide fast and reliable delivery of customized products. OrderTrust's digital order processing network, with automated links to more than 600 suppliers and fulfillment houses, provides a similar solution to emerging Internet merchants.

➤ Hybrid Clicks and Mortar

Value net innovators generally favor neither a pure Internet nor a pure bricks-and-mortar approach. They seek a hybrid approach that combines the best of both worlds for their customers.

Several variations exist. Gateway, for example, offers its "call, click, or come in" options to customers. It has rapidly expanded its network of Gateway Country stores to provide the personal touch sought by many consumers and small businesses during the sales and service support cycle. Yet these showrooms carry no inventory, thus maintaining the cost advantage of a consumer-direct approach.

Others achieve a hybrid solution by cooperating closely with established dealer networks—but in new, more effective ways. Vauxhall shows how an automaker can work with its dealers to maximize Internet convenience and the personal service afforded by a vast retail network. Vehicle test-drives and home delivery of new cars are radical departures from the traditional buyer-dealer relationship. They also represent powerful enhancements to an Internet-only, impersonal solution. Office furniture-maker Miller SQA uses its dealers for standard selling and installation activities, but through digital technology and accurate delivery schedules, equips them far more effectively than before.

■ CUSTOMER FOCUS

Each of the innovative companies we encountered puts its customers squarely at the center of its value net activities. They differentiate their offerings to meet the precise needs of targeted customers, and they deploy advanced supply chain capabilities to enhance the service mix sought by each customer segment. These capabilities form the core of their business designs.

Customer focus contains four value net lessons.

➤ Clarify the Offer

Successful value nets do not attempt to be all things to all people. Instead, winning companies identify and define target market segments and offer value propositions with powerful appeal to those segments. Value nets then profitably fulfill the promises made to those segments.

Streamline, Miller SQA, and Cemex exemplify this point. Streamline relentlessly campaigns to deliver on its promise to busy suburban families. Its value net, from Internet ordering and automatic replenishment to The Box and unattended weekly delivery, is entirely geared to meeting the needs of a very specific segment of society. Miller SQA shows a similar degree of focus. When SQA was formed as an operating unit of Herman Miller, a distinct market segment (small- to medium-size business customers) was targeted with a clear offer: "simple, quick, and affordable." A fast and efficient value net was created to make good on the company's motto. Cemex likewise has a straightforward offer: "We deliver cement to your site within a stated 20-minute window."

➤ Use a Choiceboard as Your Customer Interface

A choiceboard's ability to accurately gather customer preferences and feed them digitally to supply partners lays the groundwork essential for customer knowledge and rapid turnaround.

Gateway illustrates effective choiceboard application. It gives computer buyers multiple points of entry to its value net. Whether the buyer walks into a Gateway Country store, calls the toll-free order number, or goes directly online, he or she will encounter a choiceboard that offers controlled choices and feeds information into Gateway's fulfillment infrastructure.

Miller SQA created a choiceboard with a twist. Its Z-Axis software not only offers furniture choices and accepts orders, but also displays an entire office layout in three dimensions. "Customers love it because it saves them lots of time," a dealer told us. "Lots of time" is an understatement; this customer interface is credited with shortening the typical order cycle from several months to a few days. Z-Axis orders are automatically rendered into bills of materials and transmitted electronically to SQA's plants, which in turn provide order-level visibility four times daily to key suppliers. The Z-Axis choiceboard provides a critical front end that supports SQA's quest for speed, reliability, and reasonable cost.

Many companies, even entire industries, still lack choiceboards. The personal computer industry is already there, as any home computer user familiar with the Dell and Gateway web sites can attest. E-commerce companies of all stripes are using them. Automakers are working on it. For managers in pulp and paper, steel, logistics services, building materials, or railcars, would a choiceboard excite your customers and feed order information efficiently into your supply operations?

➤ Compress the Order-to-Delivery Cycle

Once an order is placed, value net innovators move heaven and earth to fill it quickly. Speed and instant gratification pervade modern society, so demands for faster service reach all sectors of commerce.

For sellers of commodity products, speed can be a differentiator, imbuing quite ordinary stuff—pipes, building materials, and office furniture—with greater utility. Weyerhaeuser enjoys price premiums because of its fast, differentiated delivery cycle. The company has cut ordering times from four weeks to 15 minutes and has also dramatically reduced lead times.

Miller SQA understood the value of speed and made *quick* its middle name. It has slashed order-to-delivery cycle time from the eight weeks common in that industry to less than one week. At the same time, SQA achieves 99.6 percent reliability by means of its digitally networked suppliers, its controlled-complexity product line, and its constant attention to numerical measures of speed and reliability.

How fast is fast enough for your business? You might respond that being faster than your industry competitors is fast enough. But remember that your customers may gauge your performance by what they are experiencing from suppliers in totally different industries.

Remember, too, that the bar of expectations is moving higher. If you are setting out on a two-year improvement program that aims to match Gateway's *current* three- to five-day delivery performance, you may still find yourself trailing Gateway's performance two years hence, because Gateway continues to improve.

➤ Provide Convenient Delivery

Product delivery enjoys no boardroom cachet. Few CEOs or their plant managers give much thought to what happens after finished goods leave the loading dock. Yet the delivery experience can have a major impact on customer satisfaction, loyalty, word of mouth, brand identification, and profitability. You can engineer that experience to delight customers and tap new sources of profitable revenue.

Even mundane items such as cement and groceries can thrill customers if they are packaged with superb delivery. Cemex's formula is reliable delivery within a 20-minute time frame. Streamline's is reliable delivery in farm-fresh condition. Xerox's is equipment setup, operator training, and used-machine removal. Miller SQA's combines factory-direct shipment with dealer installation support.

Convenient service delivery is also proliferating. Progressive Insurance, the fast-growing auto insurer, has evolved its value proposition from simply fast claims settlement to focusing on the overall convenience of returning a repaired vehicle rapidly to its customer. Vauxhall's approach to selling cars over the Internet provides convenience at all stages of the process, from ordering (via a choiceboard on Vauxhall's web site) to delivery (by a dealer to the buyer's home).

If superb delivery can win customers for cement, groceries, and automobiles, the range of potential applications is extremely broad. For commodity products, delivery offers the possibility of service differentiation with a tangible value. For perishable goods, quality-preserving delivery techniques are essential. And for high-value or complex products, delivery with a capital D—meaning everything from the physical drop-off to installation, troubleshooting, and after-sales support—is a way to boost revenues, dampen cyclical fluctuations in revenue, and provide customer value.

■ OPERATING EFFECTIVENESS

Customer focus must be complemented with effective systems for production and distribution. Operational "innards" must be digitized to make good on the promise made to customers. For traditional incumbent firms, operational effectiveness usually means major role and process changes. For dot-com companies, fulfillment capability will ultimately separate winners from losers. The payoff of operating effectiveness is substantial, as the innovators have shown.

➤ Build to Order

Every value net should be designed around three powerful concepts: actual demand, speed, and customization. The "make" process should be triggered by an *actual sale* to the end customer—no more passing "guesswork" orders from one layer to another as in the old supply chain, but rather production driven by actual sales and actual specifications.

Design the net to be *fast*. Speed requires systemic, not sequential, processing. Design your operation so that incoming orders are split into major modules and assigned immediately to specialized suppliers. Modules should then be grouped or assembled on the fly, during the delivery process (as UPS does for Gateway computers) if necessary. Design where possible to eliminate echelons of distribution and warehouses filled with aging product. If customer service and logistics objectives require mixing products and consolidating truckloads, do so at cross-dock facilities that are emptied by the end of each day. These steps will increase the speed of delivery and minimize inventory.

At the same time, build the capability to give customers individualized products. Successful *customization* usually begins with a concerted drive to minimize complexity through the use of standard components and a set of constrained but relevant choices.

These design features—responding to actual demand, speed, and customization—may seem like a tall order, but they are the emerging standard for doing business, and we've offered examples of companies that have accommodated each. Gateway, for example, builds customized machines to actual orders *fast* and has eliminated traditional distribution echelons and warehouses of finished goods. Some order components are merged during transit to end customers.

Converting existing build-to-order businesses or traditional mass-production companies into fast value nets is a major opportunity in many industries. Miller SQA has perfected this new model. It builds to order, ensuring speed by clustering its suppliers around its assembly plant. These design features and expert coordination through information systems provide fast, reliable delivery and give SQA 200 inventory turns each year. Weyerhaeuser has achieved similar results with customized door production.

Executives we interviewed in businesses as diverse as heavy equipment and fashion suggest they are working hard on this issue. A senior executive at DaimlerChrysler put it simply: "If you don't think people are trying to move toward the Dell model in all industries, you're crazy." Build-to-order models will soon drive the manufacture of everything from lightbulbs to cat food. If you can design the network and the necessary tools—such as complexity reduction and component standardization—you can make it happen for your company.

➤ Select Strategic Supply Partners

Filling roles across the value net design is another key to operating effectiveness. None of the innovators we observed attempt to do everything themselves. Even the Spanish fashion house, Zara, one of the most vertically integrated companies we studied, outsources its labor-intensive sewing and assembly work to a group of small nearby cooperatives. Outsourced relationships provide efficiency, as each player specializes in its own métier. Equally important, they offer flexibility and scalability.

Biogen, the Cambridge, Massachusetts–based biotechnology company, faced a critical choice of roles and partners when it decided to launch its new drug, AVONEX®. It wanted to become a full-fledged operating company rather than license its discovery to "Big Pharma." However, the company lacked the infrastructure to ramp up rapidly once regulatory approval was received. Biogen's solution was to form a value net with a small number of partners. With this handful of manufacturing and distribution allies, Biogen was able to make product available to customers within 35 hours of final regulatory approval—a record in its industry.

SOHO, the virtual furniture company, is an even more extreme example of outsourcing. SOHO's founder believed that the secret to rapid expansion and profit growth lay in leveraging the scale and experience of trusted partners. Acting on that belief, he designed a value net that relied on external providers for just about everything. Is there a limit to the virtual model? Mahmoud Ladjevardi answered the question emphatically: "No. It can grow with you. Flexibility is built in. We can add resources easily. They can be marshaled or redirected as needed."

These examples make three important points:

1. Innovators typically restrict their *strategic* value net relationships to a few providers. This reflects the time and investment needed to develop and maintain smooth-running collaboration with outside firms.

2. *Scalability,* the ability to quickly expand and contract production, is one of the main reasons for using network partners. Biogen, SOHO, and others have leveraged the assets of supply partners to avoid fixed asset investments.

3. Strategic relationships with partners work over the long term only when they lead to *mutually beneficial* situations. This means that the outsourcer must not simply push inventory onto the supplier's books. A powerful company might get away with this in the short run, but doing so does not lead to a strong supplier relationship or mutual support.

■ DIGITIZING THE VALUE NET

Every one of our innovators is digital to some degree, and all are moving toward even greater reliance on information technology. We see three important lessons in this area.

➤ Design the Information Flow First

The first step in digitizing the value net is to reach key design decisions regarding information flow. What are the key recurring operational decisions, and which information elements are needed? Which flows can be simultaneous, and which must still respect some sequential steps? How much access should suppliers and other partners have to your operational data and processes (some of which will surely work for your competitors)? These decisions must be carefully thought through prior to wiring up the value net.

At Cisco Systems, these design decisions led to instant customer linkages and transmission to suppliers. Suppliers are treated identically to employees on Cisco's information system. And Cisco's suppliers run their operations, including quality control, on Cisco's applications. Miller SQA transmits production module requirements to its suppliers four times a day. Volkswagen provides very specific, limited sets of parts information to its logistics providers. In each case, flow patterns are designed with value net decisions, roles, and responsibilities in mind.

► Digitize Communications across the Value Net

The most obvious purpose of information technology in a value net is to achieve fast and efficient transmission of information from customers to providers. Gateway's reseller and supply partners, for example, are all digitally connected. An order received from a customer is automatically transmitted to the contract manufacturers and to the assembly floor, then to UPS for pickup and delivery.

Streamline's first digital information link is with its customers. Some 75 percent of orders are received over the Internet, and that number continues to climb as more subscribers make the Internet a part of their lives. This link adds to customer convenience and reduces Streamline's order processing costs.

Digital powerhouses such as OrderTrust demonstrate how complete networks of merchants, suppliers, fulfillers, and drop-shippers can be automatically linked. OrderTrust's computers handle 400,000 transactions each day without human intervention. Even the process of linking in new partners has been automated to speed ramp-up time.

➤ Harness Bits to Power Decision Making

Companies and their partners can achieve greater control of net activities when they adopt planning software and other decision-making tools. Many of the companies we have seen use sophisticated rule-based decision systems in conjunction with enterprise resource planning software to accept and process orders, optimize production capacity, and issue time-definite delivery dates. These make it possible to schedule most orders without manual intervention. New software, increasingly web-hosted, is bringing advanced optimization algorithms within reach of almost any manufacturer and retailer. The challenges of intercontinental sourcing and logistics, among the most thorny in any supply chain, are now being addressed through new software offerings. Ventures such as Celarix and RockPort Trade Systems have developed powerful web-based applications that provide importers with the ability to manage and optimize their offshore activities in real time.

Digital technology is the backbone of every effective value net. But technology must remain a means to a strategic end. "Apple uses SAP, i2, and homegrown technologies," says the firm's Tim Cook. "Systems help automate processes. But it's the process and the people! The systems are just enablers."

■ MANAGEMENT TECHNIQUES

As with any other business design, realizing the full potential of a value net requires strong management. Leadership at the top, buy-in throughout the organization, and the right performance incentives are essential. That said, our research has identified three principles that every CEO should observe in designing and managing a value net enterprise: Define a breakthrough vision, adopt simple and clear goals, and use an entrepreneurial team to make the transition.

➤ Define a Breakthrough Vision

One of the chief distinguishing characteristics of the value net designs we have profiled is the boldness of the vision used in making a clear break with the past. This vision is customer-inspired. Miller SQA was born, for example, from a clear vision of the frustrations that office furniture buyers faced and the conviction that meeting those unmet needs in dramatically new ways would form the cornerstone of an entirely new business. The sharp departure from a months-long process to a week-long fulfillment cycle was the embodiment of this quantum leap in service delivery.

Value nets aren't created by incremental efforts. Courage and conviction are required to promote the vision. As Apple's Tim Cook told us, "A lot of people thought we were crazy" (when Apple set out to beat Dell at the operations game). In two years, Apple had surpassed Dell on key metrics such as inventory turns. It wasn't easy, but the clarity of the vision and its call for breakthrough results were essential in communicating the mind-set change and process revolution that would be necessary.

➤ Adopt Simple and Clear Goals

The evidence from innovators is overwhelming: They have set simple, clear goals to drive successful performance. When we began our research, we were familiar with the goals typically used in supply chain management. We felt that many were inappropriate—for example, focusing totally on operating costs without considering the role of differing service levels in driving customer satisfaction. We had in mind a balanced mix of more innovative goals, such as responsiveness to changing demand or ability to manage the network.

What we learned is that successful implementers of advanced supply chain designs are single-minded in their quest. They set simple goals that are clear to employees at all levels. Miller SQA's target of 100 percent on-time shipments is but one example. The image of its operations vice president handing out $100 bills to employees who know how many consecutive days the company has hit that target is a powerful one. It indicates commitment and broad-based identification with a common goal.

Streamline also keeps employees focused on the main target, customer selection, as represented in its BSF Index (the percent of deliveries made to busy suburban families). According to Frank Britt, "If you were to walk out to our distribution center right now and ask someone, 'What was the BSF Index last week?' I guarantee that every one of them could tell you. It's *that* core to the business."

Our advice is to choose a demanding goal that can be reached only through successful implementation of the new value net design. Represent that goal in a metric that everyone can understand, and follow it day by day.

➤ Use an Entrepreneurial Team to Make the Transition

We don't think you need a new superdepartment of "supply chain management" to make the transition to a value net. Such a department is a logical ideal for those who want to integrate the functional silos of procurement, logistics, and manufacturing. But creating a single maxi-silo may worsen some interactions while it eases others. No single, specific organization structure can ensure the necessary coordination to launch and operate the new design.

The experiences of the innovators suggest that a dynamic team is the best assurance of value net implementation. At Biogen, three operations executives and a handful of other employees representing marketing, quality, and regulatory services built the network that brought AVONEX® to market quickly and successfully. They did so within an environment that largely left them free to make decisions on their own.

At CIBA Vision, the Swiss contact lens manufacturer, a small, multinational team designed and implemented the company's new EuroLogistics Center from the ground up. The team leader had no previous logistics experience. The team's power came from its combination of expertise in several functions, its knowledge of each of the European countries involved, and its dedication to making the transition happen fast.

Innovators believe strongly that a formal organization structure is not the answer to value net implementation. We concur. Instead of bureaucracy, create a small, strong, entrepreneurial team that sees the vision, identifies the goal, and works across functions to build the value net.

■ KEEP A STEP AHEAD

The previous chapters described the power of a value net business design and what it takes to create one. We have provided examples of value net companies in several industries. And we have drawn from them lessons that others can follow.

More companies in more industries will adopt value net business designs in the years ahead. As they do, end customers will experience faster, better service at lower costs. Close collaboration between supply partners will become the norm. Executives will learn new ways to design and manage their businesses. Successful implementers will enjoy higher profits, and competitors of value net implementers will feel the heat.

Having said this, business designs must be constantly renewed. The picture of value net design we have presented is bound to change in the years ahead. Customer needs and expectations will change. New and more powerful digital technologies will appear. Some of the companies showcased in these pages as exemplary practitioners may stumble or find themselves outmaneuvered by competitors with newer, more effective designs.

Sun Microsystems' Hugh Aitken captures the essence of this challenge: "You have to keep ahead of the curve. Every two or three years, supply chain design gets reinvented. And that's okay. That's what growth is all about. Mark time for an instant and you're toast."

It is a fast-changing world. Readers who have been inspired by the value net concept should think a step or two ahead of the best-practice examples shown here. The five elements of business design and the lessons we have drawn provide a guiding framework, but the inspiration and the vision are yours. It's an exciting time to be an innovator. Customers are waiting to be delighted. The door to hidden profits and new value is unlocked. Please step through.

Appendix

Value Net Self-Diagnostic

This appendix provides a diagnostic tool based on the key concepts and lessons in the book. It is designed for executives who wish to assess how a value net design might benefit their customers and their company. This self-diagnostic can serve as the first step on the path to business reinvention. If you are intrigued by the accomplishments of the value net innovators, we invite you and your management team to roll up your sleeves and begin to develop the business case for change.

Value Nets introduces a new form of business design — one in which customer choice is connected seamlessly to the fulfillment engine, creating value for customers and shareholders alike. The case studies illustrate how companies in all industries can benefit from adopting value net concepts.

Mercer Management Consulting's *Value Net Design*™ methodology helps companies translate these concepts and practical lessons into carefully crafted value net business designs. The design methodology spans three phases: value net diagnostic, value net design, and value net realization (Figure A.1). This appendix outlines an abridged version of the first of these phases: a question and scorecard-based

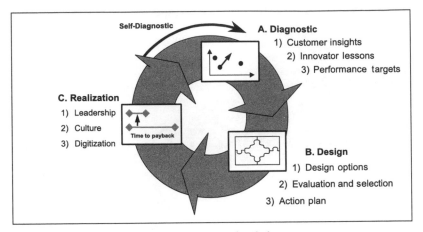

Figure A.1 Value Net Design™ methodology.

self-diagnostic. It represents a first step to determining the applicability of value net design to your company's specific situation. And it challenges management to imagine the potential results of significant change.

The self-diagnostic asks tough questions that require research, honest introspection, and discussion. We recommend a management team–based approach to the self-diagnostic. The effort involved will be repaid with an understanding of the opportunities available and initial progress on the road to crafting the value net business design that's right for your company.

■ SELF-DIAGNOSTIC

This self-diagnostic exercise is all about identifying gaps between customer expectations, value net innovators, and industry norms. It is organized around the five business design elements discussed in Chapters 3 through 7: *value proposition, scope, profit capture, strategic control,* and *execution.* The exercise is presented in two parts: management questions and performance scorecards. These will identify major gaps and suggest the design options that lead to closing them.

➤ Management Questions

The management questions are challenging. Ideally, they call for research by team members drawing on knowledge from across the organization. Several team working sessions may be required to develop suitable responses. The questions, although organized by business design element, need to be considered as an integrated whole. It is also important to keep in view how customer expectations, digital technology, competition, and globalization will evolve in the coming years so that the new value net design is most relevant and effective.

In addition to the management questions, key quantitative measures should be captured. The illustrative scorecards we'll show include performance levels for some of the value net innovators presented in the book and provide examples of the type of indicators you may wish to develop. And the scorecards come as a reminder of the performance levels achieved by value net innovators.

Value Proposition

A company's value proposition consists of product and service offerings that add value to customers. Value net innovators are the best in their industries at truly understanding and delivering on customer needs with an effective proposition that emphasizes the *service wrap*. They exploit three powerful offers: *super service* (especially speed and reliability), *convenient solutions,* and *customization,* as discussed in Chapter 3. They don't attempt to be all things to all people, but rather to craft their value proposition to match the needs of their targeted and most profitable customers. The following questions address the core of customer understanding—the three powerful value propositions and careful customer targeting:

1. How do you define your targeted customers?
2. Do you know which customers are the most profitable to serve? Is the business focused on them?
3. What are customers' goals, success factors, and service offerings in their own businesses?
4. How will customer needs evolve? How important is the service wrap becoming?
5. What impact will changes in the external environment have?
6. How do your products and services help customers achieve success? Do they address needs for convenience, reliability, speed, and customization? How are your customers' economics impacted by your offerings? Is your value proposition squarely focused on customer needs?
7. How attractive could a value net proposition be to your targeted customers?

Scope

Scope in value net design is concerned with *what* activities are required to deliver on a company's value proposition and *who* will perform them. Three categories of activities are included in the "what" of value net design: customer choice, delivery, and production. Value net innovators are creating interactive choiceboards that allow self-design by customers and efficient transmission of demand and capability information. Delivery processes are designed to be value-enhancing. Production is synchronized with the customer-facing processes and provider operations across the value net.

The "who" of value net design is about determining which processes to keep in-house and which ones to outsource. It also focuses on the "how"—the management of collaborative relationships to enhance customer value and capture profits. The value net companies highlighted in this book excel at establishing and maintaining partner relations across their respective networks. Consider the following questions:

1. Do you offer your customers choiceboards (with all four key elements—communication, demand capture, choice management, and product definition) to conveniently make customized selections based on actual fulfillment capabilities?
2. What portion of your product menu satisfies 90 percent of your customers' orders?
3. Is the delivery process fully exploited as a way to add more value to the customer? What ideas can be adapted from the value net innovators?
4. Do you use your control of the most important customer touch points to provide the best service?
5. Does production in your company respond to real demand, or does it rely on demand forecasts? Is production synchronized across the value net?
6. Have you considered outsourcing all aspects of operations except for the critical customer touch points? Is outsourcing viewed strategically or opportunistically?
7. Are your supply chain relationships collaborative or transactional? Is partner management an organizational strength in your company?

Profit Capture

This business design element entails devising the right mechanism for generating profits from a business's attractive value proposition. As we saw in Chapter 5, a value net achieves superior profits by generating greater revenues (super service and solutions) and by radically improving a company's cost and asset positions. Leading value net practitioners understand who their customers are and the extent to which their products and services add value to their customers. They also understand the cost to serve different customers. These firms minimize their inventories, simplify and digitize their operations, own few fixed assets, and grow with very little cash. They convert their value propositions to profits quickly and efficiently. The following questions probe the extent to which your company fully exploits its value capture potential:

1. Do customers place a high value on your product and service offering? Are you capturing additional profits from fast and reliable service?
2. Are you losing customers to competitors that offer solutions rather than only products and services?
3. Can you estimate the cost of missed sales when your product or service is not readily available? Are you able to employ postponement or similar techniques to ensure that product is positioned where demand is greatest?
4. Are profits being eroded by inventory stockpiles and write-downs?
5. Does a focus on "atoms" rather than on "bits" drive high operating expenses?
6. Are you growing with someone else's cash (e.g., that of customers or suppliers), or are you serving as banker? How long is your cash conversion cycle?
7. Can you gain agility, scalability, and higher profits by not owning certain fixed assets directly, but rather by accessing them through a value net?

Strategic Control

Strategic control is the element of business design that companies develop to protect their profits over time. Five common strategic control mechanisms described in Chapter 6 keep customers coming back for more: *brand, customer hook, provider relationships, innovative design,* and *low price.* Brand and customer hook create customer loyalty and provide longer-lasting profit protection. Innovation is the critical basis for much of the strategic control conferred by value nets. Low price tends to be easier to copy and offers fewer advantages. The following questions explore the current and potential strategic control points in your business.

1. What keeps a customer coming back for more? Why have some customers defected?
2. Do you have the detailed understanding of customers and suppliers needed to develop strategic control?
3. Which strategic control points can your supply chain claim:
   - Do your customers associate superior service with your company's name?
   - Do you have loyal customers and enjoy a high degree of repeat business?
   - Do you have relationships with suppliers that are exclusive or hard to replicate?
   - Is your business design more innovative than those of your competitors?
4. Have profits or market value migrated to existing competitors or to solutions providers from outside your industry?
5. What type of value net would you need to create for customers to perceive your company as innovative?

Execution

Decisions regarding the previous four business design elements acquire significance only to the extent that a company can execute them well. The successful value net companies described in this book have excelled at execution. Two simple characteristics differentiate the successful value net companies in our research: a *breakthrough culture* (vision, leadership, simple goals, and entrepreneurial teaming) and a *high degree of digitization* (shifting from atoms to bits). These questions test your company's value net execution excellence:

1. Does your company have an ambitious service-based vision, a leader who's passionate about the vision, entrepreneurial teams, and clear performance goals?
2. Are corporate goals aligned with customer preferences? Can every employee state the goals and the actual performance levels?
3. Is your team skilled in building and maintaining value nets? Are cross-functional teams a way of life in your company?
4. To what extent are traditional front-end and back-end functions integrated?
5. How fast and digitally do you communicate and make decisions?
6. Have your company's supply chain digitization efforts moved beyond connectivity and transaction automation to supporting complex decision making?
7. Are low-value-added tasks eliminated, automated, or outsourced?
8. Can your systems staff deploy information technology strategically?
9. Are customers and suppliers included in your digital network?

These management questions are intended to help you qualitatively assess the opportunities for turning your organization into a value net.

➤ Performance Scorecard

The value net performance scorecard serves as a guide to gathering the hard data needed to assess your organization's current performance. The key purpose of this exercise is to identify performance gaps against both customer expectations and industry standards, as well as against value net innovators that are showing the way in other industries.

We have assembled illustrative scorecards populated with examples of performance achieved by value net inno-

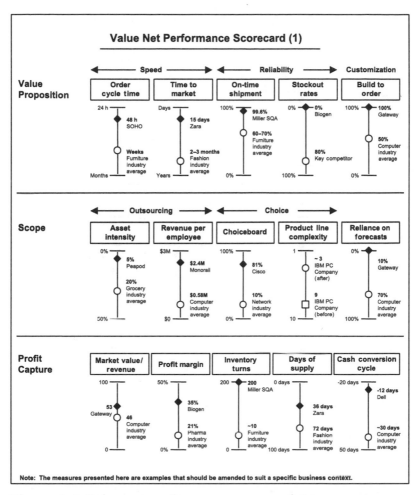

Figure A.2 Value net performance scorecard (1).

vators that we examined throughout the book (Figures A.2 and A.3). In each case, we display the value net innovator's performance level (◆) against average industry performance (○) or against the innovator's earlier performance (□). When you create your scorecard, you should also indicate customer performance expectations on the scales.

Some of the measures shown may not be applicable to your industry, and others may need to be supplemented to

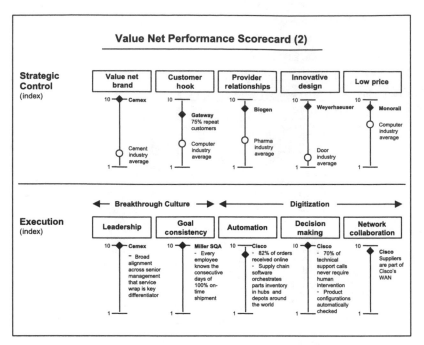

Figure A.3 Value net performance scorecard (2).

create a full picture that is suitable for your business environment. However, these example scorecards provide a good starting point for your quantitative performance assessment. Completing the scorecard gives a good visual representation of the magnitude of change required to meet your customers' evolving expectations and to open up a gap against competitors.

We have divided the sample performance scorecard into two sections. The metrics for value proposition, scope, and profit capture can be precisely measured. The metrics for strategic control and execution are based on qualitative indices and therefore require expert judgment to complete.

Value Proposition

The metrics chosen by case study companies for value proposition center on the four themes examined in Chapter 3: speed, reliability, convenience, and customization. These companies have found that it is important to take the customer's perspective when conceiving these metrics. For example, order cycle time is not the time from receiving an order to shipping product, but from the customer placing the order until the customer receives the product (possibly direct from suppliers).

Scope

Scope metrics focus on the key themes discussed in Chapter 4: *what* activities are required to meet customer expectations (choice) and *who* should perform them (outsourcing), including the quality of information your organization is using to guide these activities. Most of the example metrics presented here are well known. Product line complexity, however (part of the customer choice activity), is less common and shows that venturing away from conventional metrics may be required to capture your organization's critical performance gaps. The IBM PC Company, for example, discovered that 90 percent of orders could be satisfied with 10 percent of its product menu. Reducing product complexity can positively impact many aspects of a company's performance. Product line complexity is measured in this case as the ratio of percent of orders satisfied to percent of product menu.

Profit Capture

Innovators look at profit capture in terms of both the top line and the bottom line. The market value–to-revenue ratio (MV/R) is a key leading indicator of your company's position in its industry. If your MV/R is below 1, customers are probably finding your competitors' business designs more attractive. In addition to the measures displayed in the scorecard, specific measures used by these companies include revenue per customer, customer profitability (average, high, or low), stock price growth, and revenue growth.

Strategic Control

Strategic control measures are more qualitative than were those for the three previous business design elements. These measures reflect the five types of strategic control that value nets typically create: value net brand, customer hook, provider relationships, innovative design, and low price. Bear in mind that certain types of strategic control are far more powerful than others. The scores are determined by answering these questions:

Value net brand (high control). To what degree do customers routinely associate fulfillment service quality with your company's name (possibly measured through brand recognition studies)?

Customer hook (high control). Do you offer service aspects that induce less switching by your customers (possibly approximated through customer-retention measures)?

Provider relationships (medium control). To what extent are your relationships with suppliers, competitors, or other companies exclusive or time-consuming to build?

Innovative design (medium control). To what extent does your company's business design reflect more advanced value net characteristics than those of your competitors?

Low price (low control). To what degree do you offer the lowest-priced products and/or services in your industry?

Execution

The metrics for execution are also index-based and focus on the two key dimensions explored in Chapter 7: breakthrough culture and digitization. The gaps here are not measured against customer expectations or competition, but rather against an absolute best score of 10. Scores are estimated by considering the following:

Leadership. Is a senior executive visibly and passionately committed to implementing a value net?

Culture. Is there a shared belief in your company that a service wrap is key to customer satisfaction?

Goal consistency. Are the key goals kept simple, clear, and aligned with what customers care most about?

Entrepreneurial team. Do you have a small, cross-discipline, motivated team of executives to lead the transition?

Automation. To what degree has digital information transfer replaced paper- and people-intensive transactions in your company?

Digital decision making. How are intelligent digital tools supporting operational decisions?

Networked collaboration. Are your customers, suppliers, and other partners integrated into a truly digital value net?

■ CONCLUSION

Creating a Value Net Design for your company clearly extends beyond the scope of this self-diagnostic. Yet completing the self-diagnostic should provide you with a good understanding of the opportunities that value net thinking presents for your organization. The answers to the management questions and, in particular, the scorecards offer the insights and data you will need to build a business case for change. They will have highlighted key performance gaps that can be used to generate broad-based support for a value net design initiative. And they should have revealed the areas in which further investigation and data gathering are required to complete a full value net diagnostic. Your efforts may well be remembered as the start of a remarkable business design transformation at your company.

Index

Air Canada, competitor collaboration, 97–98
AirLiance Materials, 14
  competitor collaboration, 97–98
Aitken, Hugh, 87, 201, 243
Albertsons, 71
Amazon.com:
  customization at, 50
  HomeGrocer.com, 21
  negative working capital operations, 136
Apple Computer:
  brand power of, 159
  direct delivery plan, 10
  executive team leadership, 187
  global supply chain reform, 11
  goal orientation of, 190
  Internet strategy, 11
  inventory turnover, 9, 11
  outsourcing at, 11, 83
  product plan redesign, 10
  restructuring costs, 12
  SAP, 10
  stock price increases, 12
  suppliers, reduction in, 11
  suppliers, relationship with, 11
  supply chain management problems, 9–10
  as value net, 10–12

Apple Store, 11
Asset intensity, 150–151, 156
  low, 219
Asset optimization, 124
  inventory stockpiles, reducing for, 125–132
Assets:
  shifting toward digital information, 193–200
  of virtual companies, 84
Auto industry:
  digital consumer interface strategies, 195–197
  inventory stockpiles in, 125
  supplier collaboration in, 94–95
Automation, 194–200
  audits of, 214
  at Cisco Systems, 208–210
AVONEX®, 103–104. See also Biogen

Baldwin, Jim, 123
Barriers to entry, differentiation and innovation as, 180
Becton Dickinson (BD), customer collaboration at, 95–96
Ben-Venue Laboratories, 107
Berlex Laboratories, 105–106

Biogen, 13, 101–115
AVONEX®, 103–104
collaborative approach,
105–107
customer support at, 108–109
growth through outsourcing,
135
history of, 102
launch goal, 109–111
partners of, 107–108
profit margin, 120
results of value net design,
111–112
scope decisions, 101
supplier partners of, 162–163
team orientation of, 187–189
Blakelock, Dave, 65, 66, 68
Boeing, complexity problem at,
127
Borders, Louis, 71
Bosack, Len, 206
Brand recognition, from exceptional service, 31
Brands, product, 159
Brands, value net, 157, 159–160,
168, 250–251
differentiation and, 180
measurement of, 256
reinforcement of, 165
Breakthrough culture, 185,
251–252
at Cisco Systems, 217–218
creating, 185–186
determining, 205
entrepreneurial team leadership, 187–189
goal orientation for, 189–192
leadership vision, 186–187
measurement of, 256–257
skills for, 192–193
team-oriented approach, 188
Brindley, Martin, 195
Britt, Frank, 56, 61, 64–68, 69,
77–78, 241

Build-to-order (BTO) manufacturing, 51–52, 130–132,
234–236
Bundy, Bill, 167, 174–176,
180–181, 186–187, 190
Business design:
conversion of, 53–55
dynamic, 242–243
execution of, 31–32
innovation in, 164–165, 179
metrics for, 156, 252–257
new, 226–230
options for, assembling,
227–228
profit capture, 30
rethinking, 222
scope, 28–30. See also Scope
strategic control, 30–31
value-creating type, 26–32
as value net, 32
value proposition, 27–28
Business model, build-to-order,
51–52, 130–132, 234–236
Business redesign, 32
Buyer expectations, increases
in, 19

Capitalization:
reducing need for, 135–137
for virtual companies, 85
Carlen, Roland, 129
CarPoint, 49
Cash, growing without, 135–
137
Cash conversion cycle, 136–137
negative, 52, 151–153
Caterpillar, 22
profit generation at, 122–124
Cemex, 13, 22
brand power of, 160
delivery process, 80
production synchronization
at, 82
profit capture strategy, 30, 119

reliability policies, 43–44
technology-based initiatives
    at, 44–46
Chambers, John, 208
ChandraSekaran, Ram, 207,
    208–209, 211, 212, 213–214,
    215, 217, 218, 229
Change drivers, 18–25
Channel assembly, 52
Chemdex, 22
    digital procurement and
        sourcing processes, 198
Choiceboards, vii, 75–79, 99,
    231–232, 248–249
    for choice management,
        78–79
    for communication process,
        77
    for demand capture, 77–78,
        125
    at Gateway, 142, 148
    at Miller SQA, 175
    for product definition, 79
Chuang, Michael, 126
CIBA Vision, 129
Cisco Systems, 206–222
    brand power of, 220
    breakthrough culture,
        217–218
    digitization at, 212–217
    execution strategy, effects of,
        218–221
    execution strategy, inte-
        grated, 212–217
    history of, 206–207
    hook of, 220–221
    productivity at, 219
    scope, 208–212
    supplier relationships, 221
    value proposition, 208
Clark, Wes, 48
Clearinghouses, 98–99
Clicks and mortar, 71, 195
    hybrid approach, 230

Collaboration:
    developing and maintaining,
        237
    management of, 248–249
Collaborative partners, choos-
    ing, 114
Collaborative relationships, 76,
    93–99, 101
Communication:
    with customers, 77. See also
        Choiceboards
    for goal alignment, 190–191
Communications technology,
    22
Compaq, 26
Competition, as change driver,
    23
Competitors, collaborative rela-
    tionships with, 97–99
Complexity reduction, 236
Component standardization,
    236
Connectivity, 194–200
Consolidation, 128–129
Consumer-direct commerce,
    19
Consumer Learning Center, 64
Contract manufacturing, 29,
    83
Convenience, need for, 46
Convenient solutions, 46–49,
    54–55, 71, 247
    profits opportunities from,
        121–124
Cook, Tim, 10, 11, 12, 132, 165,
    185, 187, 190, 239, 240
Corporate performance, and
    value net design, 14
Cortefiel, 41
Cost reduction, 124
    inventory stockpiles, reduc-
        ing for, 124–132
Culture, 31. See also Break-
    through culture

Customer choice, vii, 75
  as essential activity, 28–29
  management of, 78–79
  and production, synchroniz-
    ing, 81
Customer demand:
  information about, 125–126
  real-time, 176
  traditional supply mecha-
    nisms, 3
  value net design for, 3
Customer focus, 230–234
Customer information, hook
    creation from, 161
Customer interface, see Choice-
    boards
Customer loyalty, 158, 168–169,
    250
  building, 72
  hooks for, 160–162
Customer needs, 248
  as driver of value net design,
    212, 220–221
  identifying, for strategic con-
    trol, 181
  technology and, 212
  touch points for, 46
Customer preferences, 78
Customer-provider relationship,
    4
Customers:
  alignment with, 91–92
  business-to-business, 19
  collaborative relationships
    with, 95–97
  cost to serve, 249–250
  customized offerings for, 15
  demands of, 19–20
  digitizing communication
    with, 194–197
  focus on, 48
  integration of technology
    with, 214
  leveraging, 136–137

position in value net, 4
  profitability calculations on,
    133–134
  real-time interactions with,
    76–79
  single point of contact for,
    48–49
  value proposition alignment
    with, 36
Customer satisfaction, 13,
    217–218
Customer segments, profitabil-
    ity of, 27
Customer selection, 61, 71, 248
Customization, 49–53, 54–55,
    235, 247

DaimlerChrysler, 42
  BTO design at, 51
  competitor collaboration,
    97
  customization at, 50
Daniell, Jim, 202, 203
Decision making:
  digital tools for, 201–204,
    214–215, 239
  technological facilitators of,
    32
Delivery, 75
  convenient, 233–234
  definition of, 80
  differentiation as result of,
    99–100
  as essential activity, 28–29
  and production, synchroniz-
    ing, 81
  value-enhanced, 76, 79–80,
    248–249
Delivery, fast and reliable, 6–7,
    229, 235
  and lost sales, 119
  for profit maximization, 120
Dell Computer, xiv
  as business model, 23

choiceboards at, 78–79
innovation at, 165
liquidity of, 136–137
mass customization, 50
value migration to, 25–26
Demand capture, 77–78
Demand planning, 216–217
DeMello, Timothy, 56
Demographics, and shift toward
    services, 35
Design, build-to-order, 51–52,
    130–132, 234–236
Differentiation:
    from innovation, 164–165
    speed of service as, 232–
        233
    superb delivery as, 234
Digital decision making, 32,
    201–204, 214–215, 239
Digital Equipment, 26
Digital information, 7
    links to, 238
    shift toward, 193–204
Digital protocols, 22
Digital technology, 20–23
    for demand information visi-
        bility, 125
    determining present use of,
        205
    and pricing, 96
    profit capture with, 132–
        134
    for speedy delivery, 40
    transition to, 185
Digitization, 193–194, 237–239,
    251–252
    at Cisco Systems, 212–217
    of customer communication,
        194–197
    of internal communication,
        200
    measurement of, 256–257
    of supplier communication,
        197–199

Distribution, simplification of,
    128–129
Drop shipment, 88

E-commerce, 7
    as a threat, 15
E-fulfillment, 21, 164. *See also*
    Fulfillment
Electronic catalogs, 199
Electronic data interchange
    (EDI), 198
Electronics industry, inventory
    stockpiles in, 125
eMachines, Inc., 167
Employees:
    focusing on value-adding
        activities, 209–210, 217–218,
        222
    productivity of, 219
    virtual, 211–212
Entrepreneurial team, 187–189,
    241–242
Español.com, 88
eToys.com, 84
Execution, 31–32, 184–
    185
    breakthrough culture for,
        185–193
    and digital decision making,
        201–204
    digitization for, 193–204
    performance metrics for,
        256–257
    self-diagnostic for, 251–252
    shift from atoms to bits,
        193–204
    strategies for, 204–206
Executive culture, xiv
Express package industry,
    response to customer
    demand, 19
Extensible markup language
    (XML), 22
Extranets, 197

FastParts.com, 22, 98, 199
FedEx, 19
Fingerhut:
   fulfillment and processing
     services, 29
   partner relationships at, 164
FooFoo.com:
   outsourcing, 29
   third-party order processing,
     202–203
Ford Motor Company:
   clicks-and-mortar approach,
     195
   competitor collaboration, 97
   customization at, 50
Freedom, and execution, 188
FreeMarkets, 199
Free-PC, Inc., 167
Friedman, Mel, 51, 136
Fulfillment, 231, 234. *See also*
    E-fulfillment
   capability for, vii
   decision making for, 202–203
   quick, 232–233
   web sites for, 214
Fulfillment centers, 67
Fung, Victor, 89–93, 163
Fung, William, 88–89

Gateway:
   brand power of, 159–160
   BTO manufacturing at, 52
   business model, 140–145
   cash requirements, 151–153
   choiceboards at, 78–79, 141,
    148
   customer service, 34
   execution, 145
   Gateway Country® stores, 141
   history of, 139–140
   innovation at, 165
   outsourcing at, 149–150
   production synchronization
    at, 82

   profit capture strategy, 30,
    139–155
   public face, 153–154
   scope, 144–145
   strategic control, 145
   value migration to, 25–26
   value proposition, 144
GE Medical, 121–122
Globalization, 23–25
Goals:
   in company cultures, 189–192
   nonincremental, 191–192
   simple, clear, 240–241
Gonzalez, Ferdinand, 217
Gonzalez, José María, 185
Grace, Tom, 17
Greenspan, Alan, 20
Grimshaw, Alan, 195, 196
Growth, without capital,
    135–137

Hamm, Robert, 107, 188
Hammond, Mike, 139
Hannaford Brothers, 71
Hanover Direct, fulfillment and
    processing services, 29
Hawken, Phil, 202–203
Hennes & Mauritz, 41
Herman Miller, Inc., 7, 169. *See
   also* Miller SQA
Hewlett-Packard:
   digital product processes, 199
   information sharing at, 126
   outsourcing at, 83
   postponement, 52–53
Home delivery model, 56–57
HomeGrocer.com, 21
Home grocery delivery models,
    69–71
HomeRuns, 71
Hooks, 157, 160–162, 250–251
   customer loyalty resulting
    from, 180
   measurement of, 256

IBM, complexity reduction at, 127–128
iMac family, launch of, 10
Imitation, 158
Inditex, 41
Industry reduction process, 138
Information flows:
  accuracy of, 125–126
  costs of redesign, 45–46
  designing, 202, 237–238
  speed of, 41
Information sharing, 126
Iniguez, Gelacio, 44
Innovation, 158, 164–165, 168, 250–251
  measurement of, 256
Integration:
  customer, 214
  front- and back-end, 213–214
  profit generation from, 123
Intel, inventory levels of, 131
Intelligent agents, 203
Internal communications, digitizing, 200
Internet, 20–22
  as a services medium, 35
  and supplier collaboration, 95
  for supplier connectivity, 198–199
  value of, 72
  and virtual companies, 84
Internet start-ups, venture capital investments in, 23
Intranets, 197
Inventory:
  automation of management, 216–217
  lowering levels of, 78, 124–132, 219
Inventory reduction process:
  complexity reduction, 127–128

distribution simplification, 128–129
at Gateway, 148–149
information about demand, 125–126
standard components, 128
supplier reliability management, 129–130
Iomega, information flow at, 126
I2 Technologies, 22

Jobs, Steve, 10
Johns, Doug, 166

Kraft Foods, 128–129
Krog, Hermann, 197

Ladjevardi, Mahmoud, 85–86, 236–237
LaHowchic, Nicholas, 120
Lardakis, Moira, 38, 46–47
Leadership, visionary, 186–187
Lead-time, reducing, 211, 219
Leisure time, shrinkage of, 35
Lerner, Sandy, 206
Levi Strauss, customization at, 50
Lewis, Peter, 38
Li & Fung, 89–93
  supplier relationships, 163
The Limited:
  globalization of, 24
  profit maximization at, 120–121
Lufthansa Technik, competitor collaboration, 97–98

Management, self-diagnostic questions, 247–252
Management techniques, 239–242
Mannigel, Jerry, 132–134, 190–191, 200

Manugistics, 22
Market segments, *see also* Customer selection
  targeting, 231
Market valuations, factors influencing, 26–27
Market-value-to-revenue ratio (MV/R), 255
Mass customization, 50–51
Mass production, 50
McDaid, Michael, 95–96
McGuire, Jim, 200
McNamara, Kyle, 88
Metalsite.com, 199
Miller SQA, 7–9
  brand creation at, 31
  business design, 173
  as business model, 23
  digital ordering system, 195
  goals of, 189–190
  launch of, 171
  order entry, 175
  order processing, 176–177
  price-based competition at, 167–168
  Production Metering Center, 177
  profit stream protection strategies, 179–181
  speed and reliability strategies, 173–177
  strategic control model, 169–182
  Z-Axis software use, 175
Monorail, 128, 166–167
Mullen, Jim, 110, 111, 112, 188

NetPerceptions, 51
Nike, delivery strategy, 119
Nintendo, digital connectivity, 198
Nordstrom, investment in Streamline, 63–64
Norman, Bix, 171, 180, 186–187

Online auctions, 199
Operating effectiveness, 234–237
Operating speed, 37–38
Operational activities, collaborative and systematic, 5–6
Operational world, xiv
Optimization, 239
Orders, perfect, 43
Order-to-delivery cycle:
  compressing, 219, 232–233
  focusing on, 208–210
  speed of, 6–7
OrderTrust, 14, 164, 202
  fulfillment and processing services, 29
OrderZone.com, 49
Organizational boundaries, removing, 222
Organizational structure, 185
Outsourcing, 29–30, 76, 82–93, 100–101, 236–237, 248–249
  at Cisco Systems, 208–210, 211–212
  example of, 89–93
  growth through, 135–137, 138–139
  rules for, 82–83
  strategic, 87–89
  for virtual companies, 84–87
Overhead, reducing, 200

Packaging Coordinators Inc., 107
Palmer, John, 103–105, 110, 188, 189
Paperexchange.com, 199
Paul, Bill, 63, 67
Peapod, 69
  fixed assets of, 84
Perfect orders, 43
Performance measures, 61, 192, 222
  choice of, 189

CheckOut Receipt
Carnegie Mellon University

Hunt Library
01/24/02

08:27 pm

WATTAL, SUNIL

Item:E-commerce and v-business :
business models for global success /

edited by Stuart Barnes and Brian Hunt
Due Date: 3/25/2002,23:59

Item:The seven steps to nirvana : strategic
insights into e-business transformation /

Mohan Sawhney, Jeff Zabin
Due Date: 3/25/2002,23:59

Item:Competitive advantage : creating and
sustaining superior performance / Michael

E. Porter
Due Date: 3/25/2002,23:59

Item:Value nets : breaking the supply chain
to unlock hidden profits / David Bovet,

Joseph Martha, Mercer Management
Consulting
Due Date: 3/25/2002,23:59

Thank You for using

the 3M SelfCheck System!

Items are subject to recall after 7 days!
Have a great day!

Performance scorecard, for self-diagnostic, 252–257
Personal computer industry:
  contract manufacturing in, 29
  pricing strategies in, 166–167
  product customization in, 20
  supplier reliability management in, 130
  value migration in, 25
Philips Components, customer collaboration, 96–97
Phoenix Designs, 171
Postponement, 52–53
Pricing:
  cost to serve, 96
  low, 158, 165–168, 250–251
  measurement of, 256
  for super service, 119
Procter & Gamble, customer collaboration at, 95
Producenet.com, 199
Product design:
  build-to-order, 51–52, 130–132, 234–236
  innovative, 164–165
Production, 76
  as essential activity, 28–29
  synchronized, 76, 81–82, 100, 248–249
Products:
  build-to-order, 51–52, 130–132, 234–236
  complexity of, reducing, 126–128
  customer definition of, 79
  individualized, 51
  innovative design, 158
  sequential processing, 229
  standard components for, 128
  systemic processing, 234–235
Profitable revenues, 118–124

Profit capture, 30
  with cost reduction and asset optimization, 124–137
  with digital technology, 132–134
  example of, 140–155
  performance metrics for, 255–256
  profitable revenues, 118–124
  self-diagnostic for, 249–250
  strategies for, 137–139
  traditional, 117–118
Profit migration, 15–16
Progressive Insurance:
  customer needs, response to, 46–47
  Immediate Response system, 39
  profitability of, 119
  service delivery design, 38–39
Project planning, 192
Provider relationships, 158, 162–164, 250–251
  measurement of, 256
Providers, position in value net, 4–5

Quality control:
  outsourcing, 208–209
  remote, 215
Quintiles, 84

Redfield, Carl, 219
Relationship management, 192
Reliability, 43–46
Remote sensors, 22
Research database, xv
Responsibility, sharing, 188
Retail industry, direct sales rates, 19
Revenues, profitable, 118–124
Reverse auctions, 199

Ritz Carlton Hotels, customer
    information system, 161
Rukavina, Pete, 211

Sara Lee Knit Products, 83
Saunders, Paul, 119
Scalability, 237
Schmickrath, Don, 199
Scope, 28–30, 74
    changing, 90–91
    customer choice, 75
    deciding on, 99–101
    deciding on, example, 101–115
    delivery, 75
    performance metrics for,
        255
    production, 76
    self-diagnostic for, 248–249
    and virtual companies, 88
Sehrgosha, Mazy, 96
Self-diagnostic tool, 245–257
    online version, xi
Service, *see also* Super service
    demand for, 35
    express, 35–36
    individualized, 51
    on-site availability of, 48
    rapid delivery of, 39
    third-party, 29–30
    value-adding attributes of, 28
Service sector, in U.S. economy,
        35
Service wrap, 16, 247
    defined, 35
Shareholder value growth, 14
Shift from atoms to bits, 185,
        193–200. *See also* Digitiza-
        tion
ShopLink, 70
Sinton, Chris, 216, 218
Sisson, David, 98
Smith, Erin, 111
Social values, and shift toward
    services, 35

SOHO, Inc., 85–86
    growth through outsourcing,
        135–136
    outsourcing at, 236–237
Solutions:
    convenient, 46–49
    single-point, 49
Solvik, Peter, 215–216
Speed, of super service, 37–42
Springer, Bill, 123
Strategic control:
    from brand power, 157,
        159–160
    example of, 169–182
    hooks for, 157, 160–162
    from innovative design,
        164–165
    from low price, 165–168
    with provider relationships,
        162–164
    strategy for, 168–169
Stellato, Greg, 111
Stock market valuation, and
    value net design, 14
Strategic control, 30–31,
        157–158
    and customer needs, knowl-
        edge of, 181
    performance metrics for,
        256
    self-diagnostic for, 250–251
Strategic relationships, 63
    characteristics of, 91–93
Strategic thinking, 192
Streamline.com, 49, 55–72
    accuracy of orders, 65–66
    automatic replenishment
        program, 65
    Consumer Resource Center,
        67
    customer segment targeting,
        28
    customer selection process,
        61–62

delivery process, 65–69, 80
goals of, 56
hooks of, 161–162
operating model, 57–60
service box, 64–65
touch points, controlling, 69
value proposition, 62–65
Suna, Doug, 86
Sun Microsystems, 51
collaboration with suppliers, 94
growth through outsourcing, 136
IT-based supply chain, 201
Sun Microsystems-Europe, 87
Super service, 37–46, 54–55, 247
profits from, 119–121
reliability, 43–46
speed, 37–42
Supplier ecosystem, 229
Suppliers:
collaboration with, 94–95, 130
digitizing communication with, 197–199
leveraging, 135–136
relationships with, 16, 92–93, 162–164, 169, 211–212
reliability of, 129–130
strategic partnerships with, 236–237
technology partnerships with, 42
Supply, integrated, 48–49
Supply chain:
agility of, 6
as business design, 226–227
customer-aligned, 5
defined, 17
globalizing, 23–25
indicators of redesign, 15–17
new design for, xiii

profits in, xiii
scalability of, 6
Supply chain, traditional:
profit-optimizing efforts in, 117–118
speed limitations in, 39–40
versus value net, 2–3
Supply hubs, location of, 42
Switching costs, 160–161
Synchronization, of production network, 81–82

Technical support, automating, 215–216
Technology:
as a change driver, 20–23
decision making, facilitation of, 32
Technology partnerships, 42
Third-party facilitators:
for competitor collaboration, 97–99
for order processing, 202–203
Tibey, Stephen, 129
Torrenti, Pete, 48
Touch points, 46
controlling, 71–72, 85
delivery, see Delivery
TradingUp.com, 199
Transaction automation, 194–200
Transaction-based procurement, 95
Trimmer, Jeffrey, 42, 51
TriVirix International, 86

United Airlines, competitor collaboration, 97–98
UPS:
process hook, 162
reliability of, 19
U.S. population demographics, and shift toward services, 35

Value:
adding through delivery,
79-80
creation of, 13-14
Value migration, 25-32
Value nets:
characteristics of, 5-7
customer-focused, 230-234
definition of, xiii-xiv, 1-5
indicators for need of, 15-16
new designs, 226-230
scope of, 28-30. *See also*
Scope
Value net self-diagnostic,
245-257
execution, 251-252
management questions,
247-252
performance scorecard,
252-257
profit capture, 249-250
scope, 248-249
strategic control, 250-251
value proposition, 247-248
Value proposition, 27-28, 34-36
convenient solutions, 46-49
customer-aligned, 36, 62-65,
71
customer loyalty, 72
customer selection, 71
customization, 49-53
delivery of, 181-182
lessons for, 71-72
performance metrics for,
254-255
self-diagnostic for, 247-248
super service, 37-46
touch points, controlling,
71-72
Vauxhall, digital connections
with consumers, 195-196
Venture capital investments, in
Internet start-ups, 23

VerticalNet, 49
Virtual companies, 84-87
strategic control in, 87
Virtual employees, 211-212
Vision, 186-187
breakthrough, 240
Volkswagen, digital inbound
logistics system, 197-198

Waitt, Tim, 139, 141
Wal-Mart, supplier leverage, 94
Warehousing, eliminating, 42
Web sites:
choiceboards on, *see* Choiceboards
product offerings on, 201-202
Webvan, 69
Weidert, Bill, 216
Weitzen, Jeff, 34
Weyerhaeuser, 13
Weyerhaeuser door division:
choiceboard for, 77
digital technology, 200
digitization of, 132-134
goal orientation of, 190-
191
W.W. Grainger, Inc.:
convenient solutions of,
47-49
Grainger Integrated Supply
unit, 47-49

Xerox, delivery process, 80

Yeh, Ming, 50, 195

Zambrano, Lorenzo, 44
Zara, 13
production synchronization
at, 81-82
profitability of, 119
speed of operations, 40-41
Z-Axis software, 175-176